Richard William Church

Cathedral and University Sermons

Richard William Church

Cathedral and University Sermons

ISBN/EAN: 9783743305311

Manufactured in Europe, USA, Canada, Australia, Japa

Cover: Foto ©ninafisch / pixelio.de

Manufactured and distributed by brebook publishing software (www.brebook.com)

Richard William Church

Cathedral and University Sermons

CATHEDRAL AND
UNIVERSITY SERMONS

CATHEDRAL

AND

UNIVERSITY SERMONS

BY

R. W. CHURCH

SOMETIME DEAN OF ST. PAUL'S, AND FELLOW OF
ORIEL COLLEGE, OXFORD

London
MACMILLAN AND CO.
AND NEW YORK
1893

All rights reserved

First Edition 1892. *Reprinted* 1893

CONTENTS

		PAGE
1.	THE SERIOUSNESS OF LIFE	1

"To stand before the Son of Man."—ST. LUKE xxi. 36.

Preached Advent Sunday 1874.

2. THE CERTAINTY OF JUDGMENT 16

"In the day when God shall judge the secrets of men by Jesus Christ according to my gospel."—ROMANS ii. 16.

Preached Advent Sunday 1878.

3. HUMAN JUDGMENT AND DIVINE 29

"Let both grow together until the harvest."—ST. MATTHEW xiii. 30.

Preached Advent Sunday 1883.

4. THE CONDESCENSION OF OUR LORD 43

"He humbled Himself."—PHILIPPIANS. ii. 8.

Preached Christmas Day 1880.

5. THE CHRISTMAS MESSAGE OF HOPE 55

"A woman when she is in travail hath sorrow, because her hour is come: but as soon as she is delivered of the child, she remembereth no more the anguish, for joy that a man is born into the world. And ye now therefore have sorrow: but I will see you again, and your heart shall rejoice, and your joy no man taketh from you."—ST. JOHN xvi. 21, 22.

Preached Christmas Day 1881.

	PAGE
6. CHRIST OUR IDEAL	66

"Even so we, when we were children, were in bondage under the elements of the world. But when the fulness of the time was come, God sent forth His Son, made of a woman, made under the law, to redeem them that were under the law, that we might receive the adoption of sons."—GALATIANS iv. 3-5.

Preached Christmas Day 1882.

7. THE LIGHT OF THE EPIPHANY	80

"Then spake Jesus, saying, I am the light of the world."—ST. JOHN viii. 12.

Preached Feast of the Epiphany 1873.

8. TRIAL A NECESSARY LAW OF HUMAN LIFE	97

"In all points tempted like as we are, yet without sin."—HEBREWS iv. 15.

Preached First Sunday in Lent 1874.

9. THE SENSE OF BEAUTY A WITNESS TO IMMORTALITY	115

"Who shall change our vile body, that it may be fashioned like unto His glorious body, according to the working whereby He is able even to subdue all things unto Himself."—PHILIPPIANS iii. 21.

Preached Easter Day 1884.

10. THE RESURRECTION FROM THE DEAD	131

"The Firstborn from the dead."—COLOSSIANS i. 18.

Preached Easter Day 1885.

11. THE PEACE OF CHRIST	144

"Then the same day at evening, being the first day of the week, when the doors were shut where the disciples were assembled for fear of the Jews, came Jesus and stood in the midst, and saith unto them, Peace be unto you."—ST. JOHN xx. 19.

Written for Easter Day 1886, but not preached on account of illness.

PAGE

12. **The Power of the Ascension on the Lives of Men** 154

"While we look not at the things which are seen, but at the things which are not seen."—2 CORINTHIANS iv. 18.

Preached Ascension Day 1887.

13. **The Gift of the Holy Spirit** 169

"In whom also after that ye believed, ye were sealed with that Holy Spirit of promise, which is the earnest of our inheritance until the redemption of the purchased possession."—EPHESIANS i. 13, 14.

Preached Whitsunday 1877.

14. **The Work of the Holy Spirit** . 182

"And I will pray the Father, and He shall give you another Comforter, that He may abide with you for ever; even the Spirit of truth; whom the world cannot receive, because it seeth Him not, neither knoweth Him: but ye know Him; for He dwelleth with you, and shall be in you."—ST. JOHN xiv. 16.

Preached Whitsunday 1881.

15. **Temper and Self-Discipline** . 194, 206

Two Addresses to the Clergy given in the Crypt of St. Paul's, 12th October 1880, and 16th November 1885.

16. **The Kingdom of God, not in Word, but in Power** 219

"The Kingdom of God is not in word, but in power."—1 CORINTHIANS iv. 20.

Preached in St. Mary's, Oxford, 6th November 1881.

17. **Failures in Life** 236

"For I have no man likeminded, who will naturally care for your state. For all seek their own, not the things which are Jesus Christ's."—PHILIPPIANS ii. 20, 21.

Preached in St. Mary's, Oxford, 12th February 1882.

		PAGE
18.	SERVANTS OF GOD	256

    "Paul, a servant of God."—TITUS i. 1.

    Preached in St. Mary's, Oxford, 15th October 1882.

| 19. | THE IMPERFECTIONS OF RELIGIOUS MEN | 274 |

    "Salt is good: but if the salt have lost his savour, wherewith shall it be seasoned?"—ST. LUKE xiv. 34.

    Preached in St. Mary's, Oxford, 10th December 1882.

| 20. | HUMAN LIFE IN THE LIGHT OF IMMORTALITY | 294 |

    "For our light affliction, which is but for a moment, worketh for us a far more exceeding and eternal weight of glory; while we look not at the things which are seen, but at the things which are not seen: for the things which are seen are temporal; but the things which are not seen are eternal."—2 CORINTHIANS iv. 17, 18.

    Preached in Great St. Mary's, Cambridge, 5th October 1882.

I

THE SERIOUSNESS OF LIFE

"To stand before the Son of Man."—St. Luke xxi. 36.

THE season which begins to-day turns our thoughts to the finishing and winding up of all that we are concerned with in our passage here. It turns our thoughts to the question, what will become of it all,—all that we see, all that we do, all that we are? For ourselves, at least, we know that a great break-up is not very far off. We, at least, each in his own way, —we, either abruptly, or by gradual but hardly slow decay, shall pass from the scene and appear here no more. But the interest of life, and of this present state, does not stop at this interruption. That there is something beyond it,—that what is and has been here, runs on by connections, certain however unknown, into what shall be there,—that what has been lost and forgotten here, will assuredly revive and be found in that unknown future,—that the judgments and doings of time have yet to pass under a more searching and complete light than any given us now, —this, which is the unconquerable instinct of conscience, is the assurance which comes to us from the other world. If goodness and right are more than words, if we are not deceived in acknowledging them as standards of our conduct and masters of our life, there is something to come, not only after, but out of and from what we are all of us doing here. And the word which we believe to be of God tells us, with unswerving earnestness and clearness, what that is. It is to be the completion of that law of righteousness, truth, and mercy, which here is both acknowledged and disobeyed. All things, all characters, all deeds, are to pass under the final review of that law. All that will then happen to any of us will be in subordination to the fulfilment of that perfect justice.

In that world to come a judgment waits for all things in this world ; and what is at last to happen to them, and to us all, depends on that judgment. So much was clear in the Old Testament. The Old Testament is chary of speaking of the way in which all this should come to pass. It speaks indeed, but it speaks in mystery, in suggestion, in parable. It speaks so that when our Lord came, the Jews, both the mass of them and the more thoughtful, had learned to believe in a resurrection and a judgment. Yet it speaks so that they who chose to doubt or to deny, could say that it had not forced them to believe; that its hints were not explicit enough for them. But that in some way or another, God, who made the world, should be its Judge, the Old Testament declared beyond mistake. It is the cry from end to end of the Psalms, in every tone, from the most pathetic to the most majestic and most terrible. "Enter not into judgment with Thy servant, for in Thy sight shall no man living be justified." "For He cometh, for He cometh to judge the earth; and with righteousness to judge the world, and the people with His truth." "The Lord, even the most mighty God, hath spoken; and called the world from the rising up of the sun, unto the going down thereof. Out of Sion hath God appeared in perfect beauty. Our God shall come, and shall not keep silence; there shall go before Him a consuming fire, and a mighty tempest shall be stirred up round about Him. He shall call the heaven from above, and the earth, that He may judge His people."

It was the concluding conviction in which the wise Preacher rested, who had passed before his experience all life with its emptiness, and before his mind all thought, its heights, its achievements, and its impotence. "For God shall bring every work into judgment, with every secret thing, whether it be good, or whether it be evil." I need not say that the "coming of the Day of the Lord," with ever increasing clearness in the application to a manifestation of God's righteousness and justice, is the burden of the books of the Prophets. But when that Day should come, and how God should reveal His judgment and Himself as the Judge,—of this, they were not given to teach the Church.

It was kept for the New Dispensation to tell us

the one thing more, which is the last thing we shall ever know about it while we are here. We know now, that the Day and the Judgment of Almighty God mean the judgment-seat of the Son of Man, the judgment-seat of Christ. So far, the vagueness and indistinctness naturally attending this tremendous expectation of judgment, has been limited and partially removed. The Day of God is some period fixed in the Eternal Counsels, which shall end this world. He, from whom judgment is to come over the world, its history, its generations, is He to whom the world once appointed, as His just portion, the Cross; who was crucified for the world. We, all of us, are "to stand before the Son of Man;" it may be, to be accepted; certainly to be judged.

1. Let us then keep this thought before our minds for a short time. The appointed Judge of all men and of ourselves, is Jesus Christ our Lord. The New Testament holds this before us, with a persistent definiteness, which shows that it was meant to leave no room for misunderstanding, and meant, too, to make an impression on us. "God commanded us to preach unto the people,"—these are among St. Peter's first words to Cornelius in fulfilling his new office of communicating the Gospel to the Gentiles: —"and to testify that it is He which was ordained of God to be the Judge of quick and dead." "God hath appointed a day, in the which He will judge the world in righteousness by that man whom He hath ordained," is the concluding announcement of St.

Paul's first exposition of the Gospel Creed to the Athenians who had never heard of Christ. "We shall all stand before the judgment-seat of Christ," is his argument for not judging one another, to the instructed Christians of Rome. And when he tries to bring to seriousness his beloved, but most disappointing Corinthian disciples, he holds up this before them, and before himself, as the central point of that vision of the Unseen which, in all he did, was ever before him,—that "terror of the Lord," which made him sure that, as long as he approved himself to God, men's consciences must acknowledge him, and own his truth. "For we must all appear before the judgment-seat of Christ; that every one may receive the things done in his body, . . . whether good or bad." St. Paul was but repeating the express and emphatic assurances of his Master. "When the Son of Man shall come in His glory, and all the holy angels with Him, then shall He sit upon the throne of His glory: and before Him shall be gathered all nations: and He shall separate them one from another, as a shepherd divideth his sheep from the goats." It might have been thought that words could not be found more certain and more solemn: and yet there are other words which carry us from the actual fact to the reasons in the secret of the Divine appointments. "For the Father judgeth no man, but hath committed all judgment unto the Son: that all men should honour the Son, even as they honour the Father. . . . As the Father hath life in Himself; so hath He given to the Son to have life in Himself; and hath given Him authority to execute judgment also, because He is the Son of Man."

2. Man executes judgment over man; Christ executes judgment, all judgment, "because He is the Son of Man." Bound up with mankind in all things, in man's nature, in man's humiliation, in man's trials, in man's redemption, He it is, who, having taken part with man in his hard and painful training for immortality, closes, as man's Lord and Head and Representative, this first stage of preparation. Man in life and in death, man's one Saviour from sin, man's one helper in the agony and danger of the conflict, He shall declare to men at last, what has been the issue and fruit of these long years of time: from Him, our Brother and our Atonement, we each one of us shall learn what we have done with our life, and what is the very truth about it. And so we know what all those awful auguries of conscience mean which are found even among men who have not heard the name of Christ. So we know what is meant by those unmistakable but undefined fore-warnings in ancient Psalm and Prophecy, that God should judge the world. Here, as in other ways, God is made manifest to us men in the face of Jesus Christ. "No man hath seen God at any time; the only-begotten Son, which is in the bosom of the Father, He hath declared Him." Him, who dwells in the light that none can approach unto,

and whom no man hath seen or can see,—Him, whose name is in the mouths and the prayers of children, but before whom the highest and subtlest thought of man fails and is lost, the Unsearchable, the Incomprehensible, the Infinite, whom the ancient Saints loved and worshipped amid the deeps and the thick darkness of His unknown ways and conditions of Being:—Him, not in word or hearing, but in reality and truth, Him hath Jesus Christ, one with the Father, made us to know, so far as mortality can know Him. The scattered and dispersed rays of His Divine perfection,—in the elder days scattered and dispersed and broken, though all from the one source of light,—were gathered into one perfect revelation of God, when the Eternal Son was made in time the Son of Man; when the Word was made Flesh and dwelt among us, and wrought with human hands, and spoke with human words. In Him were combined and interpreted all that before had been darkly said of the dealings of God with man. From the Incarnation, the undefined words of the Old Testament took shape and definiteness: His glory was reflected back, and lit up its shadows and darkness; in its visions His countenance, at once Divine and Human, looked forth; in the joy and experience of its Psalms, and in the lessons of its Prophecies, His voice was speaking. For had He not come from the Bosom of the Father, to make us know, as only He could make us know, the mind and will of the Father?

3. He is to be our Judge, because in Him man was meant to know God, by whom His creatures must be judged. And He is to be our Judge, also, because He is Man, our Brother, who, like us, has made the passage through life and death; who passed through it that we might be persuaded that He knows what is in man, at his highest and at his lowest: that we might believe that God our Maker "despises not the work of His own hands"; that He loves men, and pities them "as a father doth his children." He with whom we shall all of us have to do, is no unknown Judge,—one whose mind and character, and thoughts, and ways of dealing, are unfamiliar and beyond our guess. In human society, men feel it a trial to their courage when they have to appear in judgment before a stranger, far removed from them in position and habits, who sees not with their eyes, whose standard, whose purposes, whose temper they cannot be certain of: they feel the distance between him and them, the natural want of sympathy, the difference which they cannot measure, between what they think, and what he thinks. No awfulness of human judgment can give the image of the awfulness of the last of all judgment-seats.

But, upon it is seated the "Son of Man." It is that Son of Man, whose name has been to every soul of man that has heard of Him, the sign and promise of a self-sacrificing love, which in the soberest and severest earnest, passeth knowledge, passeth all understanding. It is that Son of Man whose life and ways we may all of us know so well; no stranger to us, nor speaking language which finds no echo in our hearts; but One whose words have transformed the world, and can never more pass from the households and homes of men. It is that Son of Man, who brought mercy and healing wherever He turned His steps; who was not afraid or ashamed of the vilest who came to Him, and who forgave where forgiveness could least be looked for; who accepted what flesh and blood most shrink from, who bore our sicknesses and endured our temptations, and whose love neither unthankfulness, nor failure, nor the depths of His own anguish, nor the depths of human wickedness, could quench. It is that Son of Man, of whose loving-kindness and mercy, of whose readiness to help and to forgive, we make so sure in our prayers; in whose merits we trust, and by whose intercession we plead; to whose wonderful acts in our behalf we are continually appealing; whose ever-blessed name comes first to our lips in the time of our direst need, the last hope of the despairing, the sweetest comfort to dying ears. It is that Son of Man to whom we all know that even here, we may draw so near—" He in us, and we in Him "—in the Sacrament of His Body and Blood, where to those who will, He continues, in mystery yet in truth, the special grace of His Presence;—it is He, whom in the most solemn moments of prayer, we dare to invoke by words which could only be used of One who had given all for men—" O Lamb of God, that takest away the sins of the world, have mercy upon us . . . grant us thy peace . . . receive our prayer." It is He, the Crucified, the Advocate, the Reconciler, —He who still feeds us with His Flesh and Blood, —it is He, who, we believe, shall come to be our Judge.

4. That is the law under which we are all living our lives. We are *once* really to be judged in earnest: *once* in the course of our existence we must know ourselves to be in the presence of the Son of Man. How, and with what circumstances, beyond the awful outline of what is told us, it is vain to inquire, it is impossible to imagine. When the assembled company of the dead, the multitude without number of souls, each with its own history and character and fate, stand in judgment before Christ, all will be so wholly changed in the manner of existence, that no vision framed with the materials of our present experience could adequately represent the truth. There will be unimaginable and transcendent majesty: there will be the Presence and sight of the Son of Man. There will be judgment, there will be separation. But the thing is, that before that Presence of Christ, in some way or another, each one of us has to pass, to be made manifest, to be judged.

What a thought is this, that each human life is at last, in its turn, to be brought face to face with

Christ, to be measured with His measure, to be contrasted with what we know Him to be. We know what He is, the preacher of the Beatitudes and the Sermon on the Mount, the "meek and lowly in heart," the "Holy One and the just," the Crucified for sin. Think what it must be, no longer to read of that life in a book, and look at it at our leisure at a distance, but to feel ourselves without escape, confronted with its Presence. And yet this is what is to come, if words mean anything. Think of what human lives will look like when He questions them. I say nothing of the great open sins, the great sinners, the great criminals of the world. I know nothing more awful than when we meet with them in experience or in history, to think what they will look like—the destroyers, the betrayers, the seducers, the cruel, the sensual, they who have claimed the world and human life for their selfishness, the great conspirators against the virtue, the rights, the peace, the hopes of man,—what they will look like when they stand for judgment in the Presence of the Lamb of God. I speak not of them. But what will the carelessness, the negligence, the idleness, the improvidence of our quiet homely lives look like? What is certain is that we shall have to go through a trial, most considerate and pitiful to imperfection, but most stern to deceit and neglect. We have to come to it, not with works and merits, but with a soul trained, exercised, disciplined, prepared; to come to it with a character and a life. And what shall we do that the character may show some likeness of our Master, that the life may be fruitful and consistent? Is it not so, that we too often let ourselves drift along at random, taking no trouble with ourselves to shape our course; taking no trouble to keep off the things which we know hurt our integrity; shrinking from effort, shrinking from forethought, shrinking from self-knowledge? And yet, we poor helpless souls, floating about according as the current takes us, have to face our Master's sentence on us. We talk and criticise one another loosely, without knowledge, without necessity, without restraint, knowing what He has said about idle words, and the danger of judging. We walk about the streets, we plunge into amusement, we let our eyes and our thoughts wander where they will and where they ought not, knowing what He has said about keeping the eyes and the heart pure, knowing that we are wounding our consciences, knowing that however firm against temptation we think ourselves, we are letting in what defiles the springs of life, and breaks down our self-mastery. The sin, the pain, the wretchedness, the want of the world is round us; we forget, forget for want of thinking, that there is something which we could do to help it, that Christ Himself is calling to us, in the persons of the poor and the helpless. What lives are these, so purposeless, so misdirected, so ungoverned, so left to the accidents of each day, to come in review one by one, before that Son of Man, who is so awful because He is so merciful and so true,—so awful, because He knows and feels for us so perfectly. He knows what our excuses really mean; and that men fail because they will not try.

In His three awful Parables of the Judgment, our Lord has set before us in different ways, what it is that will be accepted, what it is that will be refused. What is it that will be accepted? Watchfulness, faithfulness to opportunities, a ready eye and heart to do service to those who need it. What are the fatal signs of reprobation? It is remarkable that He does not dwell on great and open wickedness, on manifest crying sins. These need no warning. But the five foolish slothful virgins, the slack easy-going servant, who hid his talent and thought it did not matter, the people who are surprised that He should charge them with want of willingness to help Him, because they did not discern Him in common, every-day, human suffering:—these are the types of what He pronounces ruinous to hope. Is it not a very tremendous thought that they are so like the lives of so many of mankind?

We have to stand before the Son of Man—before Him whose life and labours and death, whose very coming down to be made man, and to be one of us, have made every human life so inexpressibly serious in its career and its results. A great master of science, and a great master of language, who can see nothing in this world beyond the stern powers of Nature, has imaged human life under the likeness of a game to be lost or won.[1] "Suppose," he says, "it were perfectly certain that the life and future of every one of us would, one day or other, depend on his winning or losing a game at chess.... The chess-board is the world, the pieces are the phenomena of the universe, the rules of the game are what we call the laws of Nature. The player on the other side is hidden from us. We know that his play is always fair, just, patient. But we know, to our cost, that he never overlooks a mistake, or makes the smallest allowance for ignorance. To the man who plays well, the highest stakes are paid with that overflowing generosity with which the strong shows delight in strength; and one who plays ill is checkmated—without haste, but without remorse. My metaphor will remind you of the famous picture in which the Evil One is depicted playing a game of chess with man for his soul. Substitute for the mocking fiend in that picture a calm strong angel, playing, as we say, for love, and who would rather lose than win, and I should accept it as the image of human life."—Translate Nature into the living and loving Son of Man. Substitute for the calm strong angel of fancy, the Crucified seated at the Right Hand of God till the last hour of the world; willing all men to be saved, but unable to save men against their will; with His infinite compassion and His inexorable justice; substitute for the pitiless laws of nature the law and discipline of the Spirit, the dispensation of

---

[1] Huxley, *Lay Sermons*, p. 31.

remedy and restoration, the blessed possibilities of repentance, the sweet hopes and strength of grace, and we too, I suppose, must accept that awful image as the image of human life, as it will be seen when all is over,—when we stand before the Son of Man.

May He, the all-merciful, the true, who is so boundless in His care and love for human hearts, help us in His wonderful and unsearchable ways, to clear these hearts of ours from all self-deceits and self-indulgence; these wills of ours, so wayward and unstable, yet charged with all our fate, from pretending to be weaker than they are. O brethren, we who have to do with such a Lord, and such a Judge, and such a destiny, let us not blind ourselves to what we are about now, to where we shall one day have to stand. Now, in this hour, this short hour of waiting, may that precious blood, by which we were all redeemed, win us, cleanse us, heal us, strengthen us. May it be given us, when the veil is rent, and this dream of life is passed, to see His Face, to endure His Judgment, and to enter into His Eternal Joy.

II

THE CERTAINTY OF JUDGMENT

"In the day when God shall judge the secrets of men by Jesus Christ according to my gospel."—ROMANS ii. 16.

THE Gospel, like all that we know of God's world and government, comes with the twofold aspect of mercy and severity. Mercy, not in words or notions, but in realities; severity, not in words or threats, but in certainties. On the one side, mercy beyond thought or imagination of man, such as that the Son of God, God our Creator, became man out of love for man, and died to save us; on the other, severity, as that all the evil which is so familiar to us in history and society, all that we know is wrong, all that we shrink from remembering, all our self-deceit, all our imperfections, must sooner or later really pass under the judgment of the All-seeing, the Most Just, the Most Holy. As in Nature so in the Gospel, these two great aspects of truth pass successively before us, each in its own certainty and completeness, almost as if they belonged to separate and opposite dispensations. We know that they are but different sides of the one Divine Government: we know it, but we cannot always see it. They are like the summits of mountain ranges deep below the sea; the summits rise into distinct and far-parted islands; but the foundations are out of sight under the waters, and we cannot trace the connecting links. With our limited faculties, our common inability to take in and grasp together facts and truths of different orders which seem to clash, we have to contemplate each by itself, if we wish fully to comprehend its length and breadth and greatness. Here in Church they come before us, each in its appointed season and consecrated services. Soon it will be the time to give ourselves to the thought of that ineffable grace which showed us the Maker and Saviour of mankind as the little Child at Bethlehem. Now it is the time to deepen in our souls the sense of the truth that a time is before us when the Son of God shall come to be our Judge,—Judge of all things, Judge of all men.

1. No one can read the New Testament without seeing that, to impress this ineffaceably on the convictions and the conscience of mankind, was one of the primary objects of the teaching which it records. In the definiteness and prominence there given to this announcement, it is, notwithstanding all that had been spoken by ancient Psalmists and Sages and Prophets, almost a new feature in religion. The instinct, the foreboding, the augury, the vision, —the misgiving from which there was no escape, the assured hope of a generous and loyal faith,— were now turned into explicit disclosures, coming

from the very bosom of God, and repeated without intermission by His messengers, as something which mankind had never heard with such serious certainty before. Their Master had held up this as the last and supreme part of the work He was sent to do, the upshot and close of His human ministry, the final function of His office to mankind. He, who while here on earth declined to exercise the office of judgment,—" I judge no man,"—not even him who hears My words and believes not,—" for I came not to judge the world, but to save the world;" He, when all is done, is to be the representative and minister of the Father's judgment. "For the Father judgeth no man, but hath committed all judgment unto the Son; . . . and hath given Him authority to execute judgment also, because He is the Son of Man." The Day of Christ is the explanation and realising of that ancient and awful foreshadowing of prophecy, "The Day of the Lord." The coming of the Son of Man to judgment was the solemn mysterious theme of His own farewell prophecies. His last parable to His disciples is a picture of that day, and its separations. His last words to the High Priest on the earthly seat of judgment appeal to that day, with all that it shall discover and reverse. The last voices from Heaven, when He went away, were the assurance of His coming again, "This same Jesus, which is taken up from you into heaven, shall so come in like manner as ye have seen Him go into heaven." Is it wonderful that such words roused the eager expectation, the profound interest of the first believers? Is it wonderful that they who had to tell the world what He had done, and who He was, went on to dwell, with mingled hope and awe, on what He was yet to do? Is it wonderful that, for a long while, they should have lived in immediate expectation of His return; that this awful prospect should have occurred to them as the natural check on "idle words and thoughts of ill;" as the natural support against the tyranny of evil custom? "Be patient, brethren, unto the coming of the Lord:" "Stablish your hearts: for the coming of the Lord draweth nigh:" "Grudge not one against another, brethren, lest ye be condemned: behold, the Judge standeth before the door:" Run not with the Gentile revellers to their excess of riot, heed not their mockeries, "who shall give account to Him that is ready to judge the quick and the dead:" "The end of all things is at hand: be ye therefore sober, and watch unto prayer." Is it wonderful that they reiterated with such persistent emphasis their Lord's announcement, and made it in their preaching one of the first principles and foundations of the "doctrine of Christ:" that in every record of their early sermons this stands a chief and unvarying feature: that St. Peter's account to Cornelius of the message he was charged with, is, that he was commanded "to preach to the people, and to testify" that Jesus Christ, the Crucified and Risen, "was ordained of God to be the Judge of quick and dead:" that St. Paul's argument, whether to the powerful and business-like Roman governor, or to the philosophical triflers of Athens, was still eternal judgment: men were now to repent, "Because God hath appointed a day, in the which He will judge the world in righteousness by that Man whom He hath ordained; whereof He hath given assurance unto all men, in that He hath raised Him from the dead?" Is it wonderful that it should have taken possession of a mind like St. Paul's, in all the clearness and vivid power of the idea, in its universality, its unsparing unveiling of all "the secrets of men," its hopes and its terrors, its pathetic, its tragic consequences, its glories too overpowering to think of? Is it wonderful that it should be the background of the most earnest adjuration, "I charge thee therefore before God, and the Lord Jesus Christ, who shall judge the quick and the dead at His appearing and His kingdom; preach the word;"—that it should be the basis of an appeal for patient and self-distrusting thoughts, "therefore judge nothing before the time, until the Lord come, who both will bring to light the hidden things of darkness, and will make manifest the counsels of the hearts"? Is it wonderful that his intense appreciation of its certainty, of its inevitableness, of its steady and sure approach, should have expanded into that terrible vision of the judgment of God on the corruption and degradation of mankind, on which he lays the foundation of the Epistle to the Romans? "The day of wrath and revelation of the righteous judgment of God; who will render to every man according to his deeds . . . tribulation and anguish, upon every soul of man that doeth evil, of the Jew first, and also of the Gentile ; but glory, honour, and peace, to every man that worketh good, to the Jew first, and also to the Gentile : for there is no respect of persons with God : . . . in the day when God shall judge the secrets of men by Jesus Christ, according to my gospel."

2. So thought, so lived, St. Peter, St. John, St. Paul. They thought that all that they did, and that all the good and evil of the world, now and from the beginning, was not merely the subject of immediate approval or condemnation by the Infinite and Invisible God, but was sooner or later, in some definite and awful way, to pass under the judgment of One, whom men have seen and known, whom *we* must see and know : of One who was man, as we are,— who lived and died and rose from the dead,—the most pure, most merciful, most just ; whom, once in the course of our existence, each of us is to meet face to face. The Christian Church has received that great truth, that great idea, at their hands. Except to those who deny the Christian creed altogether, there is no dispute about it.

And who denies it ? What Christian doubts it ? Ay, my brethren, but suffer the further question : who believes it ? Who, at all adequately, thinks what it means ? I am not asking whether we are continually thinking the thoughts of the first Saints of the Gospel. I am not asking whether we habitually realise, in every instant and action of life, what we shall feel when we are dying, and after death, in judgment. But so great and so certain an event in our future existence ought surely to fill a large part in our thoughts now. Without "winding" ourselves "too high" for what is possible, or real, or safe, there must be occasions without number, when such a prospect as judgment ought naturally to present itself; when it would seem the most serious and reasonable thing to ask, how will this conduct, how will this transaction, how will this state of feeling or temper look under the light of Christ's judgment? We all know what it is, for men charged with great affairs, entrusted with difficult and momentous duties, to live under the abiding sense of a grave responsibility, which is, at once, a spur and a check; which, though they do not allow it to weigh them down, is ever ready to present itself at critical moments, to direct and determine choice, to be a counter charm to selfishness or negligence. We all know what it is, when men have to look forward to explaining an entangled and dubious past before a clear-sighted and unsparing tribunal. We know how we feel, and what we think, when amid the imperfection of human actions, the perplexities and complications of human motives, a strict account is exacted from us. Conscience may be reasonably and honestly at ease; it may know nothing against us but what is fairly covered by human infirmity; but judgment, however we have to meet it, is an anxious thing; and men do not meet it here with indifference and lightness. This is, I suppose, our experience in matters of this life. Do we feel anything like it, in respect to that judgment which awaits us and all mankind, and which is as certain in the future as the Passion of our Lord is certain in the past? Is the recollection of that great day of account, that great clearing up of secrets, that great revealing of the truth, present to us when it ought to rise up before our minds, to warn, to govern, to quicken thought and word?

3. Consider one or two points. All that is past and done with now in human history, has one day to be revived and to be recalled into living and most eventful interest, at the judgment of the Great Day. All these men and women who figure in the rolls of time, whose reality seems to have passed away as if they were but mere characters in a story,—whose deeds, and purposes, and goodness or wickedness, we sit in judgment on, and dissect, and guess at, and on which without scruple we pronounce our sentence,—whose names we make free with, and cover with admiration or insult, and invest with an imaginary personality, and call up before our fancy to make us sport,—all these, the great, the noble, the saintly, the base, kings and conquerors, statesmen and rulers, famous queens and empresses, the saviours and the betrayers of nations, the mischief-makers and the peacemakers, the shadowy lords of the ancient world, Pharaohs and Cæsars, the well-

known lords of the modern world, sage and poet and artist, the discoverers of new lands, the inventors of new knowledge, the great judges and painters and satirists of man,—all were once drawing living breath as we do now, all are lying in their graves as we shall be soon. And how many of us think, and how often, that all this great multitude are surely going with ourselves to a real and final judgment? It might sometimes increase, if not the charities of history, at least the caution and soberness of history, if we remembered that beyond the tribunal of opinion, beyond the tribunal of posterity, is the tribunal of Jesus Christ. All this is not, as it seems to us, done with; what is known of it, what is unknown and uncertain, will be one day heard of again: the deed and the work, now so far separated from the doer,—the word, good or bad, wholesome or corrupting, purifying or defiling, now so far removed from its author, have still once more to meet and to be united to those from whom they came, who are responsible for them. That tremendous catalogue, "the sins of the whole world," passed away and vanished as they seem, have once more to find out the sinners who did them. All that is forgotten, from the beginning of the world, good or bad, has to come to remembrance. This is the state of things of which we too, in our generation, form a part, and have our lot, and have to remember its inexorable conditions.

4. It is not easy, unless we take pains to do so, to grasp this idea of judgment on individuals. But the

Bible puts before us another, and even more difficult side of this idea of judgment—judgment on men collectively, on nations and kingdoms and churches. It is an idea which lies at the bottom of the very structure of the Bible, the Old Testament and the New, and is closely interwoven with its teaching. National or collective righteousness and faithfulness, national sin and crime, are very real things in the Bible. Empires, cities, peoples, churches, have a character, and are the subjects of moral judgment, like individual men. The great monarchies and seats of power of the old world, Egypt, Assyria, Babylon, Rome,—pass before us, marked by God's judgment on the moral qualities and standards which appear in their history,—their pride, their insolence, their injustice, their cruelty, their dissolute luxury. The fortunes and fate of Israel hung on what, as a nation, they chose, and refused, and did. The Christian Churches of the New Testament have their distinct features, and responsibilities, and dangers, and warnings. The Apocalyptic Babylon perishes in the vengeance on her monstrous crimes. Doubtless, before the Judgment-seat of Christ, men will be judged as individuals; but among the things of which individuals must expect to give account, is their share in the collective character of the societies to which they have belonged. Even we can see, in history, the reality of national characteristics, vague as may be their outline; the bad faith of one state, the ambition of another, the craft, the profligacy, the dishonesty of a third. We can put our finger on this or that, not merely individual, but public crime. And can we doubt that the Judge of all the earth will find out a way to bring home the righteousness of His judgment to every one in his own order, whom that judgment strikes? Can we believe that Jesus Christ will take no account of the tens of thousands slaughtered by the great destroyers of mankind; of the ruin and desolation of the earth where their armies passed? And will He take account of the cruelties, the sins of an Attila or a Tamerlane, and take none of what Christians have done in their hardheartedness, their ambition, their folly? Can we believe that He whose words were so terrible against the pride of Egypt and Babylon, against that haughty insolence in men, on which not Hebrew prophets only, but the heathen poets of Greece looked with such peculiar and profound alarm,—that He will not visit it on those who, in their measure, are responsible for its words and temper, when it takes possession of a Christian nation? Can we doubt what His judgment will one day be on the cynical parade of exclusive selfishness, the cynical worship of mere dexterity and adroitness, in the sophists and tyrants of the old heathen world; and can we doubt what He will think when Christians, disciples of the Lord of truth and righteousness, let themselves be dazzled in matters of right and wrong, by the cleverness of intellectual fence, and refuse to face the question, however strongly forced upon them, whether what is so specious and so brilliant, is true and just? The history of the world proves that such public sins are no imaginary evils; they are mischiefs which always threaten, and sometimes invade, every state which is prosperous and strong. And they are as surely to be answered for before the tribunal of Jesus Christ, as the private sins of men.

Once more, then, let us ask ourselves how much, and how really, we believe in the Judgment-seat of our Lord. Before we finally reach our rest, the goal of our existence, two things have to be gone through by all,—one on this side of the grave, the other beyond it. But both are so inevitable, so real, so awful, that reasonable men may well think much about them. "It is appointed unto all men," says the Epistle to the Hebrews, "once to die, but after this, the judgment." To die, to go through dying, to feel the sundering of all the ties of life, the extinction of all earthly hope, the parting from all that we have known and loved, will be awful enough, if we have consciousness to know it. But then, on the other side, there must further be that which need not be, which certainly is not always, even in dying,—the scrutiny, the revealing, certain, impossible to hush up or disguise, of our real selves, of what we are and have done,—not in this or that department of life and duty, as now, perhaps, we choose to fancy it,—but throughout, it may be, where we least look for it. We must be face to face with perfect goodness,— with all, indeed, that we have to hope from perfect goodness, but with all that we have to fear from perfect goodness; as strong and true as it is merciful, but not to be deceived, not to be bribed.

Let us not shut our eyes to what must be. In this waiting time of our trial, amid the storms of life, or in its sunshine, let us, from time to time, seriously cast our thoughts forward; and let us lift up our hearts to our Deliverer and Judge, that His Light and Grace may help us to see clearly and truly. "We believe that Thou shalt come to be our Judge: we therefore pray Thee, help Thy servants, whom Thou hast redeemed with Thy precious blood." "In all time of our tribulation, in all time of our wealth, in the hour of death, in the day of judgment, Good Lord, deliver us." "O Lord most holy, O God most mighty, O holy and most merciful Saviour, Thou most worthy Judge Eternal, suffer us not, at our last hour, for any pains of death, to fall from Thee."

III

HUMAN JUDGMENT AND DIVINE

"Let both grow together until the harvest."—St. Matthew xiii. 30.

There are two great currents of human action going on in the world, which are represented in this parable by the wheat and the tares. And there are also two great currents of judgment on what is going on upon the stage of the world, running side by side as the world's history is unfolded;—human judgment, with all its many variations, its infinite changes in character and force, its right decisions and its mistakes, its contradictions and collisions, its returns upon itself; human judgment here below, as peremptory and loud as it is fallible;—and above, the judgment, the unceasing, all-knowing judgment of God. It must sometimes come home to us how strange, how awful, how mysterious is the contrast between these two great masses and volumes of judgment which are ever going on, never for a moment interrupted, whenever men think and observe and decide, and than which nothing can be imagined more important in what concerns mankind and individual men. Let us, for the short time we can give to it, consider it.

1. And first, of human judgment, of what I have called the great perpetual current and manifestation of man's judgment on all things round him, on his fellows, on his circumstances, on himself and his life and duty. We are always judging. It is a principal and necessary part of our thoughts, of our business, of our conversation. And it is, obviously, a principal thing in what governs and determines what happens among us; our good and our evil, our happiness or our wretchedness. As we judge justly or unjustly, as we judge rightly or wrongly, so, in a great measure, though not altogether, do things go well or ill among us. But besides this serious and effective judgment, there is a huge amount of judging which has no bearing on the course of things, which is simply futile and empty and wasted breath, because it is so idle, so ignorant, so foolish. But, all the same, there it is as a fact, asserting itself, intruding itself, affecting to settle the most difficult questions, and to pass the most irreversible dooms. Just think, as your imagination may help you to do so, of the hubbub and confusion of judgments which go up all day long over all the earth. From morning to night we are all of us passing judgment: we are passing judgment on the dead and the living, on those the most remote and the most unknown to us, and on those who are close to us, on the things we know best, and on the things of which we know nothing. Men, and classes, and nations, throw back their judgments, one at another, as if they were the

most real and unquestionable certainties, about which no one could doubt. West judges east, and east judges west,—each with equal confidence, each on grounds which are held to be clear and strong. Rich judge poor, and poor judge rich, family judges family, and neighbourhood judges neighbourhood, and party judges party. The learned judge the practical and the busy, the busy and practical the learned. Nothing escapes, nothing daunts criticism, that is, the passing of judgment about which the judges do not doubt. Judgment means the pronouncing on what a thing really is, and the application to it of a rule, and standard, and law, which we assume to be beyond dispute. To this rule and standard we are for ever bringing not only actions and opinions, but whole courses of conduct, with all their intricate train of accompanying events, and what we call dispositions and characters, with their endless lights and shades, their perplexing contradictions, their terrible or pathetic mysteries. All comes naturally within our range of judgment: on all, we seriously or lightly, conscientiously or carelessly, wisely or stupidly, fairly or unfairly, exercise our judgment. We cannot help it. It is part of our lives.

And all this makes a great noise in the world. These judgments swell into what is called public opinion,—the great force which has to do with the changes of society and institutions, which settles what shall stand and what shall fall. They accumulate into the traditions, the moral standards of a society or a generation, its governing beliefs, its tyrannical usages. And in private life and affairs, this unceasing and universal habit of judging appears in all the manifold incidents of our relations and intercourse, as members of a family, or a body, as friends, or acquaintances, as working with, or working against others, as indifferent lookers on, as in accidental contact with them. From morning to night we are judging what they do, and what they are; and they are judging us. Out of it grow our preferences, our admirations, our likings and dislikings, our life-long friendships: it expresses itself in our strong words of approval and condemnation, it hardens into our bitter animosities, our unconquerable antipathies. A case of conduct comes before us, and whether it is our duty to judge it, or only our amusement and our pastime, we judge it. A person, with all those things that make one man different from another,—his special qualities, his habits and purposes and ways,—comes before us, and we judge him. And this is not here and there, or now and then, but all day long and everywhere, as a matter of course, with every one. It is part of the necessary system of the world: we see clearly that without this exercise of human judgment, in its many forms, the world could not go on.

And a great deal of it is righteous, wise, salutary judgment; judgment which supports what is good, which directs what is just and right, which brands and confounds evil. The quality of human judgment is as various as the objects on which it is exercised. There is responsible judgment and irresponsible, there is deliberate and well-informed judgment, and there is off-hand and cruelly ignorant judgment. But besides what is reasonable and deliberate in judgment, there is a vast mass of judging with no purpose, with no control, and of which nothing is meant to come or can come, except perhaps mischief.

And *what* judging! What amazing and easy generalisations from the slenderest facts! What recklessness of evidence! What ingenious constructions put on the simplest and the most imaginary appearances! What defiant confidence and certainty, coupled with the grossest indifference to the actual truth, and the grossest negligence to ascertain it! What superb facility in penetrating and divining hidden corruption of motives for unavowed ends!

I say again, *what* judging is that of which we have so much experience, if we will be honest, in ourselves. In vain St. James warns us of what is the truth,—" if any man seem to be religious, and bridleth not his tongue, but deceiveth his own heart." In vain he exhausts every daring image to impress on us the sin that the tongue can commit, and the mischief that the tongue can do: the "world of iniquity," the "fire," which "setteth on fire the course of nature, and it is set on fire of hell:" the serpent's poison-bag of death. In vain, more calmly, he expostulates with him who takes into his hands the function of the great Giver of the Law: "Who art thou that judgest another?" In vain a greater than St. James has left on record the command which might make the best of us tremble: "Judge not, that ye be not judged. For with what judgment ye judge ye shall be judged, and with what measure ye mete it shall be measured to you again." In vain. What care we? The rushing flood of human judgment goes on in spite of it; and we are carried away, as at other times, when the temptation comes. Human judging in all its forms, good and bad, goes on its course, sometimes tested and checked by events, confirmed or falsified by them; but, in the greater portion of it, without control, too satisfied with itself to doubt of its certainty and truth, to suspect error, to need any warrant beyond itself.

2. There will come a day when all this course of human judgment will meet another current of judgment, which has been going on all the while on exactly the same things, exactly as widely, exactly as unceasingly. While we have been judging, and without check, and sometimes without care and thought, announcing our opinion,—absolving and condemning, with little doubt of our being right, God, too, has been watching, and hearing, and judging. As each case came before us, and we pronounced on it, it came, too, before Him, and He judged it. Little has in one way or another escaped human judgment; nothing has escaped His.

And He has also judged the judgment and the judges, as well as that on which they pronounced. And did His judgment agree with theirs?

There are cases, we hope not a few, where we may sincerely and reasonably trust that the judgment of man, given as he was bound to give it, and given as best he could give it, with no sparing for himself of trouble and self-restraint, with full remembrance of the law of right and truth which is above us all,— that that judgment of man was in accordance with the judgment of God. We may trust when a man judges in all things, great and small, under the control and check of conscience, when he is in the habit of remembering his words, and proportions their force or their severity to what he really knows, and what he believes to be right, that even mistaken judgments may, for the sake of their intention, receive a favourable construction from Him, who, as a great writer says, "understandeth us all, better than we understand one another."[1] But what of all the loose, random, negligent judging,—judging without thought, judging without examination? I say nothing of the cruel, spiteful, merciless judging; that is a different matter. I say nothing of the kindly, innocent, playful, harmless judging, which may go on in the unsuspicious intercourse of the gentlest and the most self-commanding. But the judging that we do without much troubling ourselves on what grounds it really rests, and whether

[1] Spedding's *Life of Bacon*, vol. iv. 10; letter to T. Matthew.

it does really answer to the truth and facts within our reach or whether it is on things which we cannot know;—what of that? How much of that agrees with the judgment of God, passed at the same moments, passed on the same things?

There will come a day when the two currents of judgment will meet, will be compared one with another. But that is not now. *Now*, we hear and know all about human judgment; it does not hide itself, it wishes to be heard; the world is full of its noise, its self-assertion. On the one hand is the loud speaking of human judgment, on the other, the silence of the Divine. And what would we give sometimes to know what it is!

A course of action presents itself, a choice of a life, and what sometimes seems, sometimes seems not, a call: or a hard question of right or wrong, a decision which may involve the good of thousands, or the fortunes of a church, which may do justice in a great wrong, or may do terrible injustice. We do what we can with our reasons, with our comparisons and balancings, with our highest motives and strongest guards against self-deceit;—but after all, what would we give to know what He thinks of it, and of us. Voices there are in plenty all round us, voices of all kinds: voices that perplex us and bid us hesitate, voices that mock us, voices on both sides, urgent and positive and clamorous, that tell us that all is clear and beyond doubt. But the heavens are silent. We know that the Judge of all the earth has passed His judgment, but what it is we know not: this is not the time to know. The rule in this, as in the lives and actions of men, is still the same:—" Let both grow together until the harvest." Then we shall know, but not before. He has left us ample means of surmising, of forecasting, of gathering, on the strongest grounds, what His judgment is. In Holy Scripture He sets before us a mirror of His judgment; He has made known to us the great principles on which He judges men. In our conscience His light reveals itself, and in the secret and deep of our heart of hearts, we may know, if we will, with a strange and mysterious assurance, what is the right thing and the best. Every man who dares to examine himself truthfully will find what real means he has for honest judgment; for judgment with which he is not afraid to ask God to judge him. Perhaps some secret sign may come, in the coincidences or events of life, which, to him, seems to convey the indication that he has been right or has been wrong. But it is to him alone, and even to him faintly and darkly. But to the outward and present world, God's judgment reserves itself. "Let both grow together until the harvest," the judgments of man, and the judgments of God.

All around is silence, while men take their great decisions, or while they waste their hours of intercourse and conversation in harsh and idle and unchecked judging, as if it were one of the indulgences and delights of life. Nature, all round them, speaks no word, the heavens look down unmoved and still, while men know, if they choose, what they are doing, while they play their part on this scene of life. They have it all their own way, if they choose to forget the things which they do not see, and the words which were spoken, once for all, by God's love and wisdom, but which are heard from Him no more. So, to the end, man will go on his way, and God's way and order remain the same. There are few more awful words in the Bible than these: "These things hast thou done, and I kept silence; thou thoughtest that I was altogether such an one as thyself: but I will reprove thee, and set them in order before thine eyes." But now, "Let both grow together until the harvest."

When we think of these two great lines of judgment together, and of their issue when finally compared and contrasted, it is impossible not to feel with anxious misgiving, what a reversal there may be at last, of many human judgments, even the gravest and the best, much more of the careless and the trifling; remembering those awful words by which our Lord warned men of the surprises of the Last Day: "Many that are first shall be last, and the last first." There is so much inevitable ignorance in our judgments now, so much mistake, so much exaggeration in what we praise and in what we condemn; so much good of which we know and imagine nothing, so much evil of which we know nothing; such strength of virtue which we never suspect, never give men credit for, such depths of sin which perhaps here are never found out:—who can doubt what awful discrepancies will, in many cases, appear between God's judgments and ours, beyond the veil? It is indeed a prospect to give us something to think of.

We go on saying our words, passing our judgments,—at length we say our last words, and we pass away from the earth: and still, He is silent. You know how anxious is the feeling of knowing that a judgment has been formed of us, and waiting, not knowing what it is, what it will turn out to be. That is our case, really, literally; with hope, indeed, and strength and encouragement; hope beyond what man's words can dare to speak, or his thoughts to imagine. But how God's judgments agree with ours we shall know one day, but now we must wait to know.

3. Doubtless as long as we live here, a great deal of human judging there must be. It is, at best, a dangerous trade, but we were meant to exercise our faculty of judging, and to form an estimate of men and things and actions. The moral atmosphere cannot be kept pure and clean, unless there is keen and fearless, and, if necessary, unsparing judgment. Yet such necessary judgment does not belong to everybody, nor to every day; and we cannot mistake what our Lord thought of unnecessary judgment, judgment which gives us no trouble, and costs us no pain, and serves perhaps to pass an idle hour. Do you think it a paradox to say that we can go

on without judging? Oh, believe it, there are persons who go through life with this restraint and bridle on their tongue, who are able to refrain from speaking idle judgments. I don't say that they never break the law of justice and charity: they would not be men if they were so happy: but they do live with it ever before their eyes, and when they break it, it makes them suffer.

But there is one thing which we can do more safely: we can turn that faculty of judgment on ourselves. We are proud of it, perhaps, proud of our penetration and sharp-sightedness: we see through appearances, we are not to be taken in with plausible shows. There is, perhaps, some character before us, among the living or the dead, which imposes on the world. We have detected its hidden unsoundness, we have unravelled its folds and disguises, we have discovered how much that is base and poor is mixed up with its attractive elements. Or again,—such and such a cause or enterprise comes before us: behind all its fair promises and noble professions, we have pierced to the secret spring, the unavowed motive and purpose, which makes it all hollow and bad. We may thus have done what is right and what is useful. But there is still something to be done for ourselves. Let us turn that light now on ourselves, that power of discriminating and illuminating judgment. Let us apply to serious questions about ourselves and our own characters, that subtlety, that shrewdness, that wise suspiciousness, that refusal to be deceived and imposed upon, which we have shown outside of ourselves. Let us turn upon our own consciences that unsparing honesty, that readiness to expose equivocations, that quick sense of unreality, which has made us, perhaps formidable, perhaps useful, to those around us. Let us, in examining our own spirits and motives, be the same clever and quick-sighted judges that we were when we judged of others. We may learn there, perhaps, what is more important for us to know than the faults and mistakes of others. There, at least, the materials for judging are within our reach.

And yet, even that inner judgment on ourselves, if it dared to be final, would be presumptuous. St. Paul bids us judge ourselves: yet St. Paul does not venture to judge even himself, as he knows that God will at last judge him. Even he, with his conscience clear, shrinks from anticipating what will be the judgment on him, when God breaks His silence. " With me it is a very small thing that I should be judged of you, or of man's judgment: yea, I judge not mine own self. For I know nothing by (or against) myself; yet am I not hereby justified: but He that judgeth me is the Lord. Therefore judge nothing before the time, until the Lord come, who both will bring to light the hidden things of darkness, and will make manifest the counsels of the hearts: and then shall every man have praise of God."

After our best and most honest judgment on ourselves, we can but appeal to Him who knows us as we are. "Judge me, O Lord my God, according to Thy righteousness." "Try me, O God, and seek the ground of my heart; prove me, and examine my thoughts."—May the great and righteous Judge, the certainty of whose coming we are thinking of to-day, and who knows the contrast between our judging and His own, teach us the secret, and give us the grace, to judge ourselves truly; and may He forgive us, for indeed it is a serious matter, all the rash, and ignorant, and bitter, and unnecessary judgments which we may have passed on others.

IV

THE CONDESCENSION OF OUR LORD

"He humbled Himself."—PHILIPPIANS ii. 8.

CHRISTMAS is a time of rejoicing, and its rejoicing is like no other rejoicing in the year. We rejoice at Easter; but at Easter it is rejoicing in the presence, and under the awe, of death. But at Christmas we rejoice as children rejoice. All looks light, and we all feel gay: we defy the storms and cold outside, and do not think of the shadows.

But still, that which is the foundation of all our rejoicing is an awful and overpowering fact,—as awful, as overpowering, as those facts which we have before us at Easter. "He humbled Himself." This most wonderful event in the course of God's dealings with His creatures, is at the bottom of all we say and think of now. It is the spring of Christmas joy as well as of Easter peace. It is sometimes almost disguised by things which appeal to our feelings as members of households and homes, which come to us with associations of all that is tender and sweet and beautiful, with thoughts of the mother and the little Child, of the angels singing in the midnight sky, and the worshipping shepherds, and the wise men from the East offering their gifts;—of the Gloria in Excelsis, and the Magnificat, and the Nunc Dimittis. But underneath all this lies this most solemn and austere of truths, "He humbled Himself." It is not out of place at Christmas to meditate for a few minutes on this truth.

"He humbled Himself." "Being in the form of God," He "made Himself of no reputation,—He emptied Himself,—and took upon Him the form of a servant, and was made in the likeness of men; and being found in fashion as a man, He humbled Himself." This is St. Paul's account of the Incarnation, of that which we commemorate to-day.

1. Now the first thing that I will ask you to contemplate is its reality. Don't think this an idle suggestion. Don't think that because you believe it to be true, you therefore have hold of its reality. To know a thing, and "to know and imagine" it, are different things. We think so lightly and so little of the inexpressible wonders of the Apostles' Creed, because we rehearse them without thinking and imagining what they mean. It was not always so. In the ancient times of the Church, men took in the meaning of the Incarnation in all the fulness of its overpowering wonder. If they did indeed believe it, it filled their thoughts and souls for a lifetime. It overshadowed every other interest. It was to them the paramount fact in the history of the world, and in the actual condition of themselves, and of all mankind. But they might realise

it too keenly, and too strongly for their faith. Its overwhelming wonderfulness might be too much for their possibilities of assent. They felt what it meant, and rejected it. One set of people saw clearly all that Jesus Christ was, as man. They understood that indeed He was One who shared their nature, and knew their thoughts, and sympathised with their pain and their trials. He was a real man, Very Man, having a history like theirs, subject to the laws and necessities and fate of their mortal nature. And they lifted up their minds to the idea of the Almighty, the Infinite, the Eternal God, and they could not accept the tremendous thought that He who was born in Bethlehem was also Very God. And another set, starting from the belief that "the Word was God," and "dwelt among us," found it just as hard, when they took in the thought, to believe that "the Word was made flesh;" that "God and man" were really "one Christ." God was indeed with us, they thought, when the fulness of time came, but it was impossible that He could be so humbled; impossible that He should stoop to be born of one of His own creatures, impossible that He should be unrecognised by them, persecuted, buffeted by them, impossible that He should really be nailed to the Cross and die. It was all but in appearance and show, it was not real : it was but a moving phantom history, to touch our feelings and take captive our hearts. Or, if that was real, which men saw and handled, then it was God dwelling in, overshadowing, prompting, animating a chosen man, —of higher mould it might be,—but who still was one of ourselves. God was one in His own essence, and Jesus Christ was another. They were one in will, one in purpose, one in work; but they could not be united in one personality. One and the self-same person could not be at once really God and man.

These were the difficulties, these were the heresies, of the early days, when men really measured the true meaning of those words, "He humbled Himself." It is a thought as awful as it is full, as no other thought can be, of blessing and hope for the sons of men. But unless all that Christian faith rests on is altogether baseless, nothing short of it is the truth. We need not fear to face it in all its reality. Christianity never could have been what it is without that reality. The Christian Scriptures never could have been written on any other faith, or any other conceivable basis of facts. The history of Christian belief, the history of Christian life, never could have been what they have been, if He who was with us, was not indeed our Lord and our God, Master of our life, and quickener of the dead: if He who was the Highest and Holiest, did not indeed humble Himself, to be in truth, what men took Him to be, to share our birth and our death. They are amazing words, but they are the reality which invites our sober and reverent thought,—" When Thou tookest upon Thee to deliver man, Thou didst not abhor the Virgin's womb."

2. All that was done was real; and what was done was, that "He humbled Himself." St. Paul exhausts his language in describing this humiliation: He emptied Himself, he says, He took on Him the form of a slave,—there was no limit to it; it was carried on even to death, the death of the Cross. At the distance at which the creature must always and of necessity stand from the Creator, surely we cannot conceive of any interposition of God in this little corner of His dominion, which would not seem to us to involve the mystery of His condescension, the humbling Himself "to behold the things that are in heaven and earth." To look upon us, to have compassion on us, to visit us, to send us help and light, to love us and care seriously about us, all this from our point of view, comparing what we are with what He is, and must be,—the Self-existent and the Self-sufficing,—is a humbling of Himself in His infinite and unsearchable goodness. We are so accustomed to take that goodness for granted that we do not wonder at any of its consequences; we almost assume them as our right.

But in that humbling which we are thinking of to-day, Almighty God has gone far beyond all this. Think of the fixed, necessary, familiar conditions of man's life in the flesh; think of all that is weak and poor and despicable in its beginnings. Think of its early helplessness, its long tracts of empty waiting, its slow lingering on the road to even the first steps of strength, the years that must elapse before it seems to be worth anything in the world. Think of its long uselessness, its long separation from any part in the real business of life, its obscurity and little account. Think, too, what our measures are of what is great, and high, and worthy of such beings as we are; of the value of time, of the importance of all that gives influence, that lightens trouble, and cuts short delays. Think, too, of what we revolt from or despise, in circumstances, in station, in the obligations and necessities of life, in reputation, in relations with other men and the rest of the world. And then consider that all this, the poorest and most wretched that man can sink to, except the depths of sin,—all this, from the rigorous necessities of its mean beginnings to its shameful and dreadful end, all this the Almighty Father chose for the Eternal Son: all this the Eternal Son of His own will took upon Himself, and went through.

We know not what high and low are in the eyes of God, but we know what they seem to men. It was not only the death of the Cross, it was the becoming in absolute and literal truth, and with all its consequences, except the taint of sin, Very Man, by which the Everlasting "humbled Himself."

3. Christmas brings with it two special lessons: the lesson of reality, and the lesson of humility.

We are not dealing with a story, or a legend, or a theory, when we offer our praises to Him who was born at Bethlehem. We are commemorating a human birth as real as our own. And if that wonderful coming down to us was not in appearance but in the most assured truth, with what a rebound does it come upon our own consciences, which tell to many of us, perhaps to most, such a story of unreality and half-truth. In our dealings with others, in our habits of conversation and speech, in our attempts at repentance and self-government, in our private prayers, in our public worship, in that secret and continual intercourse which every man keeps up with himself, what a cloud of confusion, and perplexity, and trouble, is thrown over our life by the subtleties of insincerity, by not being able to be true with our own selves. We find it so hard, even in our moments of retirement and secret thought, to shake off the empire of appearances; it is so easy, so tempting, it saves such trouble, to be content with something short of the genuine truth, in our judgments, in our arguments, in our expressions of opinion: nay, in those devotions which no man sees, which we need not offer to God unless we like, how often have we to confess that we have been satisfied,—consciously, deliberately satisfied,—with a poor make-believe of serious prayer. But in the presence of the awful reality of the Incarnation there is no room left for "shadows of religion;" and we commemorate it year by year, that we may try to impress more and more on our minds, how stern as well as how gracious a truth it is. It can be the foundation of no idle and dreamy and sentimental religion. So tremendous a fact in the history of mankind cannot be consistent with any religious system, or any religious practice, which does not feel its keenness and its force. It is too great, too definite, too solid a thing for a religion of words, and phrases, and formulas, repeated till they lose their meaning; for a religion of understandings, and fictions, and conventionalities; for a religion of mere forms, and orderly impressive ceremonies. If it has doctrines, they mean what they say. If it has Sacraments, they are no figures of things past and absent, but assurances of things present. If it has worship, it sets us before the throne of God. If He, the Lord who "humbled Himself," has promised to be with us, He is indeed with us. If He has told us anything, we must take Him at His word. And in the presence of such a fact, nothing but soundness and honesty of character can stand. It is the only hope of our manifold shortcomings and failures, but it will not allow us to act a part, or amuse ourselves with mere fine sentiments. We cannot, in our dealings with others, with ourselves, with God, suffer unresisted the continuance of what we have felt to be unreal and hollow, without learning one day how terrible it is to ignore what we claim to believe.

Oh, my brethren, the contrast is sharp enough between ordinary religion as it is at the best, and religion as we read of it in the New Testament. Don't let us do anything to make the contrast sharper. Don't let us build on the realities of Christmas, a life of forms and pretences and masks. Don't let us build on the sacrifice of Him who gave up the glory of the Father, a life of useless ease. Don't let us build on His voluntary emptying Himself of what He had in His Eternal Blessedness, a life of self-seeking. Don't let us build on the awful Humiliation, a life of pride.

4. Yes, this is the second great lesson of Christmas, the lesson of humility. It might seem to be irresistible; but we know too well that, unless we take trouble with our hearts, it will touch them, and then pass away, as it has done so often before. And we are in danger, my brethren, from our pride. We are in danger each one of us personally; and we are in danger as a nation. We have almost elevated pride to the rank of a national virtue; so far from seeing any harm in it, we extol it as a noble and admirable thing. You see it unconsciously revealed in the look and bearing which meets you constantly in society and in the streets. You see it in that tone of insolence which seems to come so naturally to many of us, in the expression of our disapproval or our antipathy; the insolent epithet, the insolent imputation, the insolent and intolerant contempt, the insolent claim of superiority and strength. It is the quality and temper of mind for which the ancient Greeks dreaded especially the jealous anger of the Gods: for, indeed, it blinds the mind, like passion, but blinds it habitually and incurably, to truth, to justice, to fact.

Oh, may He, the Greatest and the Highest, who refused not to humble Himself for men, teach us that pride was not made for such as we are. May we learn, under His impulse, the mere reasonableness of true humility: for it is the consciousness, in all reasonable men, of what they are, compared with their standard of action and principle;—in all religious men of what they are, compared with the greatness and holiness of God. It is the natural outcome of any real measurement of the distance at which the creature must stand from God; the natural lesson of our long experience of our mistakes, our ignorance, our weakness.

And there is the history of the past to reinforce the great lesson of modest and humble thoughts. There was once a great Church, as proud of its religion and its religious privileges as we are; it was the Church of the Patriarchs and the greatest of Lawgivers, of Saints and Psalmists and Prophets: it was the home of faith, it was the jealous guardian of the Oracles of God. But it was so proud, that when the Truth in visible form came before it, it could only see in Him an Impostor worthy of death. There was once a great imperial race, carrying its civilising sway over half the world, proud of its power, proud of its manliness, proud of its public spirit, proud of its justice: it knew the high arts of government; it not only conquered, it taught men law, it gave them its mighty language,—the majestic language of jurisprudence and command. It was the proudest of empires, and has never had its equal. But pride brought with it vice and cruelty and corruption, and extravagant luxury, and savage greed which could not be satisfied. The great people whose boast had been ordered freedom and simplicity of life, became the Babylon of the Apocalypse. It perished, and its fall shook the foundations of human society. We, in England, may well have misgivings when we trace among ourselves so many lineaments alike of the grandeur and of the pride of Rome.

May He, who has given us once more this blessed time, also give us grace to lay to heart its lessons. May He use it to open our eyes to see more clearly what He really did for us, and what we really are. May we see and feel all that it teaches in its wonderful story of strong and unshrinking love, of patience, of forbearance, of endurance. The world goes on its way. Great events happen; great affairs absorb men's thoughts. The old passes, the new comes. It may be for good, it may be for disaster,—men's hearts exulting in the prospect, or failing them for fear. Thus time runs its course, so full of what is immediately passing, so full of what is disguised and incalculable, so full of uncertainty, so full of perplexity. Slowly but certainly heaven and earth are passing away, and we and all flesh with them. "But the word of the Lord endureth for ever."

Amid all the outward show of this wild and restless scene, above all history, above all the turmoil of the present, above all the darkness of the future, *one* event, which really happened in the years of time, rises out of them unshaken, unchanged,—the fixed and certain mark for faith and trust and loyal hope, amid the confusion and the storms,—" the same yesterday, and to-day, and for ever." "He humbled Himself." He, the everlasting Son of the Father, "By whom all things were made, . . . for us men, and for our salvation, came down from heaven, And was Incarnate by the Holy Ghost of the Virgin Mary, And was made Man."

V

THE CHRISTMAS MESSAGE OF HOPE

"A woman when she is in travail hath sorrow, because her hour is come: but as soon as she is delivered of the child, she remembereth no more the anguish, for joy that a man is born into the world. And ye now therefore have sorrow: but I will see you again, and your heart shall rejoice, and your joy no man taketh from you."
—St. John xvi. 21, 22.

To-day we commemorate the answer which God gave to the bitter cries of suffering and sorrow of which the world is full, and which before the Child was born were so inexpressibly hopeless. Of that extremity of distress, Scripture everywhere sees the image, in those sorrows without which no life, no individual life, comes into the world. But since the Child was born, it sees in that mysterious dispensation of suffering the image of our deliverance,—the promise of much more than compensation,—the promise of a blessedness, beyond man's hope to measure. So our Lord speaks in the text. So speaks St. Paul. "We know," he says, "that the whole creation groaneth and travaileth in pain together until now. And not only they, but ourselves also, which have the first-fruits of the Spirit, even we ourselves groan within ourselves." That is the condition. But now, beside it there is the wondrous hope. "The earnest expectation of the creature waiteth for the manifestation of the sons of God. . . . Because the creature itself also shall be delivered from the bondage of corruption into the glorious liberty of the children of God."

Let us dwell, on Christmas morning, on the change which has been made in our condition and prospects, —on what we were and should be, without that Man born into the world ;—on what life and the world is, and may be to us, since He was born. This is a day on which we can afford to be real. The mercy, the love, the hope it speaks of are so real, that even in our rejoicing we may venture to face realities of another kind. The infinite travailing of the world and of our race, may indeed sober our joy, now and always. But our eyes have seen something of another world than this ; a world of wonder and grace and light, out of all proportion to all that we know either of evil or of good here ; and it is our own fault if the things of this present time, because they are so serious and so real, are allowed to damp the joy of our deliverance, or put out of sight the transcendent certainty that even here, Immanuel is come, God is with us.

1. But before the Child was born, the world and human life were under a shadow, the depth and gloom of which none of us can measure. None of us, I say ; for the common atmosphere of thought and feeling now, in our Christian times, is charged with hope and brightness even to those who deny its source. But

before He was revealed, human life was an enigma, of which no one had the key; the strangest, to those who thought deepest; the most pathetic to those who lived noblest. Man, whether high or low, at his best estate and his worst, was in the continual presence of terrible and inevitable certainties; and what the meaning of them was, and what the end, not the wisest could tell. There was the mystery of pain; of pain, not confined to the guilty or the foolish, not kept for the strong who were able to bear it, and to whom it might do good, but spread broadcast through the world, attending on all from their first hour to their last, the natural lot of the innocent and helpless little child, and binding to man by a community of suffering, the poor, dumb, irresponsible brute creation, otherwise separated from him by such an impassable gulf: pain, to all human scrutiny, causeless, purposeless, remediless. We are so familiar with it that it is but seldom that we really estimate the terrible wonder of pain. Why is it? What does it mean? What is there in mere nature to explain it? There is an end to it; but what an end! There is the end of death. And what does nature tell us of death? If it merely levelled us with the brutes that perish, that alone would be enough to darken the heavens to us, when they shine most brightly and most gaily. But that is not all. Mere nature will not leave us with the thought that we have had our day and perhaps enjoyed it; and that now it is just and fair that we should give up our place to others. Mere nature will not let us comfort ourselves, if that can be comfort, with the certainty that when we die we perish and are no more. It makes us ask ourselves, " What if there is a hereafter? What if there are unknown worlds beyond the grave, and I am to be there?" It forces us to ask ourselves whether all this wonderful growth of character, of intellect, of goodness, which we see all about us in human life, can possibly be meant to come one day to an abrupt close, and vanish like a dream. In the face of all the awfulness of death, in the face of all that seems certain and undeniable in its victory over us,—do what they will, argue as they may,—men cannot shake off, the most ignorant or the most philosophic, they cannot shake off those " obstinate questionings " whether what they see,—the motionless corpse, blind and silent for evermore,—is really the end of man. And if so, what next? From the beginning of the world, mankind have been travailing in anguish and uncertainty, in wavering hope and chilling fear, when men thought of what might be beyond, and how impossible it was for them to know it.

For they are also in the presence of another mystery,—the mystery of sin, the mystery of conscience. True, men blind themselves: blind themselves easily. Pain they must feel when it comes; death they may forget, but cannot escape. But the idea of sin, and the clamours of conscience, *can* be kept at arm's length for a lifetime. And yet, if not our own experience, the history of the world forces upon every man the tremendous certainty that sin, moral evil, is the clearest and most characteristic feature of human doings. We cannot see ourselves. We know not, except in confused and contradictory ways, the balance of right and wrong, in motive and purpose and conduct, in the busy society all round us, and of which we are part. But take any transaction you like, which we can look at in past time, at a distance, where present interests and present partialities do not disturb our judgment. Is there any, the very best, in which we do not at once discern the presence of what was wrong, the presence of moral failure, of motives veiled for the time from those influenced by them, in which we cannot help seeing the taint of selfishness and passion,—of weaknesses which really had no excuse,—of insincerities, of treacheries, of unfaithfulnesses to light;—the presence, that is, of sin, of moral evil. And if we can say this of the best, what does history show us of the "sins of the whole world?" Who, with whatever theories he may have of sin, can look back on history and not see what a fearful element of moral evil has always been present among mankind, interwoven with all that is greatest among men, inseparable from them as soon as they begin to will, to act, to strive, to conquer? Is not this part of "the bondage of corruption" in which "the whole creation groaneth and travaileth in pain together until now?"

And then, think of our ignorance, even now that

we know so much of God : much more, our ignorance, when the world was without Him who came to be our Light. Think of the darkness, which is, which must be, by nature, on the origin, the destiny, the duties of man. Think of what we are, and claim to be, as men ; what we aim at, what we do indeed achieve : the daring enterprises which have been justified by success,—the vast changes which the common and continuous efforts of mankind have made in our knowledge and powers. And then think of those very obvious, and often pressing questions about ourselves, about our life, about our bodies and souls and spirits, and our everyday actions, which we are unable to answer ; of which we know no more than the brute creatures round us. What do we know of the origin of our thoughts ? How far into the darkness can we follow the causes which make men so different—the causes of genius, of vice, of madness ? We are so made that we long to know, we even think that we have a right to know ; and it becomes part of our trial not to know. There come times when we feel like children in the dark, and not only in the dark, but alone. Nature alone cannot help us to reach to heaven above, or tell us what is there. Nature alone cannot tell us whether prayer is heard. We are like men on an island surrounded by vast gulfs of sea. Even from great portions of the visible creation we are cut off ;—in the midst of the great animal world, among creatures which live and breathe as we do, yet in all that is unseen of them, we stand apart, we stand alone. Each of us in more than half his life is isolated, a single being in the midst of the universe, living alone, dying alone. And yet, with so much inevitable isolation, nothing marks us more than our incorrigible resistance to real union,—our tendency, as fixed as fate, to division. It might have been expected that creatures like men, necessarily so separated and so isolated, would attract one another: what we see is that it is much easier for them to repel one another: or they attract up to a certain point and for a time, and then this makes the ensuing repulsion the greater.—Man, as experience shows him, groans and travails under a great moral failure. At the best, there are all the perplexing uncertainties of character, all the unsuspected faults which men never dream of in themselves, but which others see so clearly; all the strange mixtures, inconsistencies, contradictions, all the weaknesses of the strong, the dishonesties of the sincere, the ungenerousnesses of the generous, the injustices of the just,—all the combinations of opposites, none of which are impossible;—of "dissimulation with feeling," of religion and devotion with passion and laxity of conscience. And at the worst, think of what the All-seeing Eye looks upon in one revolution of day and night, in any one of our great cities.

2. And there was a time when no one could tell what all this meant,—whither all things were drifting,—whether there was any remedy,—whether there was any hope. Can words express this state

of things more truly than those of St. Paul, "the creature was made subject to vanity:" "the whole creation groaneth and travaileth in pain together until now."

There is no help,—the experience of ages attests it,—there is no deliverance, there is no ray of hope, but one; and that is the great gift of God's love which we are thinking of to-day. After the long anguish and agony of the ages, the Child was born. "When the fulness of the time was come, God sent forth His Son, made of a woman, made under the law, to redeem them that were under the law, that we might receive the adoption of sons." "The Dayspring from on high hath visited us, to give light to them that sit in darkness and in the shadow of death, and to guide our feet into the way of peace."

Why this world is what it is, except so far as it is accounted for by the fact of sin, we shall never know here. But what we do know, if we know anything, is the sympathy of God, and the redemptive mercy and healing which has come into the world. For He Himself has come into the world; He Himself has been with us; He Himself is with us. This is the message which the Church has been repeating age after age: "God is with us." God has been with us in the lowest deeps. God has been with us in our great humiliations, has visited us in great humility; God has been with us in pain, the keenest, the most terrible. God has been with us in our shame. God has been with us in death. God has been with us, Man with man, to triumph as man, over pain and sin and death; to be with us still, in pain and sin and death, not less Man than when He left us, to the end of time; to return as Man, to receive us, if we are His, for ever to Himself.

3. My brethren, the travail of the world is not yet over. We think, in our simplicity sometimes, that the clouds are passing from the sky. We count with pride, or it may be with thankfulness, our compensations for what is evil, our exemptions from what our fathers suffered from, our victories over pain. But we know quite well that, still in the background, if not forcing themselves on our notice, are those old terrible certainties, not to be escaped from,—pain, and sin, and error, and death. If in the midst of God's gifts and blessings we forget them, and our own experience does not give us warning, something will remind us from without. Some great blow to happiness, some frightful catastrophe, some overthrow of a nation's hope and peace, some cruel and causeless war, some series of ghastly crimes treading on one another's heels, bid us remember what the world is still. We think that we have secured some great advance,—placed some improvement on a basis which cannot be shaken, and from which there can be no going back, and there comes some unexpected turn of things, some great disappointment and surprise, which shows us how imperfectly we are masters of our condition.—We, in England, thought that we, at least, had mastered the arts of govern-

ment, that we had learned how to make the governed contented and loyal; that we knew better than any one, the rules and the value of fearless justice. And yet here, in the end of the nineteenth century, in no times like those of Tudors or Stuarts, we have a great and sister kingdom, disaffected and estranged, returning the bitterest hatred for great sacrifices and great risks submitted to, for the purpose, at least, of being just.

It used to be a commonplace to condemn the religious bigotry and persecutions of the fierce old days: but we too have seen religious controversy pushed through a series of consequences of which the last step was the gaol: we have seen in England the spectacle of good and earnest clergymen actually imprisoned, say what you will, for religious reasons, at the demand of their theological opponents. Some of us think these things just, and none of us can see the way out of what most are shocked at. Such things in the midst of our prosperity and peace, give us much to think of. No, my brethren, the misery of the world is not yet over.

4. We need consolations which the world refuses to give us; we need hopes, which it cannot, dare not, offer. Nothing here can secure us from that which makes all creation groan and travail until now:— pain, and sin, and folly, and ignorance, and death. As the end of all things which belong only to time, they are waiting—we know not when we may encounter them. And with all its glories, and all its beauties,

and all its changes for the better, and they are innumerable, the world would be as sad a dwelling-place as those old barbarian mothers thought it, who wept when a child was born, if it were not that, since that Christmas morning, all is changed. For then the Child was born whose pain was to hallow ours, whose death was to open to us the gates of life, and help us to die in hope.

Let us for a while forget the anguish, and rejoice in the hope of the glory of God. "For unto us a Child is born, unto us a Son is given: and the government shall be upon His shoulder: and His name shall be called Wonderful, Counsellor, the mighty God, the everlasting Father, the Prince of Peace." Now we know God's mind towards us. Now we know that He has not forgotten the earth which He has made, and His creatures, the work of His own hands. Now we know that the time will come, when the darkness and the suffering that now is, will seem not worthy to be compared to what He has in store for His creatures. "Ye now therefore have sorrow: but I will see you again, and your heart shall rejoice, and your joy no man taketh from you." It is the voice and meaning of all the Psalms which we sing day after day; trouble and danger and suffering, for a while, a little while longer; and then, the deliverance and the peace of God, the love of Christ which passeth knowledge, the joy unspeakable of the life with God—the Great, the Merciful, the True.

VI

CHRIST OUR IDEAL

> "Even so we, when we were children, were in bondage under the elements of the world. But when the fulness of the time was come, God sent forth His Son, made of a woman, made under the law, to redeem them that were under the law, that we might receive the adoption of sons."—GALATIANS iv. 3-5.

CHRISTMAS, with its tender, and bright, and touching, and humbling thoughts, brings with it the remembrance of the profound change in the nature of man, which followed on the coming of the Son of God in the flesh. God came and visited His creatures, "and was made Man." Henceforth man is what God, his Maker, has been. He has that nature, he lives that life, he dies that death, which he has in common with the awful Being who was born at Bethlehem, and is to judge him. From that time man was lifted to a level far above anything that this world of time had ever known. A new order of things began, which had not been before. It is spoken of in the Bible as a new creation, a new man. If we think of what the Bible teaches us of this great change, consequent on the Incarnation of the Son of God, and caused by it, the words, strong as they sound, are not too strong.

The results, the developments, of this great change, have, we know, changed all human history. They have penetrated far and wide into all human life, all human ideas, all human character and activity and motive. They have altered the proportions and the meaning of our present stage of being: they have made it, at once, infinitely more sacred and precious, and infinitely of less account. They have turned the eternal farewells of death into the tender commendations to Christ's mercy and peace, and into the transporting hope of the vision of God. Great, and manifold, and inexhaustible, are the workings in mankind, of that change, of which human language cannot adequately give the measure. For a few moments this morning I will say a few words about one of them.

1. Consider then what has happened since that coming in the flesh, which we are thinking of to-day, in relation to the ideal of man, the ideal of what he should be, of his character, of his perfection: the ideal of man before Christ came to us, the ideal of man since we have known Him, and He has been with us. Man has never been able to live without his ideal. The wildest savages, the rudest barbarians, have their ideal, as well as we, of what man should be. And the ideal of the natural man, of man before the great change of the Gospel, could be a high and noble one. There was such an ideal when human society rose, step by step, out of brutality and licence, into the great civilised states of

the heathen world. The love of one's fellow-men showed itself in the form of enthusiastic loyalty to that country which embraced them all: the State was the object of affection and devotion; a common citizenship, the great acknowledged bond; public-spirited readiness to do and to sacrifice anything for one's country, the height,—and who can deny that it was a very noble one,—of human goodness. Nay, there was something known even beyond that, though it was a unique and barren instance, but men had known, and learned to admire and honour, but not to imitate, one who had, like Socrates, died for the Truth, and died to do good to those who slew him. Courage, patriotism, honour, self-sacrifice for the right, and a care for all the ties of kindred and the tendernesses of friendship, were no unworthy ideals; and they were the ideals of Greece and Rome. Justice, and fortitude, and self-mastery, and wisdom, and duty faithfully and exactly discharged at any cost, were the standards already acknowledged there, by unregenerate man; they were compatible with much that lowered and spoiled them; they were often in fact associated with terrible sins; but often, to our shame and humiliation, men who knew not our Lord recognised their obligations and partially realised them. These were the ideals of the West, of those from whom we have inherited our traditions of social right and order.

The ideals which men reached to in the East were even more remarkable. Centuries before our

Lord came, there was a great religious reformation in India. We know it by the name of Buddhism. The ideal of this was complete sacrifice of all that was pleasant to flesh and blood for the sake of the soul,—to deliver the soul from the passions and slavery and burdens of mortality. And it was accompanied by two things; the most passionate enthusiasm to communicate truth, and so to help and deliver others; and a spirit of tender and all-embracing kindness, which expressed itself in the most touching language, and embodied itself in the most touching acts; which sought out the forlorn and the miserable, and which willingly associated itself with the degradation of the outcast, and with the shame and the doom of the sinner. This ideal did once exist among men, however soon it came to be alloyed and hardened into formalism and superstition; however little it actually was able to do to raise and to console men; however mixed it was with fantastic extravagancy, which we here are not able even to understand. It was a law of actions, which prescribed to itself, in spirit and will, the second table of the Decalogue; which required a man to keep nothing for himself, but to spend and be spent for others; which required him to hide every good deed, and to make the most open and minute avowal of all his faults; which demanded from the proudest and the mightiest the confession of that common lot of error, and sin, and weakness, which they shared with the humblest;

which could inspire the love and the courage of the martyrs, and give power over the hearts of men, and teach the lesson of noble resignation and obedience, and raise up a great company of preachers, as gentle and tolerant as they were earnest and unwearied. Such an ideal was before the men of the East before our Lord appeared.

These ideals, different as they are, are the greatest that history shows us in the Gentile world before the Incarnation. And there was this feature common to both of them: they almost, or altogether, left out God. Not but that the name of God, and still more the names of "gods many and lords many" were on men's lips, and the memorials of them before their eyes; not that the awful and mysterious name of God did not awaken in the thinking Greek or Roman the presage of his Maker, his Ruler, and his Judge. But his moral ideal stood by itself on its own foundations. It did not need God: it did not aspire to God: it did without Him. And to the ideals of the East, God was not even an imagination or a name. With the deep and spiritual meaning which they read into what are the commandments of the Second Table, they were absolutely and resolutely blind to the First. The world to them was empty except of evil; to those ascetics of self-conquest, beneficence, and patient humility, it was empty of God; and their highest hope was not immortality but annihilation.

Great and wonderful, and, sometimes, overpowering are these fragmentary forms of goodness, when we meet with them in the old world,—the Light shining in darkness, and the darkness comprehending It not. Let us thank God, that even to those who knew Him not, His Spirit witnessed in their hearts and consciences, to His Law and Righteousness,— witnessed for justice, for purity, for humility, for loving-kindness, for an unselfish and public zeal. Why should we not acknowledge and reverence them, though they were so evanescent, though they failed to perpetuate themselves, though they were so imperfect, though they had no spring in them of recovery and self-correction? They were for their time.

2. But God was pleased to be patient with what St. Paul calls "the times of this ignorance," till "the fulness of the time" was come. We may look back on them with silent awe, and leave them in His hands till He comes to judgment. But to us the "times of ignorance" are past. There had been an ideal of man in the world all the while of a very different kind. One family of mankind had preserved the great faith that man was the object of God's care and love, and that he was fit to be the object of God's care. Promise and legislation and history, the songs and complaints and raptures of Psalmists, the terrible lessons and unearthly visions of Prophets, had kept up this faith. One great theme, in every conceivable variation, sounds through the whole of the Old Testament, and it is this: "O

God Thou art my God: early will I seek Thee. My soul thirsteth for Thee, my flesh also longeth after Thee: in a barren and dry land where no water is. Thus have I looked for Thee in holiness: that I might behold Thy power and glory. For Thy loving-kindness is better than the life itself; my lips shall praise Thee." "Like as the hart desireth the water-brooks, so longeth my soul after Thee, O God. My soul is athirst for God, yea, even for the living God: when shall I come to appear before the presence of God?" Man was made to know and to love the living God; and the living God, who had made man, meant Himself to be known and loved by His creature. Man was lifted up from being the head of the visible creation here,— from being the noblest and most richly endowed with gifts and powers of all living things on earth, and because so great in his instincts and aspirations, and yet so weak and frail, really the unhappiest,— he was lifted up to feel that he belonged to a world beyond the bounds of mortality and sight; that he had to do with the righteousness and the love of the Everlasting and the All-merciful; that he might hope, in spite of sin and pain and death, to be of the family of the Holiest in "the land of the living." Long before our Lord came, the foundation of man's ideal was laid in the first and great commandment: "Thou shalt love the Lord thy God with all thy heart, and with all thy soul, and with all thy strength, and with all thy mind." According as man is called to do this, and is supposed capable of doing it, the ideal of man varies by a difference that nothing can bridge over.

And at last God's time came. "In the beginning was the Word, and the Word was with God, and the Word was God. . . . And the Word was made flesh, and dwelt among us, and we beheld His glory, the glory as of the only-begotten of the Father, full of grace and truth." "He came unto His own, and His own received Him not. But as many as received Him, to them gave He power to become the sons of God, even to them that believe on His name." Such a revelation, such an opening of the unseen and eternal world, could not be without a corresponding change in the standard and idea of what man was, of what he should be. It is shown in every page and every line of the New Testament.

For now, not to one family and nation, but to the whole world of mankind, was to be declared the relation in which man stood to God : that man might know God, and love God, and be knit and bound to God by the closest and most real of ties. That relation to the Father, dim in Western morality, lost in Eastern morality, was henceforth to occupy its due, and natural, and commanding place, in the thoughts and feelings of mankind. The huge gap in man's idea of his life was filled up ; man was not an orphan not knowing whence he came, or what was his destiny ; he was not fatherless, a victim of the blind forces of nature,[1] with no living love and care above him, to which he might lift up his heart, and know that he was answered. He was not simply the creature, the servant, the worshipper of the Unapproachable and Invisible, taught by His Law, visited in secret by His whispers to conscience, enlightened and comforted by the Holy Spirit of wisdom and of prophecy: for One had come to open his eyes to the realities of what he was made for, and amid which he lived; One who was like him, and spoke his words, and shared his lot. And He who thus came to him, and whom he saw and touched, was God; God who made him; God who, from everlasting, had been all in all to His creatures. Then, for the first time, he learned as he had never learned before, what sin was. Then he learned the height and depth of the righteousness of God. Then he knew what real forgiveness was. Then he learned what was waiting at the end of this mortal life. A character, not only of fresh moral force, but new in spiritual height and capacity and aspiration, appeared among men; it wrought great things in the world, it was sung by great poets,—the character, in all its manifold variations of strength and power and beauty, of the Christian Saint. Beside it the glory,

---

[1] "Tum porro puer, ut saevis projectus ab undis
Navita nudus humi jacet, infans, indigus omni
Vitali auxilio, cum primum in luminis oras
Nixibus ex alvo matris natura profudit,
Vagituque locum lugubri complet, ut aecumst
Cui tantum in vita restet transire malorum."
Lucretius v. 222-227.

the real greatness, of the heathen hero took a lower place. Goodness, not strength, became the recognised measure of action. And the thoughts of men were widened, from even the mightiest exploits on this scene of time, to the high purpose and noble pains of penitence and self-discipline, and to the ineffable joys of paradise. "The Spirit itself beareth witness with our spirit, that we are the children of God: and if children, then heirs; heirs of God, and joint heirs with Christ: if so be that we suffer with Him, that we may be also glorified together.... For the earnest expectation of the creature waiteth for the manifestation of the sons of God.... Because the creature itself also shall be delivered from the bondage of corruption into the glorious liberty of the children of God."

Could man's ideal, even the highest and the noblest, remain the same after such announcements as these? Is it conceivable that after such things as these, man should think of himself, of what he is and what he should be, as he had thought before? Is it possible to overstate the natural consequences of them? And these things are what all we Christians believe. Nothing which confines man's actions and responsibilities to the present can satisfy their claim; nothing, however great, however noble, however urgent, however touching. Beyond all, there is the absorbing truth, that this is but a fragment of a life, —not a life complete and finished in itself, but only the foreground of an endless perspective; that God our Maker has been with us to direct, to elevate, to save it; that of all man's relations to beings around him, his relations to God his Father are the greatest, to his Incarnate Redeemer the deepest.

3. Man has still to live his appointed days on earth. He must live them according to the conditions, physical, moral, social, which One greater than man has imposed upon him. He must live in society, and fulfil the obligations which social and political life imply and require. He must, if his life here is not to be a wreck and a ruin, submit himself to the law of duty, of reason, of conscience; he must tame the wild beast within him, he must crush the dull brute selfishness, which, at the very height of polished civilisation, would cut him off from his kind, in a deadly isolation from sympathy and help and love. But beyond all this he has to think of something else. He has to think of himself, as not of this swiftly passing scene, but as belonging to a vaster system, from which there is no escape by being immersed in the present. He must think of himself as taken out of the shows and appearances which each day brings with it, to be a partaker of what is permanent and for ever. He has a pattern to aim at which is not of this world, and that pattern is the life,—if we may speak so with reverence,—the character, of Jesus Christ. He has a fellowship not of this world, and this fellowship is with the Father and the Son. He has a hope and a fear beyond anything conceivable here,—the Judgment-seat of the Son of Man.

And on these things we are sometimes told to be silent. We stand before the world, which is not so much disposed as it once was, to let us off our profession of this great ideal of human life; and we are bid to realise it to the full, or to hold our peace. Or we are told that it is superfluous to preach about these things; that they have been preached about for eighteen hundred years, that every one knows them who cares to know them, and for the rest they have no interest; that it is time to attend to the real subjects of the day, to the calls of justice, to the redress of wrongs, to the wants and sufferings of the poor. Of course if these things are not true, it not only is superfluous to preach about them, but something much worse. But what if we are right in believing them to be true? Doubtless it will be a bad day for Christian preaching, when it is not moved by wrong, or forgets "the comfortless troubles' sake of the needy," and "the deep sighing of the poor," or "the patient abiding of the meek." It is always the time to do this,—it is eminently the time to do it now. But who taught us to do this? Where and when did men learn this sympathy with suffering? Who, but He who came to make us sons of God, came also the first of all to seek the lost, to preach the Gospel to the poor? Who first taught men to copy His example; and what was it that had power to keep up the tradition of His example through centuries of selfishness and sin? When, for eighteen hundred years men have done without Christ, and have risen to a higher morality, and a more disinterested benevolence, it may be time to tell us to do without Him; but that time is not yet.

But, after all, this is no matter for paper arguments. This great debate, which, in one shape or another, has been going on through long ages, and will go on when we are laid to rest, is not to be settled by them. There the great truths are, for us to take or to leave; with us it rests whether the true answer shall be given or not. The real silencing answer is the lives of men, the lives of Christian believers. The world may talk for ever, and talk to little purpose about the reality of religion. The question really rests with us whether our life is governed by such things as we are thinking of to-day; whether, whatever we have to do, the consciousness of this truth is around us like the air we breathe; whether, from believing them, we are more true, more honest, more just, more patient, more pure, more self-denying, more cheerfully helpful, more resigned and hopeful in trouble. O my brethren, be sure of this, —this, amid the strife of tongues, is the true, and acceptable, and trustworthy way of vindicating the ways of Him who has done so much for us. If only our lives will fairly stand the test which He intended they should meet, we need not fear when we speak with our enemies in the gate. The Eternal Wisdom might, if He had pleased, have stopped for ever the mouths of the gainsayer and the doubter; but He has not pleased to do so. He chose His means of victory and salvation for us, as for Himself, in the realities of life, in doing and in suffering.—May God forgive us for our miserable attempts to bring the life of faith into the life of work and business. May He forgive us, who accept such great thoughts and hopes, for being content with such poor and intermittent effort. May God help us to remember that we have been made the "sons of God," and to discern the import of those tremendous words,—" Who for us men, and for our salvation, came down from heaven, and was incarnate by the Holy Ghost of the Virgin Mary, and was made Man."

VII

THE LIGHT OF THE EPIPHANY

"Then spake Jesus, saying, I am the light of the world."—St. John viii. 12.

THIS season of Epiphany is the special commemoration of those promises of God, that at last He would bestow on the world the blessing of spiritual light. Out of all the holy days of the year it is the one which reminds us of the light which we have. Other days remind us of what God has done for us. The Epiphany reminds us, not only of what He has done, but of what He has granted us, even here, to know of Himself and of His doings. It is conceivable that He might have done His great works on our behalf without telling us so much. In former generations of the world, He loved men and watched over them, without their knowing it; He prepared good things for them, without letting them into His counsels. We cannot doubt that what Christ has done and suffered concerns, in some way, even those who have never heard His name. But for us, He has put aside, in a degree, the veil which hides from us on earth the presence and working of God, and has admitted us to know what is of the deepest interest to us,

—partially at least, as they see and know in heaven. This is what we are invited to think of at this time, —of this opening of our eyes to God's purposes and presence, this appearing to us of His very self. Things that, in other ages, neither Jew nor Gentile knew of,—things that many kings and prophets and righteous men desired to see, and died without seeing, —God has made our common heritage. This is our great and real privilege, to know that about ourselves and our relation to God, which we could not have found out, which only in our later ages was made known. Our eyes have seen indeed "the Lord's salvation, which He had prepared before the face of all people; a light to lighten the Gentiles, and the glory of His people Israel." "Through the tender mercy of our God . . . the dayspring from on high hath visited us; to give light to them that sit in darkness and in the shadow of death, to guide our feet into the way of peace." So did the expiring voices of ancient prophecy, on the lips of Simeon and Zacharias, pass into the awakening strains of the Gospel. They express the great truth that we are dealt with henceforth not as children but as men; trusted with the amazing secret of our real destiny; not merely meant for a greatness beyond all we can think or know, but told that we have been meant for it, and told of all that God has done to bring us to it. To-day we remember the first steps and stages of that great manifestation, by which we have been brought from darkness to light: and that Light was Christ.

It is difficult for us, who are so familiar with the results of that great enlightening, to take in the true measure of it, to take in the true interval between it and the darkness which preceded it, to take in the order and significance of the great process itself. What was that order, as shown in that special manifestation, which gives its name to the Festival of the Epiphany? What did that light spring from which was to enlighten the world, and how was its rise exhibited and shadowed forth?

1. The Wise Men came on their journey from the east, seeking Him who was born King of the Jews. The representatives and figures of Gentile wisdom and Gentile longings, of the thoughts, the anticipations, the deep desires of human kind, were guided to the centre of all their searching, and all their love. Ancient prophecy had promised, with persistent and astonishing confidence, in a long series of magnificent assurances, that the Divine Light should break through the clouds which seemed so impenetrable, and should rise upon all the earth. "Arise, shine; for Thy Light is come, and the glory of the Lord is risen upon Thee.... And the Gentiles shall come to Thy light, and kings to the brightness of Thy rising." They came: and "When they saw the star, they rejoiced with exceeding great joy. And when they were come into the house, they saw the young Child with Mary His mother, and fell down, and worshipped Him: and when they had opened their

treasures, they presented unto Him gifts; gold, and frankincense, and myrrh."

Thus they came; thus they offered. And what they saw was a young Child; and Him they worshipped, falling down, and presenting to Him their offerings. Was there not here the image and figure of that Divine dispensation, in which, in this world of time and preparation, all things great begin in weakness, all things most glorious begin in loss and shame? On one side were men, who, whatever they were, were personages of high name and account: there were wisdom, riches, great efforts; the earnest purpose and unsparing toil of the serious and the thoughtful, who had come from far to seek their heart's need and hope. And what on the other side? Weakness, poverty, only humble purity and innocence; only a little Child with Mary his mother. And here was the fulfilment of prophecies which had stirred and shaken the East; here was the reward, thankfully, adoringly recognised, of the anxious questioning, of the painful seeking. The question was answered, the promise was made good, what was sought for was found.

And from this point among the events of history was slowly and gradually,—how slowly but yet how certainly,—to rise over the races of man, a new illumination, a new hope, a new thought and vision of God. Age after age had repeated the great tradition of a coming deliverance;—age after age, a new, a bolder, a more rapturous inspiration had confirmed it ;—He was to come who should be the Heir of the world, King of Kings, and Lord of Lords, who should rule from sea to sea, in whom all the families of the earth should be blessed, in whom all the Gentiles should trust. And here, at last, these great lines of human hope and comfort converged ; and they converged upon that humble house in which the wise men from the east kneel before a little Child, who was in time to be known as Jesus of Nazareth.

Or take it the other way. We, on whom the ends of the world are come, have seen a great history. The greatest, mightiest, richest, most eventful act of the drama of our world is that one which has gone on during our eighteen later centuries. Say what you will of separate scenes before, wonderful, brilliant, fruitful,—these are the centuries in which the race has made its advance, has shown what it could do, and might achieve. We see in it, as its foremost feature, a great system of thought, of faith, of action ; a great discipline, and a never-exhausted spring of character and progress. We call it the Christian Church. This great system has rolled out of its old courses the movement and onward march of the world. In spite of the darkest omens, and the most formidable and threatening rivals, it fears not to claim the future, as it has controlled the past. Trace back this wonderful history, follow back the lines along which the development of society, and the unfolding of human character, have travelled, and we find them meet in that same point to which all prophecy converged; they find their way backwards, through the revolutions of time, to the inn and the manger, to the little Child for whom the shepherds praised and glorified God, and in whom the sages and ministers of a religion of eastern heathendom found the object of their search, and felt that they had come on no fool's errand, when they saw Him, and were glad. Here, in a humiliation of which words cannot express the abasement,—here, in the most utter weakness and helplessness,—was planted, unknown and in darkness, the seed, the little seed, of the regeneration of the world. Here was foreshown, in the very truth of its order and process, the event in history of the deepest, most permanent, most immeasurable consequences to mankind; the event most utterly unlike any other,—the conversion of the Gentiles, of the nations, to the faith of Christ.

And we are taught, as we are taught throughout that Divine manifestation of which here were the first rays and gleams, that profound law of the Divine working which often seems to us so strange, though it meets us everywhere, that the seed of the future is in what is unknown, unthought of, in the present. There, under the mask of the meanest and most trivial lowliness, lies in all its power and eventfulness, the Divine reality. God's greatness does not care to put on the show of what *we* count greatness. Some of the poorest and most despised things of this world are the germs of what shall be greatest in the world to come.

We little know, when we judge of the influences and tendencies round us, or of the lives and characters we encounter here, how often, and how signally will human judgment be reversed as time goes on, and discloses its strange births; how here, and much more in the eternal world, the awful rejoicing of the Magnificat will be realised: "He hath scattered the proud in the imagination of their hearts. He hath put down the mighty from their seat, and hath exalted the humble and meek." Yes, that is the law by which God raises us, by which He brings about His own works, by which He prepares in time for the eternal. Whether He makes the world, or renews the races and the life of His creations, or, from the pitiable wreck of death and the grave, exalts His creatures to immortality, or in the silence and patience of the ages, leads on and guards the thread,—from Abraham to David, from David to David's chosen daughter,—on which hung all the hopes of man's redemption, still, in dark and lowly beginnings is sown the seed of what is to be. "It is sown in dishonour; it is raised in glory: it is sown in weakness; it is raised in power:" the Divine fact is exhibited, "out of weakness made strong;" the Divine rule exemplified, "My strength is made perfect in weakness." At every step, the varied instances of this law of God's government combine to assure us that it is not what we here call greatness, but *goodness*, which is the seed of the glory which shall one day be.

2. From the first steps and order of this great enlightening, let us pass to the result. That Epiphany was the pledge and augury of a gift of true and abiding light to the world, with which it is idle to compare any disclosure to man of the knowledge which most concerns him. We, indeed, live so completely in the atmosphere which it has created, we feed so deeply, even from our mother's arms, on the truths which it has made our common portion, they have passed so subtly and insensibly into our blood and our thoughts, that we can hardly imagine what it is to be without what it has given us. We cannot disengage ourselves from the ideas and longings which it has brought from Heaven down to earth;—the thought of God, the knowledge and fear of sin, the confidence of immortality, the prospect of judgment, the hopes of repentance, the sure trust in the Divine compassion, the holy delights of love and worship, the unspeakable and adorable marvel of the life and death of the Crucified. Nothing can make this as if it had not been; those who turn their backs on it, and refuse it, in word and speculation, cannot get away from it; they cannot get away from the conditions under which they were born; and when they speak their best and deepest words, they are speaking what is not their own, what could not have been ever theirs to say, if it had not been for the Teacher, and the light, and the Divine tradition which they disown. We can scarcely put ourselves really in the place of those sitting in darkness and in the shadow

of death, on whom, unexpectedly, contrary to all that they had known and been used to, the Light first shone.

But there was a time when, whether men willed it or not, the world and life could not but seem the most incomprehensible of puzzles, the emptiest and most unmeaning of phantoms. There was a time when the alternative was *not* before them, before any of them, great or small, whether they would or would not accept the knowledge of One Eternal and most Holy; for His Name was not yet held up to them to worship, or deliberately and with grave reasons, to reject and ignore. There was a time when what seems to be the end of all things here,—the failure of the best, the fading away of the most beautiful, the overthrow of the strongest, the issue in vanity and disappointment of all promise and all hope,—could not but be taken to be what really is. God was sought for, but who could dare to tell of Him? Who could dare tell who or where He was, or what was His mind about what goes on here? Men knew that they have grief and sorrow, and infinite capacities for irremediable pain; but why they should have it, they knew not. They knew that they must die, they knew the agony of dying; but who could tell why, if they lived at all, they should have to die? Who could tell what should become of them when they were dead? Was not this "the veil that is spread over all nations?" Was not this a universal bondage, against which wish, or effort, or thought of man, could be of no avail? Was not this the lot, not of a few, but of all; the yoke that never could be broken, the darkness that none could pierce? To imagine what it was to human life and human hearts, we must imagine ourselves never to have heard those words,—I do not say, not to believe them—that unhappily we know may be, but never to have heard them,—" I am the Resurrection, and the Life:"—" It is appointed unto men once to die, but after this the judgment:"—"This is life eternal," to " know Thee the only true God, and Jesus Christ, whom Thou hast sent:"—" Come unto Me all ye that labour and are heavy-laden, and I will give you rest:"—" The blood of Jesus Christ cleanseth us from all sin:"—Who shall separate us from the love of Christ?" What measure can express the infinite distance, in all that makes the world dark or makes it light, between the times before His appearing, before those words were spoken, and the times when those words, repeated day by day by ten thousand voices, echoed in the depths of ten thousand hearts, witness of Him who offers Himself to mankind as their Lord and Redeemer, bringing into the mysteries of nature the Light of the everlasting world, the love, and holiness, and perfection which the angels worship.

3. And yet this Light, which has risen by such wonderful steps till it has overspread our sky, is but the Heavenly Light given us in such measure as we could bear it; given in the degree proportionate to time and mortality, and our stage of being; given to

men, not who have won their appointed place, but who are preparing for it. This Light, to which all that was before is darkness, is itself only the beginning and the promise of the Perfect Light to come. "We know in part, and we prophesy in part," says the Apostle. All that we have, we have but in fragments, of inexpressible majesty and glory, of perfect truth; disclosures, incomplete as yet, of the Divine counsels; the realities of the All-holy Mind as they can be manifested to men, who have but a short time to live, whose hour comes for them to depart just when they seem ripest and fittest to learn and to know. The Epiphany is a sort of figure of the way in which the Light is shown us. The Wise Men came, and looked on the King of the Jews, and worshipped Him, and then they went on their way, and saw Him no more. So it is to us who read their history. They came, we know not whence;—they pass before us, beholding, rejoicing in the supreme and ineffable wonder of this our world; they disappear, we know not whither. Such are all the disclosures of Christ's glory. They are here just long enough for men to be certain of them, and to take in what they are; and then the common course of things succeeds, and closes over them. They come like strangers into the ordinary experience of our present life, with their gracious blessing of illumination, or assurance, or warning, or strength; and having done their work, they leave us and the world to go our way.

So Christ came and went. A little while, in the world's long history, men saw Him, and their hands handled Him, and their ears heard Him; their sick bodies sprang to health under His power, their dead heard His voice and lived. And again, a little while, and they saw Him no more; He came not to stay, but to disclose Himself, and to go; and the world and mankind were left, to the end of time, to remember and to think of the overwhelming manifestation which had once been made to them. So is the light vouchsafed to us here. It is given us but in part, in broken lights, in glimpses most clear, most wonderful, most imperfect. It is given, not to sight, but to remembrance: given us to remember if we will, to forget, also, if we choose: it is the knowledge of heaven, but received on earth, and with the limitations of earth; the knowledge of One, really so near, seemingly so remote, of whom, in our deepest and truest selves we are sure, but whom, in our outer, surface life, we are unable to see, unable to point out, unable fully to prove. For the Infinite Majesty is not *here*; and it is of Him, His Person, His Will, His doings, that the reflections come down into this little life of ours.

4. Here, standing on the threshold of another year, when all reminds us of that endless current of change on which everything is embarked, and along which we all are moving,—we look back once more, for a moment, on that great break and change in the condition of the world, " the Manifestation of Christ

to the Gentiles." That break in history involved the renewal of life and society; it has brought hope where all was despair; strength, heroic strength, where it seemed vain to struggle; the energy of goodness and improvement where all seemed sold to evil. That Light from above, no unfaithfulness, no perplexity, no shortsightedness of man, has blotted from our heaven, nor can ever banish from the knowledge of mankind. Our turn has come, in the revolution of the centuries, to behold it, to be blessed with it, to be responsible for it. The new year forces on us that inexorable law of change which is the necessity of our world and life, and which, at last, turns upon us all so stern a face. But the great commemoration which accompanies the new year, teaches us to think of this law as also the condition of our greatest good. The most hopeful and forward-looking of us all cannot, I suppose, reflect without a thrill, if not a pang, that all that was theirs this time last year, can never be theirs again. And to some of us, the utmost we have to look forward to is but a little thing compared with what we can look back to. The great fact of life has become to us, that things are changed. In the slow, never-pausing voyage of life, friends have drifted apart. We pass by closed doors where once we were welcome; homes that were ours, see the ways of strangers; chairs are empty where those sat whom we dreamed we could never lose; where once we walked, our feet will never press again. And the things we liked are altered; the things we thought perfect are made light of, and laid aside; the place where we enjoyed our life, knows us no more; the faces which were about us all day long have disappeared from around us. All has been left behind, all has made way for new things, new men, new judgments.

But the reverse of all this is, that only on these terms, only on this condition of mortality, which perhaps shoots through us like a sharp pain, is there the prospect, for imperfect creatures, of higher things. We lose what we value, we leave behind what we love. It is the price we pay for the possibility of improvement, for our own approach to the perfect and the unchangeable. Woe unto us if we could not change! "Thou fool," says the Apostle, "that which thou sowest is not quickened, except it die." If better things are ever to come, the old must change and make room for them.

My brethren, we will not repine though we have to lose so much, though we leave behind, buried in the past years, what is so inestimably precious, what here, to us, can never be replaced, in the time that we have to live. We will accept the great law of ceaseless change, for the compensating power which it brings along with it, amid the vicissitudes of circumstance, of changing in character and soul, from what we are to what we would be. We will say to ourselves, "I change with all things,—I must change: this awful fact of my nature follows me everywhere, whether I will or no. But I can change within, not by necessity, but by choice. I can change from my old and dead self, to a new and higher self. Amid the wreck of what is taken from me, amid the ruins of what I was and what I loved, I can also, if I will, leave behind the restless desires, the sordid meannesses, the dark self-deceits, the miserable treacheries of the years that are past. I am meant to change, I must change, if I am ever to be what I was intended to be ;— change from weakness to strength and purity, from random carelessness to self-government, from the standard of the world to the standard of Jesus Christ. That dread discipline of change from which I shrink, is God's order for the training of the soul, as it is for the trial and training of the race. If that which He has prepared for man is ever to come to me, it must be by the passing away of all that is old,—by its passing, through the overthrow and agonies of change, into that over which change shall have no more power, —the kingdom which cannot be moved,—the everlasting peace of God."

May He, who has made all things new on earth by His revelation of Himself to mankind, and who speaks from the Throne of Heaven, " Behold I make all things new," finish in us all the work for which He has made us all. He made us for His Light, He made us for His goodness, He made us to share His Glory. But even His Light and Truth here are but the seeing in a glass darkly ; our highest goodness here is but the pale shadow of

His Perfection; our happiness and peace are but foretastes, precarious and transient, of His Eternal Rest. But we believe that verily we shall see the goodness of the Lord in the land of the living. He made us and He redeemed us, that at last we might know even as we are known. He made us that out of the shocks of change, and the decay of our mortality, He might fashion for immortality His new creation. The heavenly righteousness to which souls made perfect shall attain, is nothing less than the fulness of that love, by which the Apostle expresses the Essence of God. "The fruition of His glorious Godhead,"—this is the appointed term and goal and reward, of human kind, of those who know Him now by faith.

But oh! think of what must be before that comes. There lie between us and It, our evil ways, our besetting temptations, our poorness of soul, our hearts that cannot be trusted, the sins we know of, the sins we are blind to. There lie between the present moment and *that*, the snares, the chances, the doubts, the darkness, of the days before us; the time of our tribulation alternating with the no less perilous time of our wealth: there lie the hour of death, the resurrection of the body, the day of judgment. Through this awful interval, so hard to imagine, yet so sure to be,—along this uncertain path to the great and certain future,—through these unknown distances, these inconceivable scenes which we have to traverse, who shall guide us, who shall protect us? Whom have we in heaven but One; and who upon earth can hold our hand and keep our steps, and in the darkness give us light, but He? "The Lord is my Light, and my Salvation; whom then shall I fear? The Lord is the strength of my life; of whom then shall I be afraid?" To Him, when our hearts are full, when our flesh and spirit fail, we will commit our way, ourselves, and all that belongs to us. "We therefore pray Thee, help Thy servants, whom Thou hast redeemed with Thy precious blood. Make them to be numbered with Thy Saints in glory everlasting . . . O Lord, in Thee have I trusted, let me never be confounded." "O Lamb of God, that takest away the sins of the world, grant us Thy peace."

VIII

TRIAL A NECESSARY LAW OF HUMAN LIFE

"In all points tempted like as we are, yet without sin."—
HEBREWS iv. 15.

YES, my brethren, even in that awful condition of man's nature and life which we call Temptation, He, the Holiest, chose to have his part. It was not enough that He would be born as we are born, that He would live as we live, and speak our words, and think with our thoughts, and love with our affections, that He would suffer as we suffer, and die as we die—this was not enough. To be perfect man, He need not sin, but He *must* be tempted, and He *was* tempted "like as we are, yet without sin."

For He, the Redeemer and the Pattern of the human race must fulfil to the uttermost the law of its condition,—He must, in all things which were outside of that very inmost self, that personality which chooses and wills, and over which in Him no degenerate taint, or infirmity, or soiling touch of evil could pass,—in all other things, He must bear the burdens and know the trials, of being a man. He must be like unto His brethren, if He was indeed to be their brother. And He would be like them, that they might be sure of that which was so absolutely essential for them to know,—that they might be sure of the sympathy and answering mind of Him in whom they were to trust for everything, in that interval of waiting during which they were not to see His face—that interval of waiting and preparation for our real and unknown and inconceivable destiny, which we call our life. He drew near to them in everything that was morally possible. By the necessity of absolute Goodness, of immaculate and perfect Holiness,—incapable, for if it were, the very nature of God would be annihilated, of a shade of evil,—He could not share their sin. But as He shared the consequences of their sin, their punishment, so He would share those outward conditions which make them sin. To be able " to succour them that are tempted," " He Himself hath suffered, being tempted."

To this condition of our existence here, this law as universal and as certain as death itself, that every living soul must pass through trial, must meet that which is involved in trial, *temptation*, the time and season invite our thoughts. Lest we should faint and be discouraged, our Master and Lord went through temptation. That we might be convinced that it is God's appointed path to perfection, He was proved and tried. That we might conquer in it, He endured it and overcame. Let us fix our thoughts on this universal law of our present state; and then let us consider how we ought to behave in regard to it.

1. The soul of man, in this passage through the years of time which is the ante-chamber and exercise ground to an eternal existence, has to go through temptation. I am not going to ask why this law was imposed on human life. Till we know, not one little portion of the vast plan of God's government, but the whole of it, none but those whose thoughts are too shallow to know their own ignorance will imagine it possible to give any complete and satisfying answer. We may as well ask why God made the worlds, and made them as He has made them; why He called this or that person, you and me, into being—why at this particular time and not at another, why under these particular circumstances and not in others. These things are beyond our reach; we have to do with what we know our life and condition to be. And from the first dawn of human history, from the first beginning of each individual life, man is ever on his trial; tempted to do wrong and resisting, tempted to do wrong and falling. Man comes into life fitted and equipped to meet his trial, to meet temptation, as he comes fitted and equipped to provide for his bodily wants, to subdue the earth, to meet danger, to develop and improve the marvellous endowments of his nature. The soul comes, with reason, with conscience, with knowledge, with will, with grace; and as the day

goes on, the question is ever presenting itself, how shall it use that characteristic and unique prerogative of will; what will it choose of the things before it: how will it decide between what it ought to do, and what it would be pleasant to do; how will it decide between the present moment, and the unseen, distant, but inevitable future. And what is all human life but this; man having, in his freedom, to *choose*, to choose under all kinds of circumstances, all kinds of feelings, under the stress and force of all kinds of motives—having to choose and *choosing*,—the right thing or the wrong—going straight onward or turning aside: giving proof of what is in him, of the inmost bias and inclination of his character, of the use he would make of his freedom, of the strength and mastery over himself, by which he can make his higher self govern his lower self, by which he can make his weaker and poorer and baser wishes yield to his nobler will.

What is the whole moral side and interest of human history but this—how man bears temptation, how he comes out of his trials? Political history, social history, the advance of civilisation in its higher sense or its lower, the progress of arts and knowledge, all this is of great and undeniable interest: but there is a record and story of deeper interest still, which is only to be completed beyond the years of time; the story which tells how men have played their part as moral beings, beings accountable to that high law of right and wrong, which lifts them above everything else that they know of in the visible universe;[1] how under each new opportunity or emergency, they have been faithful to truth, to duty, to goodness, to God, to grace, or have been blind to them and have betrayed them. The beginning of the history of the First Man, the prelude and figure of what was to follow, was the history of a trial, a temptation, a defeat. The first scene in the history of the Second Man was a temptation, a victory; the type and first-fruits of what man might hope for. The Bible opens with man ensnared and vanquished. It closes with the great sevenfold promise to "him that overcometh," and with the vision of the glory of those that have overcome. And what is all that is written between the first page of it and the last, but the continued record of how, to men and to nations, there came the day of opportunity, the day of visitation, the day of proof; and how that day was met, and how they bore themselves in it, and what were its issues? What famous name in the Bible does not bring with it the associated thought of characteristic trial—Abraham, Esau, Jacob, Joseph, Moses, Job, Saul, David, Solomon, Jeroboam, Daniel, Peter, Judas, Paul? And for what does each nation come before us in its pages—Egypt, Israel in the Wilderness, Israel in Canaan, Israel in its kingdoms, Israel

---

[1] "L'homme n'est qu'un roseau, le plus foible de la nature, mais c'est un roseau pensant. Il ne faut pas que l'Univers entier s'arme pour l'écraser. Une vapeur, une goute d'eau, suffit pour le tuer. Mais quand l'Univers l'écraseroit, l'homme seroit encore plus noble que ce qui le tue, parce qu'il sçait qu'il meurt, et l'avantage que l'Univers a sur lui. L'Univers n'en sçait rien."

Pascal, *Pensées*, i. 70. Ed. Molinier.

in captivity, Israel restored ;—for what are those great names familiar to us, of mighty cities, in which were concentrated the renown of empires or the fortunes of the world—Nineveh, Babylon, Jerusalem, Rome ;—but because in them we see on the one hand, God's call, God's mission, God's gifts to men ; on the other, the use which man has made of them—the events, overwhelming in their scale of magnitude, of nations having answered to their trial, or failed in it—their growth, their decay, their rejection, their downfall? And what is all what we call secular history but the reflection and counterpart of that spectacle of trial which the Bible shows us? You watch and follow from age to age, great races, great commonwealths, great states, with their princes and their leaders ; you see their spring and mounting, you see them on the edge and balance of their fate, you see them in the sunshine and in the storm, you observe their tendencies, their inherited aims, blind as instinct, steady as necessity, measureless in the energy of will evoked by them ; you see them at some supreme crisis, making the world glorious by heroic achievement, or darkening it with a new shame by unheard of vileness and disgrace. You see all this, you may study it as a set of phenomena, you may analyse the currents of tendency and the posture of circumstances and the play of unknown or obscure influences. But, surely, the deepest interest of all is a *moral* one :—how men like ourselves bore what was terrible, or formidable, or seductive, or disappointing; how they chose between duty and pleasure, or custom, or interest, between what was excellent and what was base, between justice and mercy and truth, and the dazzling wrong which they had the pretext and the strength to do; how the slow silent course of years revealed at last what men had become under their manifold but unnoticed discipline, how they had been training themselves in faithfulness to their conscience, or had been insensibly sinking below themselves; how, in a word, they had stood the trial of what they were, stood the trial of their choice, their principle, their conscience, how they had behaved themselves in their temptations.

See man as he has been in history; see him next, in those pictures of his character and actions, whether ancient or of yesterday, which, ideal as they are, have contributed so much to make us know ourselves, the drama, the novel; you see him, when he is worth your interest, when he appeals to your fellow feeling,—a being under trial. The imagination of the ancient world, the ancient drama, represented this trial as an unequal and hopeless struggle against the iron doom of fate, an inexorable, overmastering power; yet it beheld man still put to the proof, even by the cruelty of his lot, still showing what he was, true, or weak, or brave;—holding to faith and duty, nobleness, friendship, affection, or deserting them. A higher but not less awful and mysterious idea of trial came in with the Gospel—the trial of choice and will; the trial of human responsibility and freedom, in the decision between faith and sight, between sin and God—the trial whether the soul has honesty and strength enough to break through the meshes and entanglements of pretence and plausibility, or whether in its secret hollowness it lets itself be fascinated, spellbound, blinded by evil. This is the centre and living spring of all that is pathetic, of all that is glorious and sublime in the great masterpieces of English tragedy; it is the human soul under its trial, so like our own, the human soul in the crisis and agony of temptation, yet master of its freedom to the last:—it is this which affects us so profoundly in the captive king, musing over the vanity of a world he has misused,—in the frenzy of the wronged and dispossessed father, driven to madness by his children's ingratitude and his own folly,—in that piteous debate in which the alternative is a brother's death, or a sister's shame,—in the jealousy of the husband, yielding against his better self to the fiendish treason of the slanderer,—in the growth, from small beginnings under favouring accidents, of the monstrous sin, and the terrible balancings of the sinner's conscience between murder and a throne,—in the still more terrible struggles of the sinner, who would repent but cannot, but only binds the webs of self-deceit faster about him—

> "O liméd soul, that, struggling to be free,
> Art more engaged!"[1]

---

[1] *Hamlet*, Act III. Scene iii. 68.

These were the types and images of human trial in the larger and simpler forms of earlier times; those of our own time have been more subtle and more refined but as impressive, since the greatest of German poets embodied the characteristic trial of our age in his mighty tragedy—the tragedy of man, civilised, educated man, in the presence of the twofold and combined temptations of knowledge and of passion, and staking his soul on the price of his desire. And you cannot open a novel of the last fifty years, the worst and most trifling, as well as the profoundest in its insight, and the richest and most delicate in its observation, without meeting in one form or another, high or debased, the pervading interest of human trial. They may exhibit it in false, or poor, or fantastic shapes; or they may unfold its multiplied and changing complications with that perception of the finer lines and shades of character, with that quickened discrimination of its infinite living types, with that deeper penetration into those dim recesses where the secret of its motives and its self-delusions is hid, which are as much the gifts of our time as our deeper knowledge of nature, gifts won for us by the genius of great masters and searchers of the human heart. But whether they do it ill or well, whether they teach us, or mislead and corrupt us, they equally attest the universal presence of real trial in man's life; they draw that life as one which would be without meaning, if it were not for ever meeting that which proved and tested it.

2. That is what man's life looks like, when watched from without and at a distance. But we have to do with it much more closely, than as spectators and critics,—than as the audience who look on at the play, and pass their judgment, or bestow their momentary sympathy on the actors. In this great scene,—how great, how eventful, we see clearly enough outside of ourselves,—*we* are the actors, too. We watch the game, and we forget that we see in it the image and reflection of what we are ourselves doing. But we are ourselves part of that world in which human souls are on their trial, in which each man in all the infinite varieties of state and circumstances has his task and mission assigned him by his Maker and his most Holy Judge ; his call to do or to suffer, and with all that is necessary in providence and grace, if he will, if he chooses, to do and to suffer according as God appoints him :—where each man, day by day, as the thread of his life runs on, shows in one way or another, what he is in his very self ; is made to disclose himself, the realities of his character, and the powers which bear supreme sway in his heart and shape his choice. And choose he must, moment by moment ; he knows what he ought to do, he feels what he would like to do, and with his awful doom of freedom, he can take, he is taking, which he will. We cannot live, we cannot think or wish, without this searching of intentions, this trial and revealing of hearts, going on, as, one by one, the pages of our life are turned ; and we can no more withdraw ourselves from it, or divest ourselves

of our freedom of choice, than we can escape from the atmosphere around us, or from our shadow in the sunshine. What we see in the great lives in the Bible finds place in the most commonplace of our modern lives. He was "in all points tempted like as we are." We may turn the words round, and say with reverence, that like as He was tempted, so are we, even the humblest among us—tempted, tried according to the measure of what we can bear, but as truly, and with all depending on the issue.

And this, my brethren, we have to learn, to take in the truth of it, and the bearing of it on our thoughts about ourselves. Some forms of trial round us we have no difficulty in understanding. But that *we ourselves* are being tried,—really put to the proof, —really made to show what is in us and what we are, in very earnest, as we see and read of others being tried,—that we are really tried, and sometimes to our great shame and loss,—this we do not so commonly manage to bring home to ourselves. We look on,—safe, as we think, ourselves,—with horror, with astonishment, perhaps with sympathy, on the great and strange temptations going on all round us: and well, indeed, we may. That boy or that girl, born in sin, nursed in sin, from the first dawn of reason more familiar, than with their daily bread, with evil which to us is a pollution to think of, cut off from all good, and not even allowed what we call a chance in life, have yet been sent forth on their voyage of life by the All-righteous and the All-merciful. He has

His purpose in them; they might answer to it, as others in like case have yet answered to it,—they are on their trial. But what a fate that were, if it had been ours. Or that strange combination of sickness and mischance, invading a whole family, striking down one, crippling another, sweeping off one after another the strongest and most helpful, barring one after another the openings of earthly hope, clouding all things with death and penury and pain, perhaps with shame—there is trial indeed—it is sorrow and anguish even to think of it. And, at the other extreme, we can see the trials of the too fortunate: we can see what a temptation it must be to have grown up with all things at our command, with nothing to remind us of difficulty, or duty, or want, or self-denial; taught to think that our will must be right, trifling away our time, and indulging our caprice without inconvenience or warning, knowing contradiction only to override it. There are those who have to go through such a life, on their path to the grave and the eternal world: it is not hard to see that they are on their trial.

But are we too, really, seriously, on our trial,—on our trial, with tremendous issues depending,—on our trial, as truly as the people we read of, or perhaps actually see, visibly going through the crisis which tests and proves what they are? Does temptation, in this solemn, eventful shape, really come near us too? In that quiet, prosaic round of business and domestic life, in that silent, unperceived growth in our character, of habits, and motives, and tastes, and judgments, is that heroic work really going on, of the choice between good and evil, duty and desire, the things of time and the things eternal, the grace of God and the passions of the flesh,—of resistance to temptation, of compliance with it and defeat,—which makes the glorious history of the saint, or the unutterably pathetic tragedy of the castaway? Tempted like as He was,—can that indeed be true of us?

Ah! it must be true; for every man has to show sooner or later what he will do with his conscience and his freedom and his light, what is the real rule that governs him, what is the supreme end which controls all others. You feel perhaps as if you had no concern in what we gravely call temptation. You see on one side, temptations yielded to with such inconceivable weakness and folly that you cannot even understand them. You see on the other, temptations so monstrous and revolting that you simply shudder at them; you pass on and you have nothing to do with them. No: they are temptations which are none to you; on you they have no hold, and if that was all, you might walk through life and not think of temptation. Let us leave them, only remembering in our intercession those to whom they *are* temptations, and all the misery with which they fill the world.—But *you*, it may be, have been ever kindly nurtured, and carefully brought up. You have never known want, and the mean thoughts that want can bring with it; or if you have been pinched and straitened, you have been taught, and you have had the example, to bear up bravely and work cheerfully. You have been guarded within the fence of home. Gentleness, confidence, love, have been ever about you. You have been taught to honour, perhaps to know, what is good, and excellent, and holy, in friends, in principles, in deeds. You have been kept, perhaps, from the sight and words of sin—unless, repeating the history of the first temptation in Paradise,—your curiosity has led you to search into and to learn evil which you need not know, which it was better for you not to know.—And with all these chances for you, all these blessings of God's Eternal Providence, can you suppose that you are not on your trial? What are the tempers which, day by day, you show, after all these advantages? Cannot people, with all this, yet be in their daily life selfish, ill-natured, peevish; too fond of money, unjust, untrue, unkind? Are you safe from continual, habitual, indulged worldliness, from bad temper, evil speaking, censoriousness? And will not God, for such things as these, and for what we and our characters have become in the years that we have let these things go on, will He not call us into judgment? Are not these temptations? Is there not here enough to test the soundness of our hearts, the purity, the steadiness, the integrity of our purposes? Is not this, to be on our trial?

You don't feel that you are on your trial? You find it hard to believe that temptations which you need fear, come in your way?—What about your prayers? If they mean anything, if they are anything real as between the soul of man and God, are we not, have we not been all along, on our trial about our prayers? Are you satisfied with the way you say them? Are you satisfied with the efforts you make, and with the trouble you take to say them better? Are you satisfied with the spectacle which you know you exhibit to Him who sees in secret, when you are singing His praises, when you are bowed before Him on your knees?—Ah! yes, you are unable to keep your thoughts in order, you are often vexed with yourself, you more often acquiesce in words said without meaning: but it is so hard to attend.—Yes, and what does that tell? What we are to-day, is the result and shaping of what in past days we have been. If, to-day, I am not master of my attention, if my thoughts are wandering to the ends of the earth, while my lips are speaking the most awful words that human lips can utter,—if, addressing myself to the ear of the Eternal, I am all the while dreaming without restraint of the idlest vanities of the passing minute,—if, while commending myself to His keeping, I suffer every faculty within me, to go to sleep—what is the history of this, but that in days past I have taken no trouble with myself to check the growth of carelessness and inattention; and now I am reaping the fruits of my unfaithfulness. Day unto day uttereth knowledge; the weakness of to-day is the echo of the deliberate betrayal of duty long ago, when life was still before us.—And do you say, that in the stillness of our uneventful lives, we are not on our trial; on our trial, *what we have been*; on our trial, whether, when we have failed, we will do our best to retrieve our failures?

The hour is coming which must soon decide it—decide it, and betray what has been going on, not only in those great storms of passion or adversity, those great critical decisions of will for or against what is right, to which we often confine the name of temptation, but in those secret, undisclosed, prolonged workings of choice, of effort, of self-surrender, which prepare men for what they do in public, and which are as real and as serious as what they do in public. We rise in the morning to meet what, that day, will try us, will show what we are, and touch some spring, some dormant motive deep down in our nature, revealing the truth about us to One who sees us: and as we go through each day's proof and trial, we are fitting ourselves for the event of the trial of to-morrow; and the current of our life and character is set, by unperceived and insensible influences, either towards that Eternal Life, which God has prepared for man, or towards that Eternal Death, from which there is for the soul no rising. And on this spectacle of human trial, of human preparation for the Eternal Future, the great love, may I use the word—the great *anxiety* of God, throws the awful light of that world which is not yet ours. Above the huge, appalling accumulation of human temptation, of human falls, of human victories, rises the unutterable mystery of the sympathy and partnership in temptation of the Incarnate Son, to tell us that the highest success here was not the thing which man was made for, but goodness, and truth, and love. Amid the hopeless wrecks of human history, the fatal disasters of individual lives, there is planted the Cross of Redemption and Recovery, where our shame and our hope are joined, where the Crucified stretches forth his arms to embrace and console the tempted and the defeated, in this mortal struggle for life or death.

You are weak, you are blind, you know not where you are and where you are going; you feel within you the treacheries of sin, you know how your will has betrayed you, how your motives have deceived you. Yes, but around you, and within you, has come from on high to make His abode with spirits on their trial, the Holy Comforter of Pentecost, the Strengthener, the Enlightener. He knows what you are, He interprets your real self, He responds to what is in your heart, He makes intercession for you with groans that cannot be uttered, He helps your infirmities. Commit yourself and your trial in honesty of heart to Him, that Holy Spirit of Truth, who whispers in your soul and conscience; and of one thing you may be sure; that from falsehood and insincerity of choice, from unavowed motives and disguised self-seeking, He will protect you. And *that* is what we have to fear. When our trial is over, and has to be judged, it is not our mistakes, our misunderstandings, our mismanaged attempts and ill-guided efforts, which will weigh so heavily against us—it is the treasons of our will, our palterings with sin, our disloyalty to conscience, to the voice and call of the Spirit. God, who knows that it is necessary for us to be tried, God, who knows all our weakness, and also how we may be strong, has not been backward in showing how He is in earnest. We adjure Him by the most tremendous recollections of what has actually happened, in heaven and on this earth, for our deliverance :— " By the mystery of Thy Holy Incarnation, by Thy Baptism, Fasting, and Temptation, by Thine Agony and Bloody Sweat, by Thy Cross and Passion, by Thy Precious Death and Burial ; by Thy Glorious Resurrection and Ascension, by the Coming of the Holy Ghost ; Good Lord, deliver us."—May our seriousness in thinking of what we have to do, and what we are preparing for, answer His, in His intent to help and save us ;—in appointing for us a destiny of perfection, beyond the possibility of human thought :—" To him that overcometh will I grant to sit with Me in My throne, even as I also overcame, and am set down with My Father in His throne."

IX

THE SENSE OF BEAUTY A WITNESS TO IMMORTALITY

"Who shall change our vile body, that it may be fashioned like unto His glorious body, according to the working whereby He is able even to subdue all things unto Himself."—PHILIPPIANS iii. 21.

THE Passion and Resurrection of Jesus Christ necessarily made changes, deep and enduring, in human life. Nature went on as before. The stars rose and set, and the days lengthened and shortened through years that seemed the same. "Seedtime and harvest, and heat and cold, and summer and winter" did not cease. And men were born, and lived their days, and died. But underneath this outward likeness to the past, all was new for the future. From that Easter morning the breath of the new creation passed over the earth, that seemed the same. From that Easter morning, life and death, and hopes and fears, and righteousness and sin, and good and evil, and our deepest thoughts about God and man were not—could never be again—what they had seemed before.

I will only for a few minutes this morning pursue the special thought suggested by the text. There one great change is spoken of; a change in that which we now see and know so familiarly; a change complete and overpowering in the vision it opens; a change which connects us all with the morning of the Resurrection; a change so great that it could not be, or be thought of, except by the putting forth of that power which can even subject all things to itself, and which nothing can resist, not even death, not even nature. "Who shall change,—shall transfigure,—our vile body,—the body of our humiliation, —that it may be fashioned like unto His glorious Body"—the Body, in which He is in the glory of the eternal world.

The likeness, the conformity, to Him who rose from the dead, to be the "Second Adam," the new pattern and standard of human nature, is far above all others, a moral and spiritual one. It would be worthless to look forward to being like Jesus Christ in anything that He is now, if we were not to be like Him in His holiness. But besides the great moral and spiritual change, the moral and spiritual cleansing and elevating of our nature, a change—we can only express it now—as of external and of visible form, is also spoken of. "It is sown in corruption; it is raised in incorruption: it is sown in dishonour; it is raised in glory:" says St. Paul of the resurrection of the body; "it is sown in weakness; it is raised in power: it is sown a natural body; it is raised a spiritual body." "As we have borne the image of the earthy, we shall also bear the image of the heavenly." "Flesh and blood cannot inherit the kingdom of God." "We shall be changed. For this corruptible must put on incorruption, and this mortal must put on immortality." These vast, and to us inconceivable changes refer, beyond moral change, to changes in what we can only think of as conditions of our existence. What these conditions shall be is beyond our knowledge, and impenetrable to our thought. But in Scripture we are shown as in a glass, darkly, shadows, images, likenesses, analogies, passing but vivid and piercing gleams of light, which represent to us imperfectly that awful and wondrous future. And what is shown is often summed up in the word "glory." They are but shadows, and we are told that we have not faculties for more; but they, and the word which sums them up, must appeal to, and must answer to, something in us. What is it? Is it not, so far as we can understand anything of the subject, our sense, in the largest sense of the term, of what is beautiful? Is it not our love and admiration of what is beautiful, in all its manifold and varied forms,—is it not this that points forward in us to the glory which shall follow? Is it not part of the promise and hope of the resurrection that this mysterious longing of our nature shall be at length justified and fulfilled, that the perfection which we miss here, but of which we seem to catch momentary and doubtful but transporting glimpses, shall there be, as everything there is, pure, completed, enduring?

1. We are so blinded by custom and commonplace,

that it often never occurs to us to reflect what a wonderful and most mysterious endowment of our nature, is our sense of beauty, our pleasure in it, our longing for its perfect presence. Beyond that which is useful, and that which is true, and that which is good, and that which is orderly and well-proportioned, and that which is beneficial and salutary, there clings obstinately to the soul of man this idea of what is beautiful in its infinite forms and degrees.[1] A man may not be able to explain it, but there it is. He may not be able to justify it, but there it is. He may not agree with other men about it, but there it is. And they, too, if they do not agree about the particular thing which he thinks beautiful, are as obstinate as he in thinking some other things beautiful. From the veriest savage to the highest intelligence of genius, each insists that there is such a thing, each longs to attain to it and to realise it, each admires, and finds delight in what he admires. What is it, this incorrigible, importunate, indestructible sense of beauty, which we may well find nothing to satisfy, but which we will not allow to be in vain? What is it, that fitful, capricious, fugitive thing, which none have seen in its perfection, but of which every one believes that he has seen the image; which is so variable to different eyes and hearts, and to the same at different times; but which, while its spell and charm last, fills and governs and satisfies the soul?

---

[1] See *Proteus and Amadeus*, c. xi., and a striking sermon by Dr. Dowden of Edinburgh, *The Beauty of Nature the Revelation of God.*

What is it that prompts our hymn of praise to God—*Benedicite, omnia opera Domino*—for all the glory and loveliness of the world? What is this faculty in our nature which makes us think the sunset and the dawn, the rich landscape, the noble city, the sea in its glory, lake and mighty flood and breaking torrent, the mountain pass and the snowy peak, the "pomps of midsummer," and the midnight stars; even sights of terror, the thunderstorm and the fire—beautiful? What is it that makes us find what we call beauty—infinite, inexhaustible, unfathomable beauty—in the succession and harmonies of sounds? It is not, surely, their conformity to profound rules, their mathematical subtleties of proportion and relation, indispensable conditions as these may be; but the beauty of the great composer's idea and work is something over and above, and far higher than this, and appeals to something in us which thinks not of numbers and science, though without numbers and science the work could not be. What is it that presents itself, with equal power of charm and admiration and delight, not to the outward sense, but to the "inward eye": which sees the supreme beauty, which is interpreted to it and spread before it, in mere words, read or spoken; which in human character and action, besides goodness, and force, and beneficence, and even holiness, discerns what we call its beauty, the beauty of a sweet, or a noble, or a saintly character? What is it that discerns it, amid infinite varieties of the same type, in human features and form; discerns it not merely in its ordinary vesture, in youth and health and brightness, but discerns it in the subtle play of expression, discerns it in its spring and prime, and not less in ruin and decay; discerns it even with the stamp of suffering and tears and pain; discerns it in the face wasted with disease, in the form which has lain down to die, in the lineaments of death; nay, guided by the art of great painters and sculptors, discerns its awful traces in the very embodiment of the deepest agony, in the visage of the Crucified? What is this mysterious and primary quality, dwelling in such different shapes and defying all analysis; and what are we, that we have eyes and souls to perceive it? Consider the lilies of the field, the flowers in the pastures and the wilderness, which to-day are, and to-morrow fade and perish; why this profuse wealth of exquisite but transient beauty, and why are we made so as to delight in it? Consider God's gift of light, next to His gift of life His greatest and most universal gift—the garment, with which, as the Psalmist says, He clothes Himself—and how, besides the gift itself and all its blessings, beauty is interwoven with it, adding something over and above even to its wonder; beauty on the face of the earth and in the sky; beauty in pure transparency and in the glories of colour; beauty in the water, in the stars, in the gem; and why is it, that, besides the light itself, light gives us so much beyond itself, and who can tell the secret of our delight in it, or unravel the spell of its influence? The Psalmists are thrilled with the sense of these great gifts of God :—" When I consider Thy heavens, the work of Thy fingers, the moon and the stars, which Thou hast ordained ; what is man, that Thou art mindful of him, and the son of man, that Thou visitest him? For Thou hast made him a little lower than the angels, and hast crowned him with glory and honour." " Thou, Lord, hast made me glad through Thy works, and I will rejoice in giving thanks for the operations of Thy hands ; O Lord, how glorious are Thy works ; Thy thoughts are very deep." " Out of Sion hath God appeared in perfect beauty."

2. God has given us to delight in what is beautiful, and has filled His world with beauty. But even on God's gifts man's sinful hand has come—spoiling, defacing, abusing, polluting them. We know but too well how much beauty there is on earth which has turned against Him who made it. There is beauty which is wrecked and ruined ; there is beauty which betrays and kills ; beauty which is the perverter, the destroyer. The "innocent brightness" of the child's beauty seems as if nothing could impair it ; a few years pass, and that same face is still beautiful, but with a terrible and fatal beauty, the witness, the ally, and the minister of sin. God has given to the great masters of art the power, the tremendous responsibility, of creating beauty; beauty which none have seen, which none can challenge or dispute ; beauty which is independent of human

mortality, and exercises its spell on successive generations. It is three or four hundred years since the painters of the great age were covering their walls, or their panels and canvasses; and their creations enthral and mould us still. We almost feel, while we gaze on them, as it has been said, that, "They are in truth the substance, we the shadows."[1] Art has used its power to exalt, to refine, to purify, to open our eyes and minds to truths we know not. But art has used its mighty gifts, and may use them still, not only carelessly but on the side of evil; to ensnare, to corrupt, to tempt men to admire, through the veil of beauty, what is base and bad, what left the stain of defilement behind. Art, and not only knowledge, has been, in the poet's terrible phrase, "Procuress to the Lords of Hell."[2] And, alas! we do not want art to add in this way to the wreck and waste, which sin and toil and pain have made. Watch the faces which hurry past us in succession in the crowded streets. Made in the same type, varying infinitely one from another, face after face disappoints, if it does not repel and shock; face after face tells with dreary uniformity how far, even outwardly, men are short of their ideals; face after face passes, each with its story and purpose of life marked on it; but how little in the vast procession does the eye meet with satisfaction and hope; how

---

[1] Wordsworth, "Lines suggested by a portrait," Cf. Prose Works, iii. 5, 171. Rogers's *Italy*, note, p. 366. Lord Houghton's "A Spanish Anecdote," Poetical Works, vol. ii. 281.

[2] Tennyson, *In Memoriam*, liii. 4.

seldom does the charm of expression promise to make up for what is otherwise wanting. Our glimpses and our judgments are but momentary and superficial: and there are good things there, even on the surface. There is force, there is honesty, there is intelligence, there is resolution, there is kindliness; there are faces that interest and faces which we trust; but of that wonderful capacity for nobleness and beauty, with which human features are endowed, how small is the fruit. Ages of sin and folly, and all that has followed on sin and folly, have left their disfiguring and lowering stamp, and that which was meant to be the divine image and likeness may be a pain even to gaze at.

And so we are tempted to turn away from what is real, and seek a compensation in the ideals of the imagination. It can do much for us. It can transport us into a world where we feel at ease; where things happen as they do not happen here; where we see things which we vainly look for here. The poet can make the most pathetic sorrows, the most tragic ruin, wear the fascination of beauty. The painter can show us " The light, the gleam, that never was on sea or land."[1] Higher than either, the spirit which God's grace has purified and enlightened, of saint or prophet, may pass the boundaries of this world of time, and raise itself by faith and hope to recognise, dimly and darkly, in sacrament and figure, something of what mortal

[1] Wordsworth, *Peele Castle.*

"eye hath not seen, nor ear heard," of the glories which belong to the company of the blessed. But all this is but for a moment. The realities of the present state soon reassert themselves, and make us feel how grave, yet how commonplace, are its imperfections, how vast its shortcomings, how deep its humiliations.

This is what we have, and what we have not. These are our longings and foretastes; these are our poor fulfilments, our baffled hopes and broken dreams. For we still are in the body, the "body of our humiliation;" we still bear about with us "the dying" which our Master bore. The glories and the beautiful things of our mortal state die to us, or we die to them. Death breaks in, or sin, or folly; and the home bright with peace and love, with all that brightens and ennobles life, falls to pieces and disappears. "The grass withereth, the flower fadeth. . . . Surely the people is grass. The grass withereth, the flower fadeth (beautiful as it is): but the Word of our God shall stand for ever."

3. "But the Word of our God shall stand for ever." For "Now is Christ risen from the dead, and become the first-fruits of them that slept." "Sown in weakness; raised in power: sown in dishonour; raised in glory:" that Sacred Body, scarred and mangled, and laid low, bearing the marks of defeat and ruin, of the insults of the wicked and the triumphs of sin and death, was laid in the tomb, to rise again in the

glory of an eternal victory. He rose again to fulfil "the earnest expectation of the creature," to show forth and to assure its deliverance "from the bondage of corruption into the glorious liberty of the children of God." He rose to bring with Him the perfection of human nature. He rose to recognise and to fulfil man's craving for righteousness, man's craving for immortality. And He rose to fulfil man's craving for joy and gladness, man's craving for what he can admire and rejoice in, man's craving for what is beautiful and what is glorious.

We sometimes wonder, what has all this beauty which even here meets us—these strains which seem echoes from within the veil, from a world unapproachable to us; these evening lights and summer days of which the mind seems unequal to take in the charm; this strange mysterious infinity of beauty, never in each instance the same, yet in all the same in kind—what has it to do with all that lies beside it and in contrast to it, a world of toil and monotony and pain—what has it to do with a world of suffering and death? With the sense of its excellence comes the sense of its transitoriness, and its contradictions, the shadow and sadness of the certainty of its decay, the certainty that we cannot keep it. But in this, as in other things, our Lord's Resurrection has made all things new. They may perish here; but now we know that nothing precious and nothing real is lost out of the life of man.—" Sown in dishonour, . . . raised in glory." Those mighty words authorise us to think that not in vain and for nothing we admire what is beautiful in the face of the world, in the creations of art, in the face of man, in those more subtle charms of music and speech, of expression and character. We see in it now the evidence of the riches, the magnificence of our God; but we see in it also the type and promise of what is to be, when that which is perfect is come. What is it but the actual beginning, the germ as well as the pledge, of that glory which shall follow, into which the Firstborn from the Dead is gone before us? He tells us of it, He bids us hope, He who has given its likeness and foretastes here. It must pass, as He for a moment passed, out of the sight of men, disbelieved in, dishonoured. But it passes, as He passed, to return. His day is coming, in which all that has made this stage of time beautiful will bloom and revive once more; and more than that, in which so much that we have turned away from, and in which we have seen no beauty and no charm, will shine forth renewed in the power of His glory. We watch and gaze, with mingled joy and sorrow, at beauty in the faces of the dying, of the dead, for it is of the dead who are to rise again. And shall we not be glad, too, in thinking how many of those dreary and toil-worn faces which daily meet us in the crowd and turmoil of life are one day to be illuminated with the eternal beauty, to reflect the light and perfectness of Him, on whom they wait and whom they serve, in the larger and perfect life.

4. Easter is our warrant for believing, amid its deeper and more awful hopes, that not without purpose has God endowed men with this great gift of rejoicing in what is beautiful, in sight and sound and imagination. It is the assurance of that great day of the renewed heaven and the renewed earth, which shall see the Holy City descending out of heaven from God, "prepared as a bride adorned for her husband." But just in proportion of our keen enjoyment of what is beautiful there follows a great responsibility. Surely such a gift was not given us for mere selfish ends. Close beside us, in our enjoyment, are the dark and dismal sides of human life. Surely what we can do to brighten and cheer them, to impart to them something of what is to us so precious and delightful, our very enjoyment bids us to do. We, the educated; we, who have all literature open before us and can read at leisure the books we like; we, who have been trained to appreciate and delight in what is noble and beautiful, whose eyes have been opened to discern it in its many forms, who can surround ourselves in our homes with its memorials, who search for its marvels over land and sea;—surely we have a debt to those whose life is not so brightened. That sense, that delight, are God's gifts as much as wealth, or influence, or ability of any sort; and God's gifts are not only to be used and employed; they are also to be shared and communicated. We have not only to feed the hungry and clothe the

naked; we have not only to lay the foundations of truth and justice, in the lowest and in the highest places of society, to maintain the cause of the poor, to see that such as are in need and necessity have right; but surely it is also our Master's purpose that we should carry into their hard lives something of what gladdens ours. This world has little that is beautiful for these hard lives, the lives of those whose daily toil is far from the bright places of earth and sky; who have never seen the flowers grow in the fields and woods; whose hours pass in dulness and gloom and squalidness, whose homes, when men are strong, are in dreary courts and alleys, and when they are sick and old, in hospitals and workhouses; who live, so many of them, good and patient and kindly and beneficent lives, with so little of the outward brightness that so many of us have to cheer and interest and gladden us. They have, indeed, a claim on our sympathy. It is not the least practical call and lesson of our Easter festival.

Easter makes all one, in the sense of our deliverance, in our ineffable hopes. Let us think how it may make us all more and more one, in the brightness which it brings with it, even now in our present life. Not in vain are the great festivals of our Lord's Presence with us—Christmas, Easter, Whitsuntide—become our great popular holidays. It is not for ourselves, it is for the whole body of those for whom Christ died and rose again, that for their sakes and in their name, we, in a place like this, offer to Him of our best, that we adorn His house with majesty and beauty, that we fill its courts with glorious music. For them, in such places as this, we understand that we are bound to meet their longings for what is beautiful — that mysterious sense of beauty which the Resurrection first made serious, and to which it gave a meaning. And we do well: for they have the same future before them that we have. Their eyes, like ours, are destined to open one day on "the land that is very far off," on "the King in His beauty."—But let us not stop here. Let us, by any means that we can, carry into their lives some of that keen and high enjoyment, some of that discipline and refinement and elevation of spirit, which is given to many of us in such overflowing measure. It is, perhaps, little that we can do; little that we can teach; and, compared with other greater things, of little account in itself. But if it is only a witness of our sympathy, of our wish to impart what we delight in ourselves, it carries with it a blessing. The flowers by the bedside of the sick, the dull hours made bright by reading or song, the efforts, frank, generous, sincere, after unstrained and equal intercourse, as between man and man, are the "cup of cold water" offered to those whom Christ loves; till in time, perhaps, we may do more; till we, and still more those who come after us, and are better and wiser and stronger than we are, learn more and more, and are more and more able to teach others, to see in what is most

K

delightful and lovely here the earnests and foreshadowings of that Day, when He who is the Resurrection and the Life shall make all things new;[1] when He shall change the body of our humiliation, the humiliation of weakness and disease and sin, the humiliation of the ghastliness and wreck of death, into the likeness of the body of His glory; when the promise, fulfilled in the Head, shall be fulfilled in those of whom He is the Head— "Wherefore my heart was glad and my glory rejoiced, my flesh also shall rest in hope. . . . Thou shalt show me the path of life; in Thy presence is the fulness of joy; and at Thy right hand there is pleasure for evermore." . . . "As for me, I will behold Thy presence in righteousness; and when I awake up after Thy likeness I shall be satisfied with it."

[1] Dies venit, dies Tua,
In qua reflorent omnia :
Laetemur et nos, in viam
Tua reducti dextera.
Brev. Rom. in Dominica Quadragesimæ, ad Laudes.

X

THE RESURRECTION FROM THE DEAD

"The Firstborn from the dead."—COLOSSIANS i. 18.

IN these mysterious and awful words the Apostle describes Him who, after His agony and death and burial, rose again the third day from the dead, and whose resurrection brings us here to-day. That issue and result of the dwelling of the Son of God on earth fills St. Paul's mind with its wonder and its triumph. His Master is ever before his eyes as the One Person wearing our mortal nature, who by His own power, and for the first time, broke through the immemorial, universal law and rule of death. That overwhelming event haunts the thoughts of St. Paul, and supplies a pre-eminent title by which he speaks of the Master whom he serves, and the Saviour whom he adores. He was "the first that should rise from the dead, and should show light unto the people, and unto the Gentiles." He was "declared to be the Son of God with power, . . . by the resurrection from the dead." He was "the First-fruits of them that slept." He, as St. John, too, heard in his vision, was "the Faithful Witness and the First-begotten of the dead . . . the First and the Last, which was dead and is alive." First in all things in heaven and earth, He was first to bring into that nature and that race which He had redeemed, the deliverance it had so longed for from the bondage of the grave. He, says St. Paul, in his inspired effort to realise the truth, " is the image of the invisible God, the Firstborn of every creature: for by Him were all things created, that are in heaven, and that are in earth, visible and invisible, whether they be thrones, or dominions, or principalities, or powers: all things were created by Him, and for Him: and He is before all things, and by Him all things consist. And He is the Head of the body, the Church: Who is the beginning, the Firstborn from the dead, that in all things He might have the pre-eminence."

1. "The Firstborn from the dead"—"the Firstfruits of them that slept"—how familiar the words sound; and yet, I suppose, it is not always easy to bring home to feeling and thought the real meaning with which they are charged. It is not often that they make and leave on us the impression which they made on the mind of St. Paul. For there was a time—St. Paul had known it—when, however men hoped for immortality and resurrection, their experience had seen no warrant of it. The grave closed over the dead: the Psalm of trust, "Thou wilt not leave my soul in hell,"—the assurance of prophecy, "I know that my Redeemer liveth," "thy dead men shall live, together with my dead body shall they arise"—was answered by the other voice, the wail of perplexity and uncomforted grief, "Dost

Thou show wonders among the dead; or shall the dead rise up again and praise Thee? Shall Thy lovingkindness be shown in the grave, or Thy faithfulness in destruction?" And the same spirit which inspired the one thought allowed also the natural outburst expressed in the other. The great servants of God had come and gone; had lived and died: and their sepulchres were with their children to this day, monuments of the unbroken power of death. They had hoped, they had believed; but to hope is not to possess; to believe is not to see; and men as yet had only seen what we still see of death—the visible end, the decay which cannot be arrested, the sinking in the deep waters where no love or strength can retain or deliver; the vanishing, the disappearing, the extinction. O awful mystery of death: to-day there is life and brightness and power and thought, and affection deep and strong, and character made rich and beautiful by long discipline, and the wealth of years' experience, and force to govern hearts and wills, or to turn the courses of the world; and to-morrow, all is vacancy, there is nothing there; he is never to be spoken to again; he is nowhere any more to be found; all has passed like a mist dissolving. "When the breath of man goeth forth he shall turn again to his earth, and then all his thoughts perish." That is what we see and know still. Once and again, indeed, men had been called back to life, but only again to die. Till "the Firstborn from the dead" arose, the world had seen nothing else.

"But now is Christ risen from the dead, and become the First-fruits of them that slept;" not called back by any voice of power without Him, not called back to the life of mortality. "Christ being raised from the dead dieth no more; death hath no more dominion over Him." This is the great, the immeasurable change. On this earth there has been seen, there lived and walked One who was the Son of Man, and yet was never more to taste of death; one who had borne the image of the earthly, and who had put on, while yet among us, the image of the heavenly. That of itself was enough to overpower the thoughts of men, accustomed through all generations to see everything end in death: we see and can understand what it was to those who had followed and loved Him; alternate terror and joy, perplexity and dawning bliss, such as earth had never known, doubt, incredulity, the shock of sober, irresistible certainty—"My Lord and my God." But this was not all. He, for whom had been "loosed the pains of death, because it was not possible that He should be holden of it," was not alive again for Himself alone. He was "the First-fruits of them that slept," "the Firstborn from the dead." His resurrection was no single, isolated event in the great order of His earthly ministry which it all but closed. It was the first step, the "beginning," of a new and even greater order of His ministry to the creatures whom He had made. It was the tearing asunder "the veil that is spread over all nations."

It was the opening of the kingdom of God to all believers. It was the reversal, not for one, but for all, of that supposed necessary condition of human existence, that it has to come to an end with the parting breath. It was not merely a pledge, a promise, an example; it was, for all who bear the flesh and blood which He bore, a step into a new world, with new conditions. It was a step, a real step, made, not foreshadowed, from the dominion of nature into the kingdom of grace. For He was "the Firstborn among many brethren," and He was "the Firstborn from the dead," "the First-fruits of them that slept."

2. This, if we believe that Christ indeed rose from the dead, is simply and certainly the truth. And yet we hardly feel it. And yet there are those to whom such a change with all its consequences, if believed to be real, seems hardly worthy the attention of high moral elevation and refinement. Ah, brethren, to those who have to do with death, to those who have to die, death is, after all, the sternest, strangest, hardest fact of human experience; and anything that abates the sharpness of death is well worthy the lovingkindness of God, and the deep thanksgiving of man. The writers of the New Testament believed that Christ was the Firstborn from the dead; and we see how this altered the whole face of the world and life. It enlarged almost infinitely the interest even of this present mortal life on earth by giving it a meaning and a future; but it trans-

ferred the scene of man's true and free and perfect existence, to a sphere far beyond this, far beyond the swift passage of the seventy years with their weakness and sorrow, far beyond that transitory but laborious stage, when every day, as it came and went, brought its trial, its temptation, its choice, perhaps its fall—to the sphere where all was eternal and all was accomplished. And it did this, it opened this great moral hope, as never had been done before—not for the great and elect souls of the race only, but for the obscure and down-trodden crowds, the multitudes that none can number—the slave, the lost, the abject, the miserable. For in His own person, Son of God and Son of Man, He had made the step from old things to new; and He had made it for all His brethren. As the Apostle says, We are no longer under the law, the old covenant, but under grace,— so we may go on to say, We, the children of the Resurrection, are no longer under the laws of nature, but under the laws of the Spirit; no longer under death, but under life; no longer under blind necessity and extinction, but under the living Son of God, "Who died for us" and rose again, "that, whether we wake or sleep, we should live together with Him." He who has the key to the riddle of man's being has opened the door and let in the light, the dazzling, almost blinding light of the other world on our commonplace and feverish lives, on the seeming vanity and waste of the generations of mankind. One after another, they have come, and waxed green like the leaves of summer; one after another, they have fallen and vanished like the leaves of autumn. Where are they gone, all these men who lived as we live, whose footprints and whose handiwork are about us and in all the earth, but *they* are seen no more? Have they perished? Did they begin their running with such fulness of life, only that all should be thrown away, when they laid down in the dust and disappeared? So it seemed for all that nature and experience could tell. We see "that wise men also die and perish together, as well as the ignorant and foolish. . . . Man being in honour hath no understanding, but is compared unto the beasts that perish."

"But now is Christ risen from the dead, and become the First-fruits of them that slept." But now we know what has become of them, the long-forgotten dead. No one soul in that distant, incalculable multitude has been forgotten by God Who made it. It has not ceased to be, though it has long disappeared from here. It lives and waits in its own place till its day comes, and God shall judge the secrets of men according to His Gospel of righteousness and truth. It has not lived for nought; each has had its own trial, its own great chance and opportunity, according to the "riches of God's goodness and forbearance and long-suffering," even though we cannot see how. Of each life the account has to be given, and God will render to every man according to his deeds. Life has not been in vain or an idle show: each has shown itself as it is; the fruits of to-day have gone on beyond to-morrow, on and onwards till the trial was fulfilled, and they are reaped—" to them who by patient continuance in well-doing . . . glory and honour and immortality, eternal life: but unto them that are contentious, and do not obey the truth but obey unrighteousness, indignation and wrath, tribulation and anguish . . . to the Jew first, and also to the Gentile." For " now is Christ risen from the dead and become the First-fruits of them that slept." He, first and alone, leads the great procession from the prison-house of death, from forgetfulness and nothingness—leads the great triumph of the redeemed of God; the forefathers of the human race, the patriarchs of His Church, saint and prophet and witness to the truth, all who " died in faith, not having received the promises, but having seen them afar off," strangers and pilgrims in the land which, though they knew it not, was their own; and with them, the " holy and humble men of heart " —just and good men in every nation, fearing God and working righteousness—all who, though not yet knowing their Redeemer, had the faith which followed the light within them even to death, resolved, even " though He slay me, yet will I trust in Him;" all those who, not having the law, were a law unto themselves, the blessed and accepted of Him who is no respecter of persons, and who has prepared " glory, honour, and peace, to every man that worketh good, to the Jew first, and also to the Gentile." They sleep, but they are not wasted; they sleep, but they are not forgotten: their Redeemer and ours has them in remembrance, and has shown us what they are to be in that new world which has begun for all of us. For it has begun: how could it not but begin, in reality and truth, when once the Deliverer had broken the power and the necessity of the grave? How could that world be the same, in which such a thing had happened: in which, indeed, death had given way to life? And so from thenceforward the New Testament speaks as if "the powers of the world to come" were already here, changing, vivifying, transforming all things, beginning even in time the work of eternity, even "upon earth the days of heaven." Think of what he must have felt about the facts of existence, about the light and power from above which had come to make their home here, even while this life was going on, who wrote such words as these:—"The eyes of your understanding being enlightened; that ye may know what is the hope of His calling, and what the riches of the glory of His inheritance in the saints, and what is the exceeding greatness of His power to us-ward who believe, according to the working of His mighty power, which He wrought in Christ, when He raised Him from the dead, and set Him at His own right hand in the heavenly places, far above all principality, and power, and might, and dominion, and every name that is named, not only in this world, but also in that which is to come: and hath put all things under His feet, and gave Him to be the head over all things to the Church, which is His body, the fulness of Him that filleth all in all. And you hath He quickened, who were dead in trespasses and sins ... quickened us together with Christ ... and hath raised us up together, and made us sit together in heavenly places in Christ Jesus: that in the ages to come He might show the exceeding riches of His grace in His kindness toward us through Christ Jesus." "Who is He that condemneth? It is Christ that died, yea rather, that is risen again, who is even at the right hand of God, who also maketh intercession for us."

Is it wonderful that they who thus believed and thus felt should have lived the lives we read of in the New Testament; those strangely mingled lives of pain and happiness; those lives of unquenchable and perpetual gladness; of heroic works and deeds for God; of that joyous contempt of the pangs of sacrifice, of the opinion of the world, of all that can weary or kill the body, or vex and afflict the soul, which is stamped on all the Apostolic history and on every line of the Apostles' writings? Is it wonderful that with Christ risen ever before their minds, this should have been the ordinary level of their thoughts and lives?—And then to think, my brethren, that these words are as applicable to us as they were to them. What for, but to remind us of this, does Easter come round every year, with all its preparations, and its festal splendours, and its train of following holidays? Is it not to assure us that we too, in this twilight of the world, neither dark nor bright, may have and ought to have, an inheritance with the saints in light?

3. Let us indeed humble ourselves when we think of this; but believing in Christ the Firstborn from the dead, let it not crush and paralyse us. It is but too certain a fact of experience that the average of human excellence and attainment is pitched very low; but every day there are those who are raising it, and we may, each of us, if we will, be among these benefactors of our race. Think of what one such man, of whom we have been thinking much of late,[1] may have done to raise the sense of duty, the sense of power, the willingness for a clean and true and unreserved service, in the hearts of thousands of his brethren, how—

> " The music of a lonely heart may help
> So many lonely hearts unknown to him." [2]

We have all of us to meet our Master, and he has met his. He, like all of us, had the dust and stains of earth upon him; he, like all of us, needed to the utmost his Master's forgiveness and mercy. But as far as it was possible for man to judge, and we had much to judge by, it seems that when he went from here, he went with character and will absolutely given up and trained to do what he believed his Master wanted of him; that when the Master whom he so loved met him on the other side, He met in him a servant who, as far as character and will go,

[1] General Gordon.
[2] Roden Noel, *Songs of the Heights and Deeps*, p. 186.

was ready at once for any further task—ready for unclouded communion with Him to whom on earth he had lived so near. He had given his best, and there was no more for him to give here. But what a contrast to the lives of which so many of us are conscious—of us who may have to meet the Master at any time—the imperfect, feeble, indulgent, effortless lives; the poor, ineffective and to borrow a term which but too fully expresses the truth—" malingering" service. Is that the character, unformed, irresolute, uncertain—fit to meet Him who has given us this life to prepare for His service in the other? Compare the character we have spoken of—simple, straight, complete, single-eyed and whole-hearted—with the mixtures of which we see so many, and where evil counteracts and neutralises good; high generosity with pride or bad temper, zealous industry with vain love of praise, kindliness with sloth and weakness and cowardice. What sort of preparation can that be for the further calls on us that may be beyond the veil; on us, hampered by our small or secret sins, divided in our allegiance, distracted by unconquered bad habits of self-deceit and carelessness? And yet nothing in that character which has thrilled this country as it never has been in our time, nothing in that character of simple and single-eyed Christian manliness, was above the reach of any of us. The man who had delivered an empire, and stood at bay for a year almost alone against failing hope and coming death, was but the same man who had quietly taught the ignorant, and borne with the wretched, and ministered to the sick, and tended the children, in his leisure from his professional work at Gravesend. It was no splendour of intelligence, it was no gift of power and achievement, which has made him so great and so heroic; it was the perfect heart, which rung so true for God and duty —whether duty great or small.—May He who has given us the certainty of the Resurrection to countervail the awful certainty of death, help us to that preparation of heart and character which befits those who have to do with such great realities. May He who has called us to immortality, in His mercy give us time till we are ready—ready, as far as creatures can be ready—to look up at Him, to whom they live, to whom they die. But the days are passing; let us make haste; He gives us time, but He cannot delay for long. Remember, we are of those who "look for the resurrection of the dead, and the life of the world to come."

XI

THE PEACE OF CHRIST

"Then the same day at evening, being the first day of the week, when the doors were shut where the disciples were assembled for fear of the Jews, came Jesus and stood in the midst, and said unto them, Peace be unto you."—ST. JOHN xx. 19.

THIS was the Lord's first greeting to those whom He had left stunned and hopeless. It carries back our thoughts to the promise of a few days before:— "Peace I leave with you, My peace I give unto you: not as the world giveth, give I unto you." That was the promise, solemn, emphatic, redoubled. That was the promise,—"Peace." And what followed? It was, —and they knew not yet all that it really was,—the wildest scene of storm, and war, and hate, and ruin, which the world had seen: man warring against God; man trampling fiercely, savagely, on the "peace of God." What peace was there in the restlessness of the leave-taking, in the agony in the garden, in the midnight betrayal; what peace in the High Priest's hall, before the Roman judgment-seat, amid the yelling crowds, amid the mocking soldiers; what peace on Calvary, till all was exhausted, life and hatred and hope,—till the last words of the Son to the Mother, the last forgiveness, the last commendations, the half-opened door of Paradise,—till the calm of the last sigh, and the rest of the grave, and the silence of the stupefied mourners in Jerusalem? "My peace I give unto you:" what must the recollection of those words have seemed to them, if they had strength to collect their thoughts in that tremendous overthrow? And now, when the only peace left seemed the peace of forgetfulness, there broke in on the amazed company, from the very lips which had promised it,—no longer the promise, but the very gift, the redoubled gift of peace. "Peace be unto you. And when He had so said, He showed unto them His hands and His side. Then were the disciples glad, when they saw the Lord. Then said Jesus to them again, Peace be unto you: as My Father hath sent Me, even so send I you." Peace in victory, Peace in work; Peace such as had been His in doing what the Father sent Him to do.—It was as when, on a much smaller scale, He had stilled the storm on the waters. "As they sailed He fell asleep: and there came down a storm of wind on the lake; and they were filled with water, and were in jeopardy. And they came to Him, and awoke Him, saying, Master, master, we perish. Then He arose, and rebuked the wind and the raging of the water: and they ceased, and there was a calm." Fiercer torrents than these had gone over their heads, had swept away in an instant all they cared for and rested on, had drowned the Master's life and all their hopes; and once more, in stranger truth, the storm was stilled, and there was a great calm. He was with them, who stilled "the raging of the sea, and the noise of His waves, and the madness of the people." "The Lord sitteth above the water flood, . . . the Lord shall give His people the blessing of peace." "Peace be unto you."

And so still, year by year, Easter comes to us in its due order with "Christ is risen," "Peace be unto you." Out of the battles and troubles which shake and darken life, out of the "provoking of all men and the strife of tongues,"—out of the

> "Loud stunning tide [1]
> Of human care and crime,"

Easter yearly rises, bringing with it, not the kind of joy we felt at Christmas, the joy of children, the welcome of infinite condescension, and the sight of humble innocence, — but the peace of an awful victory. Easter comes after the deepest thoughts of suffering, of gloom, of death. It comes after the darkest, dreariest week in the year. To those who have at all been affected by the memories and the reflections of that week, it is the taking off of a prolonged and trying strain; Easter meets them tired, depressed, weighed down with having had to look so closely at sin, and pain, and bitter death; and it wipes all this out like a bad dream in the triumph it has led to, in the reappearance of the Great Deliverer, —the same, though so changed, unharmed by the power of evil, alive for evermore.

[1] *The Christian Year*, St. Matthew's Day.

There are two points on which I will say a few words, in the peace of Easter.

1. It brings to us the peace of conviction and belief. Belief is something more than acquiescence in a conclusion. After thought has done its work, and led the mind through all the array of arguments and proofs to a position with which reason is satisfied, it has not necessarily brought it to the point of real, active belief. We know that we shall die; but we can keep that certainty at arms' length the greater part of our lives. There is a further effort, a distinct act of will, a distinct stirring and rousing of the sluggishness of the soul, a distinct exertion and rising up of the inner powers of consciousness and imagination, to make us feel what yet is so certain, to take hold of it by real faith; for faith not only accepts conclusions, but "sees the invisible;" it brings with it the power to transfigure and illuminate reason into insight. We Christians think that there is no event in the condition and history of mankind, more certain than that our Lord rose from the dead. It seems to us established with a majestic solidity, which became the corner stone of the great Gospel of the Love of God. Except on the hopeless, the unverifiable argument, that *it could not be*, it seems like flying in the face of all human experience, of all that we know of the ways and goings on of men, to conceive that we should be mistaken in what is so attested, and has, as a matter of fact, been the source and spring of such consequences. Without it, we have to account

for not only the greatest, but the most salutary and the most hopeful changes in the progress of human society. It, alone, arrested the ruin, the imminent wreck and foundering of Western society; and with Western society must have gone the hopes of mankind. It, alone, was equal to support a moral and religious revolution, of which the forces are not yet spent, and which act with the greatest intensity on numbers who now refuse to recognise in the darkness of the past, the Power from which those forces have originated; who cannot see in Christ risen, the seal, the only seal, of that "mind of Christ" which, so often in disinterested service—often with heroic self-sacrifice—they recognise to be the greatest ideal possible to man. It alone has been the basis of what none can look back to without wonder, the perpetual advance of all the centuries of our modern world: centuries which with monotonous and inconsistent mixtures of good and evil, yet never—or only once perhaps, in the tenth century, and that with much that was hopeful,—never went back in those conquests, specially necessary for men in mere human society, of larger and truer ideas of justice and mercy and beneficence. Christendom has much to answer for, but it has done that which no other social phenomenon in the world, political, moral, religious, has ever approached to, has ever conceived of. We can see how it should, as well as that, in matter of fact, it did, flow from Christ's open tomb. Those who think differently must believe that the memory of an obscure Syrian devotee, poor and miserable and ruined, floated up by accident, by the chances of an age of Oriental fanaticism, no one can tell how, to the summit and control of all those forces which shape the world; that it gained them, and kept them, and developed them, indefinitely,—and was, in fact, the inspirer of the greatest and noblest times the world has seen, the inspirer of the enthusiasm and worship of its greatest children.

We live in times of energy and unquiet and change. Around us, familiar to us, are questionings on every conceivable subject of human thought, challenging every human belief, every human law, every human hope. As we walk through life, we cannot help hearing these awful voices on all sides of us, threatening what is best and dearest, implanting doubt, terrible in their seriousness. Don't let us weakly complain of what is inevitable, as this is; God can bring abundant good out of danger and evil, if only men are true. But it is indeed a blessing to pass out of the fevers and anxieties of the day into the calm of Easter. It is not less a blessing to pass out of the dull heavy pressure of custom, into the presence of such an awful opening of another world, as Christ risen from the dead. For, do not let us deceive ourselves, it is most awful; it has no fellow in all that has happened in time. It is the living reality, on which depends the fate of mankind; it is this or it is something we dare not think of. It is idle indeed to think of toying with ingenious guesses about forgeries, or allegories, or legends affecting and poetic. It is not such things that can bear the weight of Christianity—of historical Christianity, much more of spiritual Christianity.—And to this, Easter leads us. It invites us to make that step of which I spoke, from intellectual assent to the effort and living energy of faith. We are brought close to the very centre of that vast system of witness by which we know of Christ. And if we will yield to its gracious influences, if we will stir ourselves up to see with the inward eye what our words declare, if we let love and devotion, and awe and reverence and hope, have their due scope, Easter will bring us, in the midst of perplexity and trouble, what St. Paul calls "peace in believing:" we shall know in whom we have believed. It will bring the peace of conviction, of belief, of faith.

2. And next; Easter, by its wonderful memories, and its gracious persuasions, invites to peace of conscience. Christ's Resurrection, I need not remind you, has been, from the first, the great call, and the great power, to newness of life.—" Raised again for our justification." "As Christ was raised up from the dead by the glory of the Father, even so we also should walk in newness of life." This is a familiar line of thought in the New Testament, echoed in the services of our Prayer Book. And so Easter is the natural start for correction, for amendment, for learning and facing the truth in our lives, which are always drifting and straying from the standard which we acknowledge. Easter is the natural

beginning of a renewed and purified conscience. The past time of reflection and repentance has, we may hope, opened many eyes, torn asunder many self-deceptions, filled many souls with goodwill and hope and courage, in their efforts against sin ; has brought home to many, the misery and the darkness of living apart from God, or in rebellion against Him. And now Easter comes to send them on their way rejoicing, to make new and straight paths for their feet, to breathe over them, for their further work in life, the peace, the strength, the living hope, of which the Resurrection is the fountain. Only let them keep themselves pure. Only let them jealously guard, as their best treasure, their Easter peace of conscience. Only let them remember that nothing will keep it pure—neither thoughts, nor feelings, nor prayers, nor even sacraments, much less the outward environments of a religious life—without the continual activity of a watchful and honest will. The man's self must do it by the grace of God, not things outside him ; where he is, in what he chooses and does, there God's grace will meet him : where he is only passive, and lets circumstances decide for him, he cannot hope for the conqueror's crown, or for the disciple's peace.

I might, I think, appeal to a wide experience in saying that there is one condition of the religious conscience, where all seems fairly right, except one little uneasy, unhealthy spot, never really healed, but intermittent in its mischief, which seems at times to disappear, and then breaks out again with its old life. It is not for nothing that an Apostle has given to the language of morals as well as of religion, the profound thought and the phrase of a " besetting sin," "the sin which doth so easily beset us." And he gave it to religious men, to men like so many of us here, surrounded by the memorials and the gifts of religion. It may be any sin,—impure thoughts, uncharitable judgments, evil speaking, selfishness, insincerity, cowardice, slackness, inattention, irreverence in prayer : but it comes and goes, is repented of and returns, and conscience knows it but too well. And there is one feature characteristic of this ill-satisfied conscience, where all would be honest and well but for this one reserved dark corner,—that it seems to be pursued, dogged, haunted by appeals and warnings, from unexpected quarters, and with startling force, in which it cannot help believing that it hears the voice of God. The touch of nature is one, and it makes all the world kin. Do not all who know something of a besetting sin, know something of this experience?

When conscience is thus uneasy, everything round it, like the fragments of a mirror, seems to multiply the reflection of its unsound condition. The consciousness that we are not quite true to God and duty, the consciousness of the "unlit lamp, and ungirt loin," gives a meaning and colour even to trivial accidents ; we see in them our own story, our own portraiture ; and the eye of the portrait is ever upon us, and meets us whenever we look up. It is the little rift in our loyalty: it is, as St. Paul calls it, the "little leaven," endangering the whole lump. And where it is, peace cannot be in its truth and wholeness. God's merciful warnings hinder peace.

And yet, Easter was meant to bring us peace,—peace of conscience, peace in the depths of heart and will. And Easter confronts, with its tremendous and majestic certainties, our poor little make-believes. How do they look, those ugly, pertinacious, mean disobediences, next to our Lord's victory, next to Christian truth and hope? Can we be the same persons, who exult with kindled souls in the one, and palter fitfully with the other? Cannot we use the sincerity of our faith, our devotion, our rejoicing loyalty, to beat down these despicable treacheries of our lower nature?

Easter calls to newness of life. Easter calls to just those efforts which we need to make to reach "the conscience as the noonday clear." Easter calls to purge out the old leaven. Easter calls our feet into the ways of "sincerity and truth;" into the "ways of peace."—May its blessed work be fulfilled in us. May we so walk now before that King of Glory, whose triumph we rejoice in, that He may be with us when we die, with His parting blessing "Peace be unto you:" that He may meet us, when we shall die no more, with the greeting which made the disciples glad on the first Easter morning, "Peace be unto you."

XII

THE POWER OF THE ASCENSION ON THE LIVES OF MEN

"While we look not at the things which are seen, but at the things which are not seen."—2 CORINTHIANS iv. 18.

THIS contrast, in what we have to do with here, fills, so to speak, the atmosphere of Ascension Day. All day long the voice pursues us, "Lift up your hearts;" "He that descended is the same also that ascended up far above all heavens," ascended "that He might fill all things;" "Set your affection on things above, not on things on the earth;" "Your life is hid with Christ in God;" "The things which are seen are temporal—for the time,—but the things which are not seen are eternal."

This great contrast is part of the necessary condition of our human being, if there is any religious truth in the world. The things that are seen, that are now, are indeed of the deepest interest, most precious and most eventful, of far reaching, incalculable influence. Duty, and faith, and love, and goodness, and justice, and mercy, have to do with the things that are now, the things that are seen: who can measure their greatness, their value? But when all that has been said, realised most amply, felt most keenly, still it remains true that man was made for a life, for a sphere, even greater than the greatest we can know here; that all that is seen is but for a time; that the things that are not seen are eternal.

And Christ our Master went up on high out of our sight to draw our hearts after Him, to make us feel that, in spite of all veils and shadows now, in spite of all interests and all duties now, the end and goal for which we live and think and will is beyond all that we can ever know here—to make us *feel* it, to make us *imagine* it. *Know* indeed we do, and we bless His name for what He has shown us: but we know, we can know, only in part; we know as those who are encompassed by inscrutable, unfathomable nature, and between whom and the unseen hangs the curtain of death—death, silent, final, without answer. We know as those who have known the mystery of the Incarnation, and have seen the dawn of Easter, and who "look for the resurrection of the dead, and the life of the world to come:" and yet that is little to what we shall know when we know even as we are known. But this at least is part of our knowledge, that what we are here is but a little fragment of what we were made for; and that Christ is gone up to the throne of God to warrant us in going up there too, in heart and mind continually, in hope, in rejoicing, in wonder, in adoration; in the persuasion that though He is there, He is yet also here, always with us even to the end of the world.

And to Him we owe our supreme loyalty, and duty, and devotion, and boundless trust, as to our Lord and our God. The love of Him, the union in affection and will with Him—that is what we profess; that, when it is in reality and truth, is Christian religion.

The world is full of other religions: I do not mean here of other professions and forms of religion, the varieties of belief and worship and religious custom, which divide the world, Christian and non-Christian. I mean religion in the sense of what a man's heart owns to as most mighty and most irresistible in all things round him; what he bows down to and sincerely worships in the secret sanctuary of desire and will; what he holds highest and most precious, most excellent and most Divine in what he knows and thinks of, most worthy his homage, his labour, his interest, the spending his life for. That is truly a man's religion the object of which fills and holds captive his soul and heart and mind, in which he trusts above all things, which imposes on him reverence and awe, which above all things he longs for and hopes for. It is that which possesses and fascinates all that is most real in the man's self; that which in his real self he is devoted to, of all things within his range and all the things among which he may choose. "Covetousness," says the apostle, "which is idolatry,"—worship of an idol, which stands between the soul and God, making itself the soul's real god, appropriating all faculties and all movements of thought and will which belong to God. Such religions there are among us, active, energetic, consistent religions, which place something before the soul which is short of our Lord and God, and which in their sincerity and reality put to shame the dulness of Christian faith, and the slackness of Christian devotion. Their objects are things in the world: some of them bad and hateful; some of them the gifts, the creations of God Himself, but which are made to take His place, and are thought of, and prized, and extolled, as if He was not. We sometimes wonder what to us instructed, reasonable Christians, who cannot conceive ourselves, even in imagination, bowing down to a graven image,—what can be any longer the meaning and lesson of the Second Commandment, "Thou shalt not bow down to them, nor worship them." What is the use of repeating it? Can we even imagine the temptation to do so? But are there no other things, the idols of refined and civilised men, no other "likenesses" than were known in old time, "of things that are in heaven above, or in the earth beneath, or in the water under the earth," to which worship is done, subtle, profound, and absorbing,—idols which occupy the place of God, or perhaps profess to represent Him,—idols which meet us at every turn, and which need and justify the reiterated command, "Thou shalt not bow down to them, nor worship them."

1. For instance, God is all-powerful, almighty, and we worship Him who is the Maker and Ruler of all

things. But the world, as we know it and have to do with it, is full of forces and necessities, whose origin and law is lost in darkness, which we cannot trace beyond a little way back, which seem self-originated and self-acting.[1] They are awful,

[1] Am Meer, am wüsten, nächtlichen Meer,
 Steht ein Jüngling-Mann,
 Die Brust voll Wehmuth, das Haupt voll Zweifel,
 Und mit düstern Lippen fragt er die Wogen :
 "O lös't mir das Räthsel des Lebens,
 Das qualvoll uralte Räthsel. . . .

 . . . . .

 Sagt mir, was bedeutet der Mensch?
 Woher ist er kommen? Wo geht er hin?
 Wer wohnt dort oben auf goldenen Sternen?"
 Es murmeln die Wogen ihr ewiges Gemurmel,
 Es wehet der Wind, es fliehen die Wolken,
 Es blinken die Sterne, gleichgültig und kalt,
 Und ein Narr wartet auf Antwort.
               Heine : *Die Nord-see.*

> How summer-bright are yonder skies,
>   And earth as fair in hue !
> And yet what sign of aught that lies
>   Behind the green and blue?
> But man to-day is Fancy's fool
>   As man hath ever been.
> The nameless Power, or Powers, that rule
>   Were never heard or seen.
>
>   . . . . .
>
> The years that made the stripling wise
>   Undo their work again,
> And leave him, blind of heart and eyes,
>   The last and least of men.
>
>   . . . . .
>
> But vain the tears for darken'd years
>   As laughter over wine,
> And vain the laughter as the tears,
>   O brother, mine or thine,

tremendous, irresistible, irreversible. They seem blind and aimless. We are powerless in their grasp if we oppose them; if we can use and direct them, it is still as blind and deaf and unchangeable and senseless forces. They bind us fast in their chain; they cut across the field of human will and feeling and purpose, reckless of the havoc they make,

> For all that laugh, and all that weep,
>   And all that breathe are one
> Slight ripple on the boundless deep
>   That moves, and all is gone.
> "The Song," in Tennyson's *Ancient Sage*.

> Pur tu, solinga, eterna peregrina,
> Che sì pensosa sei, tu forse intendi,
> Questo viver terreno :
> Il patir nostro, il sospirar, che sia ;
> Che sia questo morir, questo supremo
> Scolorar del sembiante,
> E perir dalla terra, e venir meno
> Ad ogni usata, amante compagnia.
> E tu certo comprendi
> Il perchè delle cose, e vedi il frutto,
> Del mattin, della sera,
> Del tacito, infinito andar del tempo.
>   .   .   .   .   .
> A che tante facelle ?
> Che fa l' aria infinita, e quel profondo
> Infinito seren ? che vuol dir questa
> Solitudine immensa ? ed io che sono ?
> Leopardi, *Canto d' un pastore dell' Asia alla Luna.*

> "Ma da natura
>   Altro negli atti suoi
>   Che nostro male o nostro ben si cura."

>   " Misterio eterno
>   Dell' esser nostro ! Oggi d' eccelsi, immensi
>   Pensieri e sensi inenarrabil fonte,
>   Beltà grandeggia, e pare,
>   Quale splendor vibrato

of the hopes they disappoint. In the onward roll and tide of what seems a boundless ocean, comprehending all things, from the hypothetic atom or the microscopic cell and germ to the farthest sun, the moral world, as we know it, seems swamped and lost. They care neither for good nor bad. They bind us with bonds which oppress and crush us.[1] This tremendous side

> Da natura immortal su queste arene,
> Di sovrumani fati,
> Di fortunati regni e d' aurei mondi
> Segno e sicura spene
> Dare al mortale stato :
> Diman, per lieve forza,
> Sozzo a vedere, abominoso, abbietto,
> Divien quel che fu dianzi
> Quasi angelico aspetto,
> E dalle menti insieme
> Quel che da lui moveva
> Ammirabil concetto, si dilegua."
> Leopardi, *Canti* (Firenze, 1876, pp. 117, 155, 158).

[1] TO NATURE

(In her ascribed character of unmeaning and all-performing force).

> O Nature ! thou whom I have thought to love,
>   Seeing in thee the reflex of God's face,
>   A loathed abstraction would usurp thy place,—
> While Him they not dethrone, they but disprove.
> Weird Nature ! can it be that joy is fled,
>   And bald unmeaning lurks beneath thy smile,
>   That beauty haunts the dust but to beguile,
> And that with Order, Love and Hope are dead?
>
> Pitiless Force, all-moving, all-unmoved,
>   Dread mother of unfathered worlds, assuage
> Thy wrath on us,—be this wild life reproved,
>   And trampled into nothing in thy rage !
>
> Vain prayer, although the last of human kind—
> Force is not wrath, but only deaf and blind.
> *Sonnets by Emily Pfeiffer* (p. 29).

of nature is an idea which enlarging knowledge has brought home to our generation with a sharpness and definiteness never recognised before. It fills and occupies minds, till even the consciousness of will becomes overshadowed and cast into the background, a phenomenon, or a doubt. And with this dread image before men's minds there grows up a terrible religion of despair, a religion which men accept, and believe in, and assert. Nature in its garb of fate and necessity has shut out God; and men with hearts and consciences and affections, bow their heads before it, and resign themselves, some-

---

On which the late Mr. Mark Pattison, Rector of Lincoln, wrote to the authoress (*ib.*, p. iii.): "I think the most striking and original of your sonnets are those which are inspired by the evolutional idea—an idea or form of universal apprehension, which, like a boa, has enfolded all mind in this generation in its inexorable coil. Try as we may, we cannot extricate our thought from this serpent's fold. Its pressure upon the soul forces our spirit to cry out with a Laocoon shriek; but though the inspiration of despair, it is inspiration, and poetry is its natural vent. You seem to give it vent with great power. Perhaps I could have wished for a more profound agony in the feeling at times. But the calm contemplation of our fate as helpless victims is perhaps the most just mental attitude. I select especially the three first sonnets to 'Nature,' which seem to me noble and powerful expressions of the sentiment. . . . The last line in the second sonnet[1] is wonderful, and still haunts my memory—

'And darkly blundered on man's suffering soul.'"

---

[1] "Thou art not calm, but restless as the ocean,
  Filling with aimless toil the endless years—
  Stumbling on thought, and throwing off the spheres,
  Churning the universe into mindless motion.
  Dull fount of joy, unhallowed source of tears,
  Cold motor of our fervid faith and song,
Dead, but engendering life, love, pangs, and fears,
  Thou crownedst thy wild work with foulest wrong,
  When first thou lightedst on a seeming goal,
  And darkly blundered on man's suffering soul."

times with a light heart, sometimes with piercing agonies which they cannot suppress, to a world in which they can see nothing but pitiless *fact*.

2. Again, it may be said that there is a religion of literature. Literature, the record and image of the thoughts, impressions, and feelings of men, in the most diversified conditions and in the most diversified expression, is one of the gifts which have been made to our time: a gift, a real and inestimable gift it is; a strange and new one, distributing without stint to the many, what used to be the prerogative and treasure of the few; opening more and more the inexhaustible wonders of the intellect and the character of man; placing within increasing range, access to all that is loftiest and wisest, most perfect and noblest, in what men now and before us have thought and said; leaving us utterly without excuse if, with the very highest placed within our reach, we choose the refuse and the vile. But it is a dazzling gift, a gift which makes men think that there can be nothing to match it, nothing beyond it. To know what great minds have spoken; to feel elevated by being in their presence and in sympathy with them; to put our footsteps into their tracks of thought; to see true and deep things said in the most perfect and most living words; to feel the mind awakening, expanding, glowing, gathering light and enthusiasm and strength, from contact with the power and insight of minds greater than itself; to understand

the opening of the eyes and the unlocking of the heart and its dim secrets, as new ideas rise above the horizon and open before them ; and still more, not merely to receive, but to *create*, not merely to be a listener and disciple, but to be conscious of being a master and a teacher ;—this carries with it a charm which, as we know, has often been able to make other pursuits seem tame, and other glories pale. It seems so pure and noble ; it seems so full of good ; it seems so to exalt and refine ; and under its influence nothing else seems equally capable of exalting and refining, nothing else seems to bring with it good, so to inspire and fortify, so to calm and sober and enlighten. Why should men look beyond it ? Where would they be likely to find deeper and more abundant and more various truth ? Where would they find truth expressed in more adequate, in less limited or less repellent forms ? Where will they learn to think in more dignified or consoling fashion of even the hard portions of our lot, pain and disease and death ? Is not this enough for the heart and soul of man, of man at least, cultivated, civilised, instructed, enlightened ? Is it not enough for his meditations, his aspirations, his secret acts of devout homage, and devout uplifting of the spirit ? Will not the religion of great books and great thinkers, the religion of genius and poetic truth, be a sufficient religion ?

3. Once more. There is a mysterious power in the world, a mysterious endowment given to man, one of

the most wonderful and lofty of all his prerogatives—the sense of beauty. The world, we know, is full of things which, when they address themselves to eye or ear, or, without the intervention of eye or ear, to the inward mind and soul, produce on us the effect which we speak of as *beautiful*. Endlessly various, in form and light and colour, in feature and expression, in voice and tone and ordered sound, in word and suggestion, and in all that is called into invisible existence by the powers of feeling and imagination and thought, it comes before the human soul as one of the chief sources of its brightness and joy, one of the chief things which exalt and gladden life, the spring within us which never dries up of admiration, delight, rapture. Where does it come from, this strange, irresistible sense of what is beautiful ; so different according to our measure with all of us, yet with all of us confessed to be so certain and so clear—this perception, which seems to be the crown and glory of the gifts which set man at the head of all that lives : where does it come from, and what is it ? Who can define or analyse it, in its infinite shapes, which agree in nothing else but that we call them all—sunrise and sunset, storm and peace, mountain and river, picture, and sculpture, and music, and building, and poem, visible features and invisible character—all we agree to call beautiful ? Is it anything real, this thing that we call beauty ; or is it a mere spell cast over us, a glamour, a delusion of eye and brain, imposing on us a show without substance ? It is something which appeals to us, in what is highest and purest and noblest in us; again, may be, it is something which captivates and fascinates what is meanest and lowest in our nature: yet still we speak of it as beauty. Is it indeed surprising that a faculty and endowment so subtle, so charged with varied and mighty power, so full of ministry to the joy and happiness of life, should so fill human souls with its treasures and wealth as to shut out all other interests, and become to them all in all, the standard by which everything is measured, the supreme longing and rule of their lives? Is it surprising that art should almost become a religion—a worship and an enthusiasm in which the wondrous shadows of God's glory take the place of God Himself, in His holiness, His righteousness, His awful love? It is not surprising: but alas for us if we yield to the temptation. The love of beauty, in work, and speech, and person, was the master-passion of the reviving intelligence of Italy: it attracted, it dominated all who wrote, all who sang, all who painted and moulded form. Out of it arose, austere and magnificent indeed, yet alive with all instincts of beauty, the *Divina Commedia*, the mighty thought of Lionardo and Michelangelo, the pathetic devotion and deep peace of the Lombard, the Tuscan, the Umbrian schools; but to whole generations of that wonderful people—from the fresh sonnet-writers and story-tellers of the closing middle age, Guido Cavalcanti and Boccaccio, to the completed refinement of the days of the Venetian masters and Ariosto—

the worship of the beautiful, as the noblest, worthiest devotion, stood in the place of truth, of morality, of goodness, of Christian life. And this idolatry of beauty brought its own punishment, the degeneracy and deep degradation both of art and character.

4. Yes; the world in which we now pass our days is full of great powers. Nature is great in its bounty, in its sternness, in its unbroken uniformity; literature and art are great in what they have created for us; beauty is great in its infinite expressions: but these are not the powers for man—man, the responsible, man, the sinner and the penitent, who may be the saint —to fall down and worship. They are to pass with the world in which we have known them, the world of which they are part; but man remains, remains what he is in soul and character and affections. *They* at least feel this who are drawing near to the unseen and unknown beyond; they to whom, it may be, these great gifts of God, the spell and wonder of art and of literature, the glory and sweet tenderness of nature, have been the brightness and joy of days that are now fast ending: *they* feel that there is yet an utter want of what these things cannot give; that soul and heart want something yet deeper, something more lovely, something more Divine—that which will realise man's ideals, that which will complete and fulfil his incompleteness and his helplessness—yes, the real likeness, in thought and will and character, to the goodness of Jesus Christ. " My flesh and my heart faileth; but God is the strength of my heart,

and my portion for ever." Man has that *within* him which tells him, in presage and parable, of greater and more awful things than anything he can admire and delight in yet: he has that *without* him which certifies him that his hopes and aspirations are justified; that when these precious things of the present must pass, with the world to which they belong, there is laid up for him what "eye hath not seen, nor ear heard, neither have entered into the heart of man, the things which God hath prepared for them that love Him:"—sinlessness and strength and peace, and the vision of God. Cannot we indeed, believers though we are, sympathise with the doubting poet, who realising his thought, and comparing what is now with such hopes, was overwhelmed by it: "*Are not these things too good to be true?*"[1] Yes, indeed, if any one else had told us except He who loved us and gave Himself for us, He "who for us men, and for our salvation came down from heaven, and was Incarnate by the Holy Ghost of the Virgin Mary, and was made Man," who "died, and rose, and revived, that He might be Lord both of the dead and living." Too good to be true for mere

---

[1] Robert Burns: see Currie's *Life of Burns*. Compare Browning's *Easter Day*:

> "Remembering any moment Who
> Beside creating thee unto
> These ends, and these for thee, was said
> To undergo death in thy stead
> In flesh like thine: so ran the tale.
> What doubt in thee could countervail
> Belief in it? Upon the ground
> 'That in the story had been found
> Too much love! How could God love so?'"

guesses and hopes; not too good to be true for those for whom God withheld not His only Son; not too good to be true, in all its unimaginable wonder, if the Conqueror of death has been here " to seek and to save that which was lost." " He that spared not His own Son, but delivered Him up for us all, how shall He not with Him also freely give us all things?"

XIII

THE GIFT OF THE HOLY SPIRIT

"In whom also after that ye believed, ye were sealed with that Holy Spirit of promise, which is the earnest of our inheritance until the redemption of the purchased possession."—EPHESIANS i. 13, 14.

WE celebrate to-day the greatest gift ever made to man. I am not speaking of things done for him, and without him. I am not speaking of the gift of the Father's Eternal Son to be man's Redeemer, Brother, Atonement, Pattern. But the gift of to-day was the greatest change that was ever made in what man is in himself, in his powers and spiritual endowments, in what he can himself become. There have been other great revolutions in his history; crises and epochs which made things henceforth new, in the various stages of that order by which God has been bringing back the world unto Himself. There was the Law, the long discipline of Prophecy, the Cross, the Resurrection, the Ascension. There was the opening message of the Gospel to the Gentiles, the breaking down the middle wall which had separated mankind, the transformation of the Synagogue into the Church Universal. Of course all these profuse outpourings of God's bounty have altered indefinitely our condition, our hopes, our motives. And there were, besides them, other gifts belonging to what we call the sphere of nature, put into the hands of man, which make him what he is: the homely and familiar arts which so touched the imagination of the ancient poets, and raised their wonder more than they do ours; the discoveries, the capacities, the knowledge of later times, at which even we who possess them, stand amazed.

But here is a gift of a different order. It brings with it, indeed, light; it brings with it truth. But the essential and characteristic part of it is, that it brings with it changes within us,—changes unthought of,—in the moral and spiritual nature and capacities of man. It is a gift, altering and raising the powers by which he chooses, and wills, and acts,—the affections, the heart, the character, which make him a moral being, with power to do right, to feel right, to wish and desire right. It is the gift which opens to him, in a degree unknown before, the life of holiness, the life which makes him really like God, really able to know God, to love Him, to live with Him. It is the gift which, in the language of Holy Scripture, has renewed, has created afresh, our nature as men. Christmas is the commemoration of the birthday, the new birth in time, of the Only-begotten, the second Adam, the Head of redeemed Humanity. Pentecost is the commemoration of the birthday of the new birth of Humanity itself; of the day when a new divine power came into the very inmost souls and beings of men, changing them from their old selves, filling them with new energies fresh from the very heart of God, begetting them anew from the deadness of sin, giving them, by a new birth through the Spirit, the power to become the sons of God.

1. We know the power which new and great ideas have in giving a fresh start to the life of men, in remoulding it, and redirecting its course. The promise, the gift of the Holy Ghost, as it shapes and colours the whole language of the New Testament, is such a great idea. The very thought of such a thing, of a Divine Presence in the souls of men, enlightening, strengthening, elevating them, in a new and living way unknown before, could not form, as it does, the characteristic feature of a great faith and a great teaching, without producing the effect of great ideas when they take hold of the minds of men. However vaguely held, however imperfectly grasped, the belief that there was such a communication between God and the soul of man, that this was the fruit and largess of the Lord's Ascension, must have of itself awakened men from the routine of custom, and opened to them new prospects of the possibilities of improvement. But the gift of the Spirit was not merely an idea, it was a real power from the unseen world—the very power and working of God. It was the coming of a Divine Person, one with the Father and the Son, into these very souls of ours, to work in them His most incomprehensible, but most certain and blessed work. It was something more than the disclosure of truth, the

communication of light and of holy influences drawing and governing the heart. That which was the special promise of our Lord before He suffered, that which He solemnly guaranteed after His Resurrection, that which He sent down and shed abroad after His Ascension, was no less than a sacred, permanent, indwelling in human souls, of One who was God with Himself, continually to guide and teach them; day by day to restore and purify them; at last to fashion them into the likeness of the Son of God, and to fit them for the eternal and perfect life. Here in the very centre of our being, in the centre of our wills and affections, here where we love, and desire, and choose, and act, where we are tempted, where we conquer, where we sin—here is One who does more for men than the great Master could do for His disciples when He was with them; One, who makes known to us all that Christ really is, all that Christ really means; a Comforter, an Advocate, who is to abide with us for ever; One, whose presence brings with it holiness, and divine love, and peace, in a way in which they never were in human souls before; One, under whose guidance we are going through our discipline, and learning to shape and present our prayers; One, who knows our deepest and most inmost needs, and deigns to associate Himself in wonderful, unspeakable, sympathy with our yearning supplications; One, who in the awful words of Holy Scripture, makes us one in union with the Father and the Son; One, whose presence with our spirit, is the pledge to us, while still in the flesh, of the still greater gifts which our Father reserves for us in the world where sin and death are not.

This is the answer which our Father has made to the obscure, but deep and unalterable longings of our fallen nature;—fallen, but not content with its defeat and fall. In the religious history of man, two great cries for help, for deliverance, meet us throughout, in infinitely varied tones. One is the cry for forgiveness, for the wiping out of the dread and unknown debt of sin, for the averting of those incalculable consequences on which conscience dwells so obstinately, and with such terrible forebodings. That cry has been heard and answered. What the forgiveness of sins by the Most Holy and the Most Just can mean, is a mystery which the human mind can fathom as little as it can any other mystery of God's existence, or God's working. But One has come to us, from the throne of Godhead, saying to the worst and most hopeless of sinners, " Thy sins be forgiven thee ; " One has hung on the Cross, of whom it is written, " The blood of Jesus Christ His Son cleanseth us from all sin," He hath made " peace through the blood of His Cross."

But the cry for pardon is not the only cry of the soul. There is the cry for goodness, the cry for the power of doing right, the passionate cry for deliverance from the miserable weakness, the shame, the bitterness, of always doing wrong. " To will is present with me ; but how to perform that which is good I find not. . . .

O wretched man that I am! who shall deliver me from the body of this death?" St. Paul is the spokesman of innumerable generations, of thousands who never heard his name, from the East and West, of representatives of thought and feeling far removed in time and character from his. Who shall breathe into man's soul the spirit of a new life? Who shall invest him with a new power, not to admire and sympathise with what is good, with what is Divine—that he has; not to shape fruitless wishes and struggle to them in vain—that he knows too well: but to take the Divine light into his own heart of hearts, to make it his own, to seat it on the throne of his soul, as the ruler and commander of life and thought and motive? God has heard that cry too. In the fulness of time, with the Eternal Son, the Saviour, the Healer, the Deliverer, came also the Eternal Spirit, the Lord and Giver of Life, working in men's very selves the amazing change which they could not work themselves, opening their eyes to the great truths which they lived with but saw not, raising their thoughts to high and heavenly things, endowing them with the strength, the courage, the purity, the perseverance, of Saints, making in the moral world "all things new."

2. We call the new life which came into the world, the new and original types of character which we have in the New Testament—the burning love, the unstinted self-devotion, the infinite compassion, the sweet and beautiful innocence, the high ambition to spend and be spent for God—we call all this the

fruits of Christianity. In more exact words, all has flowed from the great gift of Pentecost. It was this great change, this answer to the cry for righteousness, this new indwelling in human hearts of the Father's Eternal Spirit, which made all this holiness, all this moral and spiritual elevation possible; which wrought in and with the spirits of men, according to the effectual working of His mighty power,—converting, enlightening, comforting, sanctifying.

And that Power, that Presence, that In-dwelling, is with us of to-day as it was with the first disciples on the day of Pentecost. It is with us still, "a Power from on high, transforming into sanctity, from without and invisibly, yet with inward efficacy and evident tokens."[1] It is still with us, pledged to us in that Divine Society which it "called out of the whole world unto faith and holiness;" that Body and Temple built of human souls "to be an habitation of God through the Spirit." It is still with us, visiting us, blessing us, in those great mysterious actions, in which the Church communicates and conveys to men on earth the heavenly gifts which she is charged to guard and to dispense—the Divine Word, the Divine Sacraments. They are outward things, but they are much more than merely outward things. A power dwells in them, and works in them, which never dwelt in such things before. Nothing can be merely outward, which the Risen Lord ordained in the New Dispensation of the Spirit. They are, for all the ages, in

[1] Bp. Andrewes' *Devotions*, Day IV.

calm permanence and regular continuance, what the vision of Pentecost was in that first rushing storm and fiery lightning flash, in which the Christian Church was born,—the tokens, the evidences, the outward veils and garments of the invisible Presence. It is still with us in the washing of regeneration, in the laying on of hands, in the Communion of the Body and the Blood. It is with us, too, in ways, in times, which none can know, none can understand, but those whom He so visits. He may come to the soul, we know not whence; He may come we know not how; He may speak in a voice audible to one heart, one conscience, alone. He may open to the soul thoughts which words cannot interpret; He may show it visions which it cannot utter or explain. He is the Eternal, Illimitable Spirit; all the depths and heights of holiness, of wisdom, of love, are in His hands; none can circumscribe, none can follow out His working; to every man He divideth severally as He wills, in what way He wills. Infinite variety of gifts, with perfect unity in their source and purpose,—this is what St. Paul teaches us to believe. And what wonder that the manner and the range of operation of such a Divine Person, Infinite in Holiness, Infinite in Love, should transcend all human intelligence. Let us bless and thank Him for what we know He does, for what we see that He has done; it may be, for what we are sure of, though we can tell our secret to no one, for our own selves. And then, let us remind ourselves that He is that Spirit of God who filleth the world; who owes no account to men for what He is pleased to do; who is not bound to tell us whence He comes and whither He goes; whose goings forth we cannot follow, whose ways "are past finding out."

Surely it is not useless for us, with our imperfect characters, with the words and cares of this world ever about us, to dwell on these high themes, of which St. John and St. Paul are full. It is not useless; it is most necessary. Only let us remember that we may dwell on them uselessly. It is useless merely to talk and think of them; it is useless here in this working day of trial merely to admire and praise. The greatest or the most joyfully devout among us, must come down from filling his thoughts with the contemplation of these wonders, of that Divine communion of the Spirit of God with the spirit of man, which has renewed the whole constitution of our nature,—must come down at last to the earth, our present home, to its prosaic necessities, to those homely duties, which are the actual trial and touchstone of our fellowship and union with the Spirit of Christ and God. It is there that we must find the safest, surest witness of the Spirit, that we are in truth, what we are in calling and title, the sons of God.

I do not say that there is no other inward witness of the Spirit. I do not say that He may not vouchsafe to His chosen ones, favours of assurance, and blessed confidence, incommunicable to others, and which others cannot judge. But He has left us under no uncertainty of what is the ordinary witness of His influence and guidance. The works of the Spirit are the witness of the Spirit. "The fruit of the Spirit" wrote that great Apostle, who was so impressed with the overwhelming importance and mightiness of the new work of the Spirit among men,—"the fruit of the Spirit is love, joy, peace, long-suffering, gentleness, goodness, faith, meekness, temperance." Nothing can make up for the want of these as evidence of the presence of the Spirit; for it was to train the heart of man to these, to plant and nourish these virtues in his soul, to make these graces the strong and permanent elements of his character, that the gift of the Holy Spirit within him was vouchsafed, that this wonderful change was made possible in the powers and capacities of man's nature. A new heart also will I give you, and a new spirit will I put within you. . . . I will put My Spirit within you, and cause you to walk in My statutes, and ye shall keep My judgments and do them." Here was the purpose, the great moral purpose, of the promised gift. The great army of the Saints of Christ has shown how it has been fulfilled, in that variety of goodness and holiness which the world never saw before.

Let us then, not at Church only, amid the exultation and glories of praise and worship, but at home, amid our tasks and our duties, think seriously and worthily of our condition as men to whom a really new power, not of nature, not of our own creating, has been given by the unutterable gift of God's Holy Spirit. We have sung the *Veni Creator* hymn in Church; let us repeat, in deepest earnest, its invitation and its prayer, in our secret chamber, in the thick of our work, amid temptation, amid trouble, amid rejoicing. He, whose presence was sealed to us in our Baptism, in our Confirmation, He who has come to us in many hours when we thought not of Him—the Inspirer of good thoughts, the Clearer up of doubts, the Strengthener of true and pure resolves—He is ever at hand to be appealed to, to give us light, to save us from the evil which hangs over us, to teach us what to pray for and how to pray, to infuse His own energy and purpose, and "fire of love" into our dreamy and wavering devotion. Waste not such blessings and such gifts by not believing them, by living as if they were not, by hollow praises, by unreal words. Ask Him humbly, ask Him unceasingly, to teach you to understand more and more the purpose of His coming; that He came, that He is with us, for the great work of renewing men to the image of God, "in righteousness and true holiness," that without Him "nothing is strong, nothing is holy." If you can only learn this lesson all His other blessings will follow. He will kindle our dark and dead knowledge into living meaning, He will accustom hearts and wills to recognise and welcome the will of God. He will shed abroad in our souls—how or whence we cannot tell—the growing and deepening love of Christ.

He will make trouble endurable by His comfort, and temptation even a blessing by His support. Toil, with Him to uphold us, will be light, and sacrifices easy; with the heat and burden of the day, He will bring refreshment and rest; disappointment will have its recompense, and tears their solace. With Him as our guest, and loyal to Him as our guide and light, we shall go on from strength to strength, till He brings us safely, in peace, in hope, in due preparation, to that brink and great dividing line, when all behind us shall be closed, when this world shall be over, and we have nothing but the next before us.

So may He guide, and bless, and have mercy upon us. May He have mercy upon us in our course and trial, one by one. May He have mercy in time of perplexity and trouble on that Church of ours which He has so wonderfully quickened to a sense of its calling and its responsibilities. May He, the Spirit of light, of truth, of unity, dispel our ignorance and misunderstandings, raise our souls to the height of His teaching, draw estranged hearts one to another, teach us all to forbear and to be patient, to trust one another and to hope. May He who is also the Spirit of strength and fortitude, teach us to have courage, when necessary, to say the truth that is painful to say, to accept the duty which is hard, to bear the pain which it is right to bear. May He, the Spirit of love, of wisdom, of soberness, of concord, overrule all our mistakes and all our jars, swallow up all our discords in His own Divine harmony, chasten our presumption, tame our pride; till at last, not by what *we* do, but by His Supreme guidance, God's work is done on earth, His purpose, for our days, fulfilled, His Church fully animated by that Divine Spirit which alone can make it one; and each one of its members, according to his place and measure, has found in it, under the same blessed Teacher and Comforter, first his true work, and then his rest.

XIV

THE WORK OF THE HOLY SPIRIT

"And I will pray the Father, and He shall give you another Comforter, that He may abide with you for ever; even the Spirit of truth; whom the world cannot receive, because it seeth Him not, neither knoweth Him: but ye know Him; for He dwelleth with you, and shall be in you."—St. John xiv. 16, 17.

THE world we live in,—in which we are appointed to pass our present probation,—is so very different from the world unseen, that world which *must* be about us on all sides, encompassing the earth on which we dwell, that all that comes to us from it can be but dimly and partially understood. How could any one, who puts the two things side by side, the world of our experience, and the world of which we have no experience, possibly suppose that it could be otherwise? That world, which must exist, or else this one could not,—that world beyond us of which the evidence is, up to a certain point, certain even to our senses, in sun, and sky, and starry universe, though that is but the smallest part of it,—we shall never know here, whatever else we may know. There it is, a certainty, yet impenetrable as death: and here is our world which we are familiar with all the days and all the nights of our passage through life. We cannot make one the measure of the other. The two touch one another—nay, must be most closely and intimately united: but to our sight and sense it seems as if, between it and us, there were "a great gulf fixed," so that they who would pass from hence to it cannot, neither can they from thence pass to us.—It seems, but it is not. They have passed from hence to it, who are the innumerable majority of those who have breathed the breath of life here on our earth; they are passing in numbers over all the earth, now, at this moment, while we are speaking and listening: and we too, when our day comes, shall pass. And they too, from thence, have come to us. God's ministering and immortal Hosts come, perhaps at any moment, to do service to the heirs of salvation.

But twice there have been special and wonderful openings of the unseen world,—two great occasions of communication between it and us, which stand before all others, which stand before everything else in the things that have happened here since man dwelt on earth. Twice the veil has been drawn back; twice they who belong to that world have been among us here. One of these unveilings of the unseen belongs to the past—to what we call the past;—on earth it is far away, far back in the roll of centuries, though above, it is no past event, but an ever-living reality. Once, from the heights and depths of the eternal world, there came forth One, into this world of time, who appeared among us, who was made

Man, and died, and rose again, and ascended to sit on the Father's right hand. And He was the everlasting Son of the Father, God of God, very God of very God; yet He lived with us, and men saw Him, and heard Him, and their hands handled the Word of life in the reality of man's flesh and blood. Then the invisible became for the time visible: then that which is essentially of the heavenly and the eternal came under the conditions, the familiar conditions, of the only experience which men have here.

But that was followed by another opening and unveiling of the other world; by another visitation and appearance of its powers in this life; by the disclosure and the coming of another Divine Person to be with men, to be over them, and among them, and in them. But this time the invisible was not made visible; on the other hand, that Presence was not to be only for a few years, and then to become to man's sight and appearance a thing of the past; it was to be a new, but henceforth ever-present, continuing fact in the moral and spiritual condition of mankind. We know the other world by the coming of the Son of Man. We know the other world by the coming of the Holy Ghost.

1. To this great change in our condition, the Presence of the Holy Ghost, to-day turns our thoughts. And I think it must sometimes occur to us to ask, why, considering what is said in the New Testament about it, it is so much, so to say, in the back-

ground of our thoughts. Obviously, with most of us, part of the reason is evident. We are accustomed to live by sense and sight, and we find it hard to bring strongly and really into our lives that which we do not see. And it is still harder when it is not only that which we do not see, but that which we cannot trace, or comprehend, or imagine; that which, though it is in this world, so near to us, and so mighty, yet belongs so entirely to the unknown, unvisited, invisible world. We are afraid of it, afraid of mistakes and illusions; afraid of confounding it with unrealities. Of the Incarnate Son we can think and conceive, however imperfectly. He has intended that we should do so; He became like us, that we might, in our measure, understand and follow Him; He left us the detailed story of His words, and deeds, and ways, that we might receive the image of Him in our hearts and affections. But the Blessed Comforter belongs to the spiritual world; and we are still in the flesh. We know Him by what our Master has told us of Him; we know what He must be in His goodness and love to men; we know His power and what He has done. But Him we know not, as we know our Lord Jesus Christ. He opens His hand and fills the world with His gifts. He gives and maintains our spiritual and moral life. But the mystery of His Person and His Being we have not faculties to penetrate. And we are apt to forget what He does, because we are unable to realise what He is.

But that is not the way in which the New Testament teaches us. It does not pretend to give us a glimpse of the manner of His Divine Being; but His presence, His work, His power, are everywhere in it. And naturally; for that Presence and those gifts are the last and emphatic promise of our Master to His Church. Think how from first to last, in all that we read about the new Dispensation in the New Testament, the Presence and action of the Holy Ghost are presented to us:—think how mysteriously and how persistently, He is associated with, (if we may so speak with reverence,) the great moments and events of the Incarnation, the Birth, the Baptism, the Temptation, the Anointing, the Resurrection: think how in all His attributes of novelty and wonder in the moral world,—as the Comforter, the Enlightener, the Guide to truth, the Strengthener, the Judge, and Witness, and Convincer of the moral apostasy of the world,—He is the subject of the last great closing discourse of our Lord before His Passion: think how a new age, a new order of hope and revival of sanctity, begins for the world at Pentecost: think how, when we follow the opening and development of that new life, in all its manifold circumstances and applications, in the Epistles of St. Paul, the key of it all is seen to be the ever-present, infinitely manifold energy and ministration of the Holy Ghost: think how St. Paul startles us with what he takes for granted in his appeals and arguments, "Know ye not that your body is the temple of the Holy Ghost;" "The Spirit itself beareth witness with our spirit, that we are the children of God;" "Grieve not the Holy Spirit of God, whereby ye are sealed unto the day of redemption." Follow through the New Testament, the uninterrupted, the unstudied, and, as it seems, matter of course references to the personal and definite intervention of God the Holy Ghost in the guidance of the Church, and in the purification and discipline of souls;—and we must judge, I think, that if we forget Him, if we think only slightly and intermittently of His Presence and His Power, we do not think as they thought, who speak and who write in the New Testament.

2. For, indeed, the coming of the Holy Ghost was as much a new thing in the world as the Incarnation and Sacrifice of the Eternal Son. Each is equally a part of what, in our human way of thinking, appears to us as God's supreme effort, in the infinite seriousness of His love, to recall and reclaim His creatures which had gone astray. It was not enough that man should have before him, visibly manifested before his eyes, the perfect image of the goodness, the wisdom, the stainless beauty of the love and holiness of God. Our own hearts tell us too well that *that* may be before our eyes and minds in vain; may be gazed at and not felt; may be felt and not loved; may be loved, but with a wayward, fickle, and barren love. Something more was wanted than even the life of the Incarnate Son, than even the thought and the story

of the Crucified, if hearts like ours were to take in their lessons. The whole history of the race, until the fulness of time came, shows how little resource men had in themselves for keeping up, much less for raising the standard of purity, of faith, of truth. What they needed, what they had not, was power within them, and not only lessons without them. And that power, that new and unknown gift to man, from his Father in heaven, was the promised gift of the Holy Ghost. Almighty God had come to him in the flesh: Almighty God came to him also in the spirit. Man found that he had a light and strength within his soul, which not only made the look and value of all things new, which not only gave him, as he never had it before, the higher aim, the better mind; but which enabled him, as never before, to fulfil it, to tread down sin and resist temptation.—The history, the proof, of this astonishing moral revolution is written in the Epistles of the New Testament: compare with that, anything that was known before, of man's attempts at righteousness, and you feel that you are passing into a new condition and idea of life, new in purpose, new in hope, new in realisation. Compare the civilised world of Horace, and Virgil, and Cicero, with that enthusiasm for goodness, for holiness, for likeness to Jesus Christ, which set in after Pentecost in the early Church, and never was altogether quenched again—and which, mistaken and ill-directed as it often has been, is one of the most marvellous facts in the history of mankind; and no one can say that the change is an imaginary one. Whence, but from Him, those new features of human character—new, at any rate, and absolutely unknown before in the whole Gentile world, which followed the coming of the Holy Ghost; that new faculty, that new idea, so familiar to us, so unheard of till He came, except to the Psalmists of Israel, which we call, the love of God; that new readiness, that new passion of unselfishness, which led men like St. Paul to spend and be spent for love of the souls of men?

All about the working of that Divine Comforter was wrapt in mystery, except the fruits. How He made His Temple in man, how He imparted His light and His truth to His creatures, how He strengthened the vacillating, and spoke without words to the inward ear, and raised the fallen, and won back the wanderer, none could trace, none could know. The wind bloweth where it listeth: the ways of the Spirit are unsearchable. It is vain to imagine how that Heavenly Person associates Himself with our spirit, becomes to us the source of light and strength, and of the desire of good, making His work our work too, overshadowing, protecting, guarding our souls, giving us thoughts above our own thoughts, surprising us into an earnestness so unlike our common selves. Why should we expect to be conscious of His Presence? Why should we expect, such as we are, to recognise and discern clearly what is of God? But the effects of His Presence were soon recognised in the world, and have never ceased to be recognised since. They were seen in those two contrasted lists in the Epistle to the Galatians, of the works of the flesh and the fruits of the Spirit, —of what the moral world had been and was, without Him, and of that new phenomenon and substantial fact of character which had shown itself beyond denial since He had come.

3. And as He was the power which made St. Paul and his disciples what they were, so has He been in the kingdom of God ever since, so has He been in moulding the varied holiness of the innumerable saints of Christ;—so is He, to all that is good, and noble, and strong, and pure, and loving, among men now;—so is He, if we have any good or hope in us, to each one of ourselves. There is no other source spoken of in the New Testament of that which is to make man's nature what God meant it to be: the New Testament teaches us to turn to Him for help in the great trust committed to us, the keeping of our own soul. We are too apt to forget it. Let us use this day to revive what ought to be continually present to our minds. It is as certain that we depend on Him for our advance in goodness, as it is certain that we are not given to understand how He works in us and with us. It is as certain that He is the Divine Comforter, One with the Father and the Son, and yet a real Person, to whom glory and adoration and faith are due, as it is certain that unless we approach Him continually in serious and

deliberate prayer, we shall forget One, who to our imagination and understanding is lost in the unfathomable mystery of the invisible world. Yet if we are Christians, He not only "abideth with us," but "He is *in* us." And He belongs to that world to which we too belong, if only we could see it; which one day, not far off, we too shall know by experience, as we know this one.

We are sometimes told not to think too much of heaven, but to keep to our duties, our services, our business on earth. We are bidden emphatically to remember that to labour is to pray. Certainly we do wrong, if we neglect our earthly duties, under pretence of giving ourselves to the thoughts of the other world. But unless we are only for this world, the links which connect us with the other ought to be to reasonable men of the deepest interest. I don't think we are apt to err in excess by thinking too much of that which is, after all, to be our lot for ever. But the Presence, the ever-continued assistance of the Holy Ghost, unearthly as it is, is yet a thing of the immediate present,—of the present shaping and improvement of life, of present growth in depth and reality, and elevation of character. If ever we rise above what is of the earth, earthy, above what is of time, transitory,—above what is of this world, fugitive, unsatisfying, corruptible,—it is to Him that we shall owe it. Shall we let ourselves forget such a Person, in our thoughts and in our prayers? The Church does not forget Him. The

New Testament for ever reminds us of Him. It is our idle and carnal hearts, dulled and cramped by custom and indolence, which are too laggard to do justice to His Divine Glory, and to the part which He has in the restoration of mankind.

My brethren, we are really living under this wonderful and awful dispensation of God's care for us. What it would be if we had the dearest and wisest of friends, most severe and yet most tender, ever at our side, to warn, to prompt, to kindle;— that it is which St. Paul, and St. Paul's Master, tell us that we have, only "very nigh" to us, in our very hearts and minds. We have, all of us, often felt ourselves over-matched in our efforts to be better men, to do what was right, to know the truth and to obey it, to realise where we are and why, and where we are going. Have we sufficiently remembered our promised strength,—Him, who throughout the Bible, definitely in the New Testament, not obscurely in the Old, is set forth to us as the Friend and Helper with whom our spirit is in perpetual contact, no mere influence but a living Person, who cares for us and loves us as God does? It was no vague poetical fancy which dictated the great Church hymns to the Holy Ghost, *Veni Creator*, *Veni Sancte Spiritus*, and the like. It was no mere feeling of symmetry which inserted in the Litany the petition, "O God the Holy Ghost, proceeding from the Father and the Son, have mercy upon us miserable sinners."—Let us in our troubles, our failures, our blindness, turn to Him who, we know, so sympathises with us,—who, as St. Paul teaches us, helps our infirmities, and takes part in our poor imperfect prayers, and makes intercession for us with "plaints unutterable,"—yes, identifying Himself in unspoken words with the sorrows and longings of His creatures. Let us try to place clearly before our minds the reality of His Presence with us, and His Help. He will teach if we will listen He will inspire if we will receive. He will bring to mind if we do not shut Him out. We shall hear His voice if we do not harden our hearts. If in earnestness and sincerity we yield ourselves to His discipline, He will end by bringing us nearer and nearer to the likeness of Jesus Christ, by preparing us for that new world, where those who are to be happy in it, must be holy.

XV

I

TEMPER

An Address delivered to the Junior Clergy Society in the Crypt of St. Paul's, 12th October 1880.

IN the few words which you expect me to say to you, I suppose that you look for some suggestions to be offered to your consideration touching practical things—our hopes, our risks, our difficulties, our temptations. It is obvious that anything that can be presented to you in this short time can be but in the way of thoughts, questions, hints, left with you, to be dealt with by yourselves afterwards.

I will venture so to offer to you the subject which I will call—I will explain myself further—the subject of *temper*. And by this—this curiously ambiguous but expressive word, meaning at once the restraint of feelings and the very reverse—I mean, not temper, as we call it, shown in the intercourse of society, nor temper shown in argument, nor temper under provocation, nor temper under the troubles and disagreeables of life; but temper, in our habits of mind and thought and feeling, towards the facts and circumstances which surround our condition, which affect our opinions, our position, our conscience, our duty, and with respect to which we have to exercise judgment and choice. I mean the permanent and recurring impatience and irritation sometimes produced in the mind, by a state of facts which continually cuts across our wishes, jars with our tastes, upsets our theories, or baffles our practical efforts; which seems to us wrong or absurd, but which we cannot alter; which mocks and defies our reason, or our sense of right, or our good feeling, but also defies our strength. Examples of what I mean are to be seen in the chronic irritation of large classes of mankind at the inequality of conditions; or, to take a different subject, in the impatience felt by some good men at the impossibility of putting down war altogether among men professing to be reasonable as well as Christian. The Psalter, which knows and reflects every phase and shade of human experience, knows this—" I was sore troubled: I said in my haste, All men are liars." ... "My feet were almost gone, my treadings had well-nigh slipt. And why? I was grieved at the wicked; I do also see the ungodly in such prosperity.... Lo, these are the ungodly, these prosper in the world, and these have riches in possession; and I said, Then have I cleansed my heart in vain, and washed mine hands in innocency.... Yea, and I had almost said even as they; but lo, then I should have condemned the generation of thy children. . . .

Thus my heart was grieved, and it went even through my reins." It is the state of mind of which the expressive picture is given us in the story of the prophet Jonah, who tried to evade a service in which he thought he might be used, and then discredited; who quarrelled with God's mercy because it did not square with his own prophecy; and who, in answer to his Master's twice-repeated remonstrance, " Doest thou well to be angry?"—bitterly insisted, " I do well to be angry, even unto death."

This habitual allowance and nourishing of temper and irritation at a state of facts is plainly a characteristic of some minds, and some minds, too, of the highest order. It is an entirely different thing from simply the presence or the bursting forth of indignation and wrath. To be in the presence of unquestionable injustice or baseness, and not to feel wrath burn at it, is not to be of the mind which the Bible reflects. And there cannot be the seriousness and earnestness and zeal which are essential to all high human character, to say nothing of all high Christian character, without a man chafing and being provoked, when he finds stupidity, or selfishness, or laziness, or insincerity, in his way. Nor am I speaking of that energy, that determination, that fire of hostility, which may animate a great spirit against a great abuse, or a great enemy of truth and goodness against the truth and goodness which he would destroy, or a great fanatic against the barriers of reason and good sense which thwart his course. In the great conflicts for good or for evil alike, strong hatreds must play as large a part as strong enthusiasms. But I am not speaking of this. I am speaking of what we all understand when we speak of a man *showing temper*; or having that weakness and defect, in his way of dealing with matters, which we know by the name of temper, whether irritable, or querulous, or acrimonious, or despondent and gloomy.

And I think no one can read history, or watch contemporary action, without observing what a part this plays in affairs, quite apart from differences of view or object, and without seeing that this is a distinct characteristic of some men, and makes the difference between them and others like them, or engaged on the same side, or influenced by the same general principles. It may be affectation: just as there are people who think it fine to be out of health, there are people who think it a mark of being deep, or honest, or conscientious, to show temper at what they find out of joint in the world. It may, of course, be something infinitely poor, mean, peevish, captious, childishly perverse; but the thing is, that it need not at all necessarily be this. It may be the quality of an elevated, not to say of a really noble nature. A man of such a nature, otherwise strong and generous, may be so out of harmony with certain fixed conditions of things round him, may be so possessed by a fierce abiding wrath against certain classes, or institutions, or arrangements which clash with his ideas or stand in the way of his objects, he is so much at the mercy of a chronic irritation against them, that the notion of an equitable judgment from him on anything connected with them is simply ludicrous, and the mere mention of them is sure to call up the expression of his antipathy and scorn. The contrast between temper, in this sense, and the patience and self-control opposed to it, is sometimes very marked in men who start together on the same course. I will venture to refer to two examples which occur to me; and I will take them beyond the sphere of our own communion. Some of you may have seen two recent biographies of men who left our communion in the storms of forty years ago, Mr. Allies and Mr. Sibthorp. They were both men of high honour and purpose, and their stories—an autobiography in one case—are both of much interest. But the one, while showing ready self-sacrifice for principle, the loss of much that men prize, to follow what seemed the call of God, is marked, as it seems to me, from first to last, by temper, blinding the eyes, embittering controversy, giving no chance to justice. The other, a story, too, of strange vacillations of opinion, is *as* marked by patience, sweetness, equity—the power and the bands of sympathy lasting unbroken, when the agreement in principle and conviction, and the ties of habit and association, were shattered. The other instance of what I mean is from the French Church. At the beginning of the second quarter of the century the Abbé Lamennais seemed to have roused the French

Church from intellectual slumber and political servility. He struck a chord of response in many hearts; among them of one who was to be the greatest of modern French preachers, Lacordaire. But things did not go smoothly with these daring spirits and logical reasoners. Stubborn facts rose in their way, even where they most looked for support. They found, baffling or threatening them at every step, the fears, the jealousies, the fixed traditions, the wise caution, the convenient understandings, the accommodations, the inertness, the diplomatic craft which were the growth of a thousand years in the Roman Court. Strong and sanguine as they were, these powers were stronger. Then began the trial of temper—the trial of seeing brilliant theories more and more in disaccord with realities, of seeing authority making short work of logic, of meeting distrust and disapproval of what it had cost them so much to offer, of being reminded at each turn and in all sorts of indirect ways that they were practically wrong. Lamennais's was not a character which could stand such a trial. From the first, passion—eager, headlong, scornful passion—had been as strong with him as his powerful and ambitious intellect. And when with his acknowledged successes he still found that he could not move the world as he would, that the latent necessities of a system and its intangible powers of resistance were too much for him, a fierce bitterness of temper, increasing by perpetual indulgence, took possession of his soul. Not Rome only, for which he had invented new arguments, nor the Pope, whom he would have made absolute over the modern world, but Christianity, but religion itself, were at last enveloped in his disgust and despair. Lacordaire, too, made up his mind. I don't know how far he avowedly gave up theories which he found would not work; he always maintained a very independent though not a recalcitrant, or disobedient position; but he learned to devote his life to adorning, as best he could, the Sparta which had been given him as his lot. One man's temper, it is impossible not to see it, was the leading influence to intellectual change, and had much, if not all, to do in breaking up his position; it drove him from his moorings, and sent him adrift into the "wild and wandering sea" of doubt. The other, more patient and self-commanding, it may be more yielding, when he found what he could *not* do— create an ideal Papacy —tried what he *could* do. He was content to accept, without quarrelling with it, a state of facts which he did not like, but could not alter: to work in the harness provided for him by an ordering which was not his own: to merge his personal mortifications and disappointments in larger interests to which he had devoted life. And he stirred, as no other preacher had stirred, the religious heart of France. Perhaps to us here the stormy career calls forth the keener interest. In view of the Master's judgment-seat, who commissioned both, it is a different matter.

Great and difficult questions are round us, and are likely to increase in proportion as we realise what words mean and what things are with which we have to deal. These, then, are days when we have all of us to watch against the insidious influences of temper, which often comes in a noble guise, as generous indignation, plain-speaking, the courage of our opinions. None of us are likely to find the actual state of facts round us quite what we should like.—There are limits, for instance, to our knowledge of what it is most important for us to know; and we fret against these limits. Why should not questions have been answered which a word might have settled? Why should we not be *certain*, when we *must* act *as if* we were certain? Nothing is so trying to the temper as untying knots; and men are sometimes led to declare that we have not the knowledge which we *may* have, because we cannot have the knowledge which we desire.—Theology, again, the result of the continued action of human minds and hearts on the wondrous revelation of God's mind, so definite here, so impenetrably dark there—theology, with its necessarily technical apparatus and language, with its hard outlines, with the audacities, the pettinesses, the refinements, the extravagances, which have as necessarily accompanied its development among creatures like ourselves, not only repels some minds, but is a subject so uncongenial to the taste of the day that it disturbs their equanimity and their good sense. We see in their judgments about it the unmistakable stamp of temper. They have not patience to examine the use of what has occupied some of the mightiest and most devout of human intellects. They do not ask how we could have done without it. They contrast its dryness and subtlety with the freedom and poetry of Scripture. They might as well accuse Newton's *Principia* for not of itself evoking the feelings called forth by the starry heavens on a summer night; or expect from a scientific treatise on Harmony what they get from the compositions of Handel or Beethoven.—Again, it is very trying to many minds to find the facts of our social order so hard to deal with; or, again, to find the reality of the Christian Church so unlike the ideal. It has been and is a sore trial to many to find that an institution like the Church is not as saintly, or not as consistent, or not as free, or not as keen in inquiry, or not as comprehensive, or not as definite, or not as improving as they could wish. It is equally a trial to others that society will go on in customs which cannot be defended in argument; that people will stick to conclusions when the old reasons for them seem gone; that they will not open their eyes to truths which to the improvers seem self-evident. Men engaged in these discussions have reason to be on their guard against the gradual growth and the constant unfelt presence of temper, all the more in proportion as they feel deeply, and are disinterested and sincere.

It may easily come to govern them—that is, to cloud their judgment, and disable their capacity for fairness and truth.

Noli æmulari; Μὴ παραζήλου; *Fret not thyself*—is the Psalmist's thrice-repeated burden in Psalm xxxvii., when he contemplates what Bishop Butler calls "the infinite disorders of the world." *Noli æmulari* should be one of the most oft-repeated watchwards with us, who have to deal in our time and sphere, as best we may, with these disorders. We may need it, when honestly constructing a plain and intelligent theory of the things that most concern us and our work, and when the actual facts of history and life give us trouble; for whatever our theories, we shall be sure to meet with something inconvenient and perplexing, which we could wish out of the way. We shall need it in our practical efforts after improvement; for, take what line we may, we shall be sure to meet with hindrances which we cannot account for, and checks which we had not expected. We shall need it when we are going with the flow and rise of the tide. We shall need it when, perhaps, our part of the work is done, when we find ourselves on the defeated or failing side, playing a losing game, fighting for what seems a beaten,—its enemies, sometimes short-sightedly, call it—a lost cause. And this is likely to happen to most of us, if only we live long enough;—if only for this, that things get out of date; and what was young becomes old; and arguments, theories, books, once fresh and attractive, are left behind, worn out and used up, at least in their old forms, with the friends who are gone, and the scenes we have done with; and new ideas and assumptions and ways push aside and take the place of those with which we began. Any one, I suppose, who has gone through the ups and downs, the successes and failures, of great political, or social, or religious movements, and has the courage, looking back at a distance upon its course, to see not only its victories, but its false steps, its follies, and its mistakes, will place, foremost among these mistakes, the mistakes of temper. He will see how often things *right* were not *rightly* done; how often, in heat and exasperation, matters were pushed to needless extremity and violence; how often accidents were raised to the dignity of essentials, and trifles blown up to the importance of principles; how often, for the sake of a present advantage in argument, a gross exaggeration was snatched at, and an extreme or perilous position fought for, bringing on those committed to it disaster and trouble. He will see what mischief has come from that *splendida bilis* which at the time seemed so natural and so grand; how much has been lost by not allowing for the mere slowness, the ignorance, the perplexities of others. These are common, if not inevitable, concomitants of great efforts and conflicts in the greatest causes, when men are the fighters. They should not make us desist from the war against the manifold evils of the world; they should not make us regret having had our share, if so be, with all the mistakes, in such conflicts, in which we now see how many things might have been much better done. They are not a palliation for faintheartedness and hanging back, when it is plain that ventures must be made for Christ's sake. But they help those whose experience reflects them, to see new force and meaning in the Psalmist's warning—*Noli æmulari.* I remember seeing, in a country house of Catherine de Medicis, near the Loire, roughly scratched on the guardroom wall, probably by some English or Scotch attendant, or messenger, or soldier of her bodyguard, who had witnessed what had come of St. Bartholomew and the wars of the League, the words—" *The yre of man wyrketh not the justice of God.*" It was a strange inscription for such a place. It was like an echo from the sixteenth century itself, from the very centre and depths of its darkness and cruelty, bearing witness to the eternal truth which, more than any other age, that century set at nought and trampled on—which we know in the familiar words, " The wrath of man worketh not the righteousness of God." No, indeed ; the wrath of man may be God's scourge and punishment. But the work of God's righteousness, the work of that Infinite Wisdom and Infinite Charity, whose servants we are, and whom we are now going to meet in the Holy Sacrament, needs cool heads and self-commanding spirits, as well as pure hearts and unflinching purpose, and zeal that counts not the cost.

II

SELF-DISCIPLINE

An Address delivered on the Day of Devotion for the Clergy, appointed by the Bishop to be observed at St. Paul's, 16th November 1885.

YOU have heard this morning of the place which *Sympathy* must occupy in the Ministry of Grace:[1] in the Ministry of that Gospel, of which the leading note is the sympathy of the Creator with His creatures in their terrible distress, and in their strange aspirations — the wonderful sympathy of Him, who though He is so high, yet humbleth Himself to behold the things in heaven and earth, and despiseth not the work of His own hands—the awful sympathy of the most Holy, who for love of us refused not "to be touched with—to sympathise with—the feeling of our infirmities;" to be "tempted like as we are, yet without sin;" to win "the power," by suffering temptation Himself, "to succour them that are tempted." A minister of Christ cannot think too much of the demands or of the power of sympathy.

Sympathy is going out to others. I will ask you now for a few moments to enter into yourselves,

---

[1] The subject of Bishop Claughton's address.

and consider something of what we have to do at home, to fit ourselves for our hard and exacting work abroad. I will ask you to give some thoughts to the subject of *Self-discipline.* St. Paul opposes to the "spirit of fear,"—that δειλία, that meanness of heart, that coward and craven shrinking from responsibility and effort, which is pourtrayed in the unprofitable servant who could find nothing to do with his one talent—St. Paul opposes to this, that triple characteristic of all high action on human souls—"the spirit of power, and of love, and of a sound mind"— δύναμις, ἀγάπη, σωφρονισμός — energy, charity, discipline in its work and its results. And those whose work in life is to discipline others in the ways of truth and holiness must begin by taking much heed to the discipline of themselves. Vigour and activity are always in danger of becoming imperious or absorbing. Love may degenerate imperceptibly into self-pleasing dreaminess. Both need the corrective of a manly severity, at least with ourselves; of the spirit of sober self-command—what our version calls "a sound mind."

Each heart and conscience knows well where it needs this self-discipline most: whether to curb temper, or to conquer sloth and hatred of trouble, or to brave the face of man and endure without flinching under his words and scorn, or painfully and hardly to keep down the thoughts and imaginations and seeds of evil, sown in the soul by the sins of long ago against purity and light, and never perhaps to be quite extirpated while we live. Will you forgive me, if I venture to suggest a few points, by way of sample, of that self-discipline which our calling requires.

1. Most clergymen have, by the necessity of their position, besides the great and paramount interest of their vocation and ministry, secondary and subordinate interests running along side of it. Some of these are the inevitable outcrop of a clergyman's employment and activity. Some of them are in their measure and degree, legitimate. If he is doing his work well, he cannot well help feeling one of the greatest pleasures in life, the pleasure of good work for good work's sake, the pleasure of doing his work according to the aim and desire of his heart. He cannot help having the pleasure which a really great commander has in the risk and hard work of a well conducted war, the pleasure which the artist, or the thinker, or the discoverer, has in those exercises of power and energy, which though full of toil and perhaps mixed with disappointment, yet answer to the purpose and effort of the soul. Then, as he is still tied to life and society, there are the interests of his family, and of those he cares for; his social position, the sphere which he would like to fill, the fair openings to influence and power, his character in the world, the kindness with which others think of him and treat him. These secondary interests cannot but have a place in our thoughts. There is

no one who has not to do with some of them. Most men have to reckon with a great many. And yet we all know—it is written on the history of the Church—how these secondary interests, these inevitable, and some of them, legitimate companions of our highest activities and our indispensable occupations, may by their very familiarity, their humble, every-day necessity, steal away our hearts, and, almost without our knowing it, really take the place of the one master interest of a clergyman's life. We of all men need a vigilant self-discipline against that selfishness which, in one form or another, is ever lying in wait for every human being: the selfishness which makes an idol of our very activity, of our very affections, of our very duty; which welcomes the secret elation of success, which allows itself to dwell on the worldly prospects of that success, which cannot tear away thought and imagination from the flattering consciousness of having preached well, or written well, or acted well. I say nothing of the grosser temptations of worldly interest, though few men are strong enough to make light of them and undervalue them. I say nothing of the tendencies which carry the strong, the resolute, the practical, into impatience and mere self-will: the love of having their own way, and doing everything by their own hand. I say nothing of the perils to the man himself of that combination of high intellect and high enthusiasm, which makes even the world attend; of that power over the secrets of hearts, that gift of piercing to the roots, of seeing and holding up unsuspected truths, which has often put to shame the preacher himself, when he thinks what he has said, and made him feel that among the things he will least like to meet at the last day are his own sermons. It is not these only, but the humbler and more unobtrusive by-interests of our lives, which make a demand on us for vigilant self-discipline.

2. Again, we need self-discipline, amid the sweet and tender and softening influences, amid which many of us live, and from which even the hardest life among us is not entirely cut off. Family life is a noble and blessed thing, with its sacredness, its venerable associations, its solemn, even eternal bonds, its ties and affections wrapped round our heart of hearts, its holy or touching memories, like no other in the world: but surely it is a thing in which a clergyman needs to think a good deal of self-discipline. And besides this, a clergyman, if he is doing his work well, if he is deeply in earnest and is recognised as being so, if he can speak to men's hearts and souls, can help them to see light in the darkness, can elicit from them the response of conviction and sympathy, is in time surrounded by an atmosphere of affection and reverence, very helpful to his great objects, but not quite safe to himself. He has to deal with people, many of them very dear to him, who love and admire and largely, perhaps boundlessly, trust him—trust him with all they value —trust him even to the grave. Besides the strong,

there are the weak. Besides the rough, there are the gentle, the enthusiastic, the tender-hearted, the confiding, the devout. Besides men, there are women. He who has to be all things to all men in their needs, has to think of all. And now more than ever, God be thanked for it, the ministry and service of women is become one of the established parts and helps of a clergyman's own ministry, part of the regular system of a well organised parish. He has to do largely with them, as sufferers, counsellors, workers ; with invalids and troubled in mind ; with widow and fatherless ; with district visitors, with nursing sisters, with ladies, well-born perhaps and cultivated, who have given themselves to reclaim the lost, to serve the penitent, the miserable, the poor. In spite of all terrible realities of hardship and stern endurance, this presents the soft, the tender side of religious service. Surrounded by it, looked up to for inspiration and guidance, a clergyman has to keep control over himself, that only its wholesome influences affect him. He *may* let it be too much to him. He may accommodate himself unwisely to it. He may allow it too much power over his judgments. He may let it insensibly give a bias to his teaching and his thoughts. He may let it steal away something from manliness and sober strength. Such undue yielding of the stronger to the weaker is no uncommon sight anywhere, and it has been seen in the history of religion. The highest purpose, the highest purity, the most austere self-denial, has not always kept off the touch of the sentimental or the effeminate. It was an abatement on the majestic sweetness of Fénélon. It was not always absent from the steady and masculine strength of Port Royal. A clergyman has need of self-discipline, lest all that is tender and consoling round him tempt him into softness, and weaken the fibre of character, of doctrine, of conscience, even of devotion and worship.

3. To take another point. We are called to be busy men, to be critical men, to be faithful men in witness and rebuke, to be outspoken, to be staunch to our trust, to resist evil. What offices these, calling for severe and honest self-discipline. How easy, from being busy, to become bustling, officious, fussy. How easy to see only our own field of activity, and forget that there are others as important beyond it. How easy, from being justly watchful for strictness and duty, to become censorious, one-sided, hasty in blaming. How easy, from being zealous against error and falsehood, to become unauthorised meddlers with the business and the burdens of others, intolerable disturbers of the liberty of others, accomplices in injustice, self-satisfied denouncers of what we have not taken the trouble to understand, stupidly malignant in our narrow and shallow dogmatism. How easy, in our fear and hatred of compromise, and of betraying principle, to be stiff, hard, impracticable. It is the old story; our faults and blunders mask under the disguise of our noblest duties. But the very gravity of our

office, the necessity laid upon us to judge, to condemn, to take a strong line, to guard our sacred trust, to make no peace with evil, makes it all the more our duty to bridle, not our tongues only, but our hearts; to strive after that calmness and breadth and equity which ought to be in all clothed with authority; that self-command which belongs to all sound human judgment: that large considerate forbearance, that ἐπιείκεια, which was one of the favourite virtues of the most fiery of men, the apostle St. Paul.

4. Once more:—we live in a time of great conflicts of thought and opinion, amid the rapid growth of new, daring, ambitious ideas, which challenge submission, or at least inquiry. And not only new ideas, but some of the oldest and most familiar appear in new aspects. A recent writer has marked the difference when a man passes from "what he knows," to what he "not only knows, but *imagines.*"[1] Great ideas may lie long dormant in our minds, known and conventional—the ideas of a miracle, of sin, of eternal righteousness, of the forgiveness of sins, of the Atonement, of the Incarnation, of God:—then all at once, the reality of their meaning bursts upon our thoughts, and they astonish us by their stupendous and unearthly wonder, to which nothing here, nothing that we deal with, is like or commensurate. And the unveiling is sometimes overpowering: the mind staggers under their awful great-

[1] The phrase is Mr. Kinglake's.

ness.[1] Again, on all sides of us, in the teeming literature of the day, appealing to our love of truth, soliciting our assent, defying our disproof, touching our sense of consistency, taking certainty for granted, displaying the attractions of bold, and strong, and clear, and complete exposition, are theories, systems, philosophies, criticisms, histories; pictures, drawn by science, illuminated by imagination and poetry, of society, of religion, of nature and the world. Shut ourselves out from it all, of course we may, if we choose: but they are the things which interest and influence the living people who are the objects of our charge. In the face of all this, does not mind and imagination, and thought need the help of serious, careful, self-discipline? that inner guard over impressions and assent, that combination of mistrust and frank candour, which will make us proof, not against the claims of truth, but the snares of plausibility: which holding fast to proved convictions, will let us keep our mind open to the light. We need, many of us, a steady consciousness of that failing, which makes us perhaps the slaves of the last argument, the captives of the last ingenious paradox or brilliant novelty, or else, silent and helpless and despairing under the stress of assertions which we know not how to contradict, and reasonings which we cannot answer. We need to remember that time tries arguments as well as men, and is as truly an element in deep and sound conviction, as conscious

[1] See Mozley's Bampton Lectures, pp. 3-6.

and recognised and producible processes of thought. And yet, we need also to keep in order the fear of what is new, *because* it is new to us; the dislike of trouble,—and the greatest of all troubles to some people is the trouble of thinking,—when a serious demand is made on our fairness and attention. Again, in times of unsettlement and change and new departures, we are liable, according to our temperament, to be shaken in different ways. To one set of minds, the adventurous and the hazardous will always have an attraction of its own. Such minds will see special marks of truth in what is uncompromising and thorough-going and fearless of consequences. They like strong language and sweeping statements, and to feel that they are brave: and if the apparent moral loftiness of a view is combined with something of imaginative grandeur, the homely and prosaic testing of grounds and objections is impatiently put aside. And on the other hand, these new aspects, and these revolutions of ideas produce on other minds the effect of panic. The temptation comes to think that things threatened are lost; to think that because things are injured, they are utterly ruined. Men talk wildly and exaggerate danger, because they are frightened. Some years ago there appeared a work, which professed to be an elaborate demonstration that Supernatural Religion is in reason impossible, and historically false. Some of us may remember the alarm it produced. Serious men really spoke at the time as if it had made a new and bad breach in the defences of religion; as if Christians must look about them in earnest, if they were to save anything from the storm; as if the difficulty of believing and maintaining belief had been gravely and sensibly increased. A truer measure has since been taken of the book. Whatever its force may have been, the alarm was out of all proportion to it: but there *was* the alarm, and it was not worthy of wise and reasonable men. Surely, we may remember that, after all, be the strife of tongues what it may, there is as regards religion as well as morality a vast body of history behind us, of solid thought and conviction around us, unshaken and untouched by the novelties of ingenuity or the fashions of thought in the passing hour. In matters of inward thought and imagination, as well as in matters of desire and conduct, we have need of self-discipline. We need to take trouble to rule our spirits, to awaken our sluggishness, to question honestly and courageously the ideas that throng into our minds, to look with a steady eye on difficulties and risks, to resist the temptation of short cuts in argument, of hasty impulses in choice and conclusions; to resist the temptation to go beyond reality—that reality of which our inward consciousness is witness—in what we say, in what we admire, in what we profess, in what we fear.

> "Prune thou thy words, the thoughts control
> That o'er thee swell and throng;
> They will condense within thy soul,
> And change to purpose strong."[1]

---

[1] Newman's *Verses on Various Occasions*, LXXXVIII.

"The spirit of power, and of love, and of a sound mind," are the words of the apostle. A poet has varied but not altered the combination—"Strength, and humility, and largeness of heart."

"*Fortezza, ed umiltade, e largo core.*" [1]

I have ventured to speak to you of one of these great requisites for a clergyman's eventful work, the "sound mind," which is the spirit and the fruit of self-discipline, and which is also the truest and most genuine form of manly and noble humility. For it implies the true acknowledgment to ourselves of our shortcomings and mistakes, and when they continue, as they so often do, the courage and the patience to bow ourselves to the task of self-correction. Of all the work that we do, the work with our own spirits and characters is to ourselves the hardest to judge of; with some of us, the most disappointing. But the reality of all our work—I do not say the outward success—must depend on the reality of this. And if we go on with it in faith and honesty, surely it will not be in vain, even if less than we hoped for. For there is One whose Divine help is promised and pledged to us, if we are honest and true; One whose hand works in His own secret and wondrous way, who is the source to men of insight, and wisdom, and counsel, and strength; the Holy Spirit and Comforter, to whom we were solemnly committed at our Ordination. To His mighty power and guidance let us again commit ourselves. Confiding in

[1] Dante (?), Sonnet 55.

His help, our fathers trained themselves to be the guides, the pastors, the comforters, of His flock and people. The task of conquering ourselves, of governing ourselves, may now seem to us, as doubtless it seemed to them in their day, "toilsome and incomplete." "Toilsome and incomplete" it seemed to them at the time, in the doing. But they now look back with other eyes on their efforts after self-discipline, from their place of rest. Let us pray the Holy Spirit of Truth, who helped them, to give us the single eye, the fearless heart, the dread of self-deceit, the love of what is real, the hatred and horror of what is showy and insincere. May He give us grace not to lose heart, to have patience with ourselves— and to draw from the necessity of having patience with ourselves an argument for having patience with our brethren. "What a man cannot amend in himself or in others," says the great master of the honesties of self-discipline, the author of the *Imitation of Christ*—" he ought patiently to put up with, until God orders otherwise," and he adds—" If thou canst not make *thyself* that which thou wouldest be, how canst thou expect to have thy brother according to thy wish "—" Si non potes te talem facere qualem vis, quomodo poteris alium ad tuum habere bene placitum ? "

XVI

THE KINGDOM OF GOD, NOT IN WORD, BUT IN POWER

"The Kingdom of God is not in word, but in power."—
1 CORINTHIANS iv. 20.

OF him who wrote these words, these words are plainly true. Of St. Paul it is as certain as anything can be, that this contrast expressed the truth about the business to which his life was given. It was, in the first place, not a name but a thing, not a profession but a conviction, not an opinion to be talked about, but a truth to live and die for. But there is more than this. Beyond the opposition of mere words and professions and names to reality, there is the opposition between things which are, and our theories and speculations about them. And here, again, St. Paul held to his contrast. The Kingdom of God had come into the world of experience, and work, and fact, and was come to take its part there. The Kingdom of God was not a philosophy, not even a divine philosophy, but a living force, to try its strength against the other forces, coarse or subtle, of human life. It was not merely a great idea, but an imperious and self-acting law to each man's life; not a speculative system of the universe or of morals, co-ordinating causes, accounting for results, but the weight and power of an actual movement, outside of man, which could change and govern wills, and acts, and events. It was not something within the domain of human thinking to shape and deal with, but something apart from all thought about it, with a substantive and independent existence of its own.

There are such things—we know them, and he knew them. The kingdoms of this world, the empire of the Cæsars, the forms and organisation of society in his day, were not in word but in power. You might dispute about them. You might hate, or you might admire and praise them. You might acquiesce in them, or resist them. But, after all said and done, you were but a thinker and talker about them, and they were the things that are. Such to St. Paul was the "Kingdom of God," the "Gospel of Christ," the "Church of God." Nature is not in word but in power. The family is not in word but in power. Morality is not in word but in power. Law is not in word but in power. Take them away, and it is a different world—not a world that we know, not a world which we can well imagine our knowing. True, we are accustomed to them; but beyond custom, nature is, and the family, and morality, and law. And so to St. Paul's life and convictions was the "Kingdom of God." It was the necessary complement to all that was in the world. Once, he had known the world without it: henceforth he could no more know the world without it than a blind man whose eyes were opened could know the world without the light.

Except to the few who knew what St. Paul knew, and thought as he did, it was, at the time, a bold saying; not too bold for what he put his conviction upon, but bold according to the appearances of the time. But, indeed, it was not a whit too bold. The course of events has amply verified his belief. As a fact in the history of the world, the "Kingdom of God" which he preached, has been, if ever anything was, "not in word but in power." And mankind, unbelieving as well as believing, have not ceased wondering at it.

May I, then, invite you to consider for a few minutes this very obvious and commonplace subject, contained in St. Paul's words, that "The Kingdom of God is not in word, but in power;" it is not a supposition, but a fact; not a theory, a speculative system, but a reality, which we cannot help and cannot undo, and which we cannot make to be just what we like, in the existing order of things which we know. There is use, sometimes, in bringing ourselves face to face with assumed, and obvious, and accepted things. We are always in danger of straying away, under the temptations and interest of thinking, from plain, rude reality. Our ingenuity builds up, or develops, or destroys, forgetful that what we are operating upon, as we think, so skilfully, goes on its way, not heeding our thoughts about it any more than the suns which rise and set. You argue triumphantly that a thing is this way, or that way, or that it cannot be, that it is dead; and lo, in spite of all that ought to follow, it lives. *Eppur si muove.* The things which we least notice, because they are so familiar, so undoubted, are often the things that most need and deserve our attention.

The contrast between the reality of a thing and men's thoughts about it runs through all our life in every department of it. Every one, according to the place which he occupies, is conscious of it. The merchant, the lawyer, the man of science, the engineer, the sailor, all know it well, when they come into contact with what is outside their own world; but the contrast is not limited to merely professional or technical matters. Whenever men touch real things, there is seen and felt the difference in knowledge and mental attitude. Take the way in which we think and speak of a person whom we know by books or report, and then the difference, when we come to know the living man by face, and expression, and voice, and behaviour, in all the unimagined variety of the shades and hues of his character, all the compensations for what we disliked, all the abatements from what we admired, all the changeful play of affections or of mood, all the richness, if the life is a long and active one, of inventiveness, of adaptability, of surprises, all balancings between strong tendencies; and, finally, all this harmonised into a complete whole in a way which might beforehand have seemed impossible. Here you have words opposed to things, speculation opposed to life in action. Take the different look that a system, philosophical or religious, wears, when we know it only by its name, and when we come to see what it is inside its own borders, and what it has to say for itself; and even if we condemn it, how different a shape our condemnation takes. Or again, take the way in which most of us think and speak of poverty, and wretchedness, and pain, and sin, in a wholesale sort of way, using the words like cyphers and counters, and compare that with the knowledge, various, strange, terrible, overpowering, of one who really goes in and out among the crowds, and knows them in their homes and haunts; and, further, with the idea which so much knowledge as this gives of the apparently infinite extent beyond, unknown, unfathomable, of misery, and suffering, and evil—all the varieties and families and complications of wickedness; all the forms of disease and wild anguish beyond what most of us think or dream — "*plurima mortis imago*"—moral and physical. And so, when we talk of the terrible things which the earth has seen, its wars and battles, its famines, its plagues, the gathering of all kinds of sickness in a great hospital; or again, some huge institution of customary wickedness and cruelty—the Roman games of the amphitheatre—the Inquisition of the Middle Ages—the slave trade of our own—what a difference, when we toss the mere words about, and when we make ourselves acquainted, seriously acquainted, with the very things that happened, with all their surroundings and consequences. There you have words, unreal, shadowy generalities, contrasted with things; the pale, vague aspects of things contrasted with the things themselves. Or, once more, contrast the idea beforehand of a life such as that of a university or a camp —I suppose it is the same with a life employed in great public affairs—with what it proves to be in actual result—the indistinct, childish, ignorant anticipations of the schoolboy, or the outsider, often so grotesque and so positive, with the real, manifold experience when it comes. That is the kind of difference between words and things; between untested words, unexplored, superficial notions, and a system actually at work in its various functions.

So with Christianity—with the religion which St. Paul called the " Kingdom of God." We may talk about it, for, indeed, it is impossible to keep it out of our conversation. But we may talk about it as an ordinary landsman talks about the management of a ship, or the qualities of seamanship; or, with the ideas of a fashionable trifler about the poverty of the poor; or, with those of a schoolboy about the work of a Cabinet. We may talk with a mere external thought of it, as an expression necessary in political, or philosophical, or social writing. We may not only talk but speculate about it, with interest and ingenuity; yet, with all our ingenuity and interest, deal with it as theologians and preachers sometimes unhappily deal with the great theories and conclusions of science in a way which scientific men justly resent as impertinent ignorance, knowing as they do how solid, and vast, and difficult a thing science is, how thorough in its processes, how firm in its grounds, how wide-reaching in its powers. Indeed, it is not every one who has a right to speak, even of what he most dislikes or distrusts, in science. But religion, too, is a deep and substantial thing—much more than a matter of words and superficial notions: and it, too, must be *known*, if it is to be spoken of reasonably and justly and wisely, as all that greatly interests and affects mankind may expect to be spoken of.

For, indeed, Christianity is not speculation or anything speculative. "The Kingdom of God is not in word, but in power." It is not satisfied even with abstract truth. It must be life, or it is nothing. It has of course, it must have, a philosophy. But the moment it is treated merely as a philosophy the idea and meaning of it perishes in our hands. The "Kingdom of God," if it is the Kingdom of God, is a religion, a loyalty, a power, an influence, a service; conquering, quickening, stimulating, controlling man, his soul, his will, his character, his fate and history. Independently of our thoughts about it, it is every day working its work among the consciences, the aspirations, the anxieties of thousands of men. While we are judging it, it is judging us. Whether we are for it or against it, whether it perplexes us, or attracts us, or irritates us, it goes on its course in a path beyond our reach, beyond our calculation. It has gone on for nineteen centuries. It is going on still —"not in word, but in power"—not as a theory, but as one of the elemental forces in the life which we know—perhaps as mysterious and inexplicable beyond a fixed point as they, but at least as much a fact.

A fact, obviously, in its outward aspect, as no one denies. It is taught, it is preached, it is professed, it governs. But it is for much more than because it manifests itself in public institutions, that the "Kingdom of God" is one of those things which are "not in word, but in power." It is not because it bears itself so loftily among the things of men. It is not because its cross is on the crowns of kings and the banners of great nations. It is not because its claim is allowed on man's substance and man's time. It is not because it has educated generations in great schools and universities. It is not because it has moulded the worship of civilised men. It is not because it is enshrined in cathedrals, and has also hallowed God's Acre and God's House in the poorest hamlet of the obscurest corner of Christendom. All this may go—hard as it is to imagine it—as it has come: it was not once; again, it may not be. Nor again, what is more, because when we look over the history of the greatest and most fruitful times of the human race we see what it has done. The footsteps of the Kingdom of God are among us. In that long line of chequered but undoubted progress since it made its home with men, in those struggles after better things, often so misplaced and futile, but still so obstinate and unrelaxed, which have marked the centuries since it came, we see the signs of what was not in the world before. We men of the West, surely we are not mistaken in claiming, on a large view, a superiority over the quick-witted races of the East, over the great races which preceded us, and gave us so many of our most prized possessions; but a superiority, not surely in intellect, but in, what we call, character, in our wider and nobler and more manly view of the conditions and facts and government of life. And where did we learn this? The Kingdom of God has not been with us in vain. It has not been idle among us. At least it has left its monuments with us.

But there is more than this. It would be little if only its monuments were among us. "The Kingdom of God is not in word, but in power." It is in its hold, so tenacious and so eventful, on the inner life of men, that these words are verified. I venture to say that they are as true at this moment as they were when they were first written. I venture to say that there never has been a generation since they were first written, when they were not amply verified. There rises up, indeed, before our memory and imagination all the inconsistency, all the unfaithfulness, all the lethargy, all the consummate hypocrisy, all the abandoned wickedness in high and low, which has neutralised or perverted

Christianity—the Kingdom of God. It is an awful, a portentous vision, in what it is, in what it threatens. But, beside it, is the no less certain truth, that in the worst and most fatal storm, the hopes of the Kingdom of God, its power over men, its spring of recovery, have never been overwhelmed. How could they be? Man is so made, so "fearfully and wonderfully made," that the thrill which Christianity sent through him at first, it sends through him still. Without a rival it has the key of his heart—his longing, wavering, suffering, doubting, suspicious heart. It has come, not only into the outward world of sight and speech, but into the invisible world of souls; and there it has set up its throne, and rules as nothing else does, except the passions which it combats. It has brought a new language into the world, the interpreter of the affections, the emotions, the ideas which it has opened to the human soul; a language not for the few, but for the many, a language which all understand who "travail and are heavy laden," who sin and who suffer, who weep and who die, who pray and who hope; a language which makes the things beyond time and the grave to be the common food of daily life; a language in which the men who have passed away ages ago communicate and sympathise with the men of to-day, and which is understood all over the world by races and classes which have nothing else in common. Now, as in the Middle Ages—now, as in the catacombs, or in the desert—now, as in the first days—the cry *Kyrie Eleison*, Lord have mercy on us, goes up from the depth of men's souls. The love of the cross is their hope in extremity. The prayer to Our Father in the many languages of man, sums up their petitions and self-dedication. It has penetrated everywhere, where men feel most strongly, most tenderly, most really, where they think most seriously. It has sent its fibres so deeply into the structure of civilised life, into marriage, into education, into mourning, into the chamber of death and separation, that life, as we know it, is unintelligible without it. Every book that we open, of friend, or foe, or neutral, bears witness to its pervading and intangible power. The great prophets of human thought and human character, Shakespeare and Bacon, reflect in every page its ideas, speak perforce and naturally the language it has taught them, acknowledge and bow down before its presence, as they do before the law of right or wrong, as they do before the realities of joy and pain and death. And its words and thoughts come as naturally to the souls of the humblest, in those hours which teach truth to men, and which make all men equal before the facts of life.

For it answers to three things in us, which, as long as men are what we know them, we never shall get rid of, and against which both speculation and passion beat in vain—the consciousness of evil and sin; the recognition of righteousness as our true law and standard; the longing for love. They are elements latent wherever you can trace the rudiments of a moral being, as we know moral beings; but the coming of the Kingdom of God, in the person of Jesus Christ, has quickened and developed them as they never were before; and it is by its hold upon them, while we are discussing it, defining it, doubting it, that it rules in consciences and hearts, and creates a new and enduring life, which it is idle to deny, in the bitterest moment of hostility and despair. It rules in the tremendous and mysterious idea of sin, that idea so hard to analyse and to follow to its roots, but which is stamped on the face of history and society, and which each man's self-knowledge is compelled to recognise. It rules in the idea of righteousness, of a reality of goodness, to which the eyes of even the worst can be opened; of a recovery from the delusions and the waste of evil; of endless hopes of moral elevation and improvement. It rules in the idea of holiness, in the idea of purity, in the idea of truth. They are ideas belonging to the essential furniture of the soul, not utterly lost even in its debasement and blindness. It rules in the idea of forgiveness and mercy. It rules in the inextinguishable idea of final judgment. And then it rules in the Person, and life, and death of Jesus Christ; of Him, who, "though He was rich, yet for your sakes became poor, that ye, through His poverty, might be rich."—"Who loved me, and gave Himself for me:"—while those words haunt the memories of men, the soul, after all its wanderings in search of something to trust to, of something to love, of something to love it, will find them waiting for it, will feel that they are like nothing else in the world, that they are irresistible. " Not in word, but in power," have been the countless lives of charity and sacrifice, lives of every various order of obscurity and splendour, which have been lived in the faith of that Son of God, and have repeated on a humbler stage and in narrower spheres the lesson of the Cross of Christ.

It is one of the dangers of human life, amid its keen and varied interests, to lose sight of one or other of the standing and primary realities by which it is surrounded, and which cannot be forgotten without loss and risk. The utilitarian forgets that there is such a thing as poetry and passion, and the mere sense of what is beautiful. The practical man cannot think how so much time is spent on literary training or abstract speculation; the thinker, absorbed in a great philosophy, wonders at the fascination of politics or commerce. Yet all these things belong equally to the great facts of the world, whether we remember them or not; they don't depend on our observing them; they go on and work and tell upon the world; and it is we who are the losers, if we are too busy or too narrow or too blind to take account of them. And so, whether we forget it or no, whether we appreciate it or no, the Kingdom of God, the Gospel and the Church of Jesus Christ, with all their wonders, *exist*: exist, not in books or theories, but in fact—exist, "not in word, but in power"—exist, prior to all views and speculations about them—exist, really, and widely, and inexhaustibly, animating and governing human life—exist, after the long testing of time and experience, after the fiercest hostility, and the most merciless criticism—exist, after enduring everything that undermines and kills ideas and institutions—exist, as really, I do not say as worthily, but as really, as they did at first, in that which is their true seat, the convictions and the affections of the souls of men.

If that which is best in us is not to be maimed and cramped, we have need to take full account of this as much as of the facts of nature and society. We shall be living, if we do not, in an imaginary and unreal world. We must meet the Kingdom of God. We find it here, and we must meet it, either as friend or foe; for it is a practical thing; and however much we may dispute,—and, while we are disputing, men are born and are dying,—men sin and suffer, and need but too deeply all that can be done for them. In this world, which is often in its reality so startling a contrast to what we assume in our speculations and imagine in our dreams, high practical truth many a time, even in the hurry and distractions of our rush through life, comes to us like the Sphinx; it requires an answer, and, alas for those who give the wrong one! But we must give an answer. In such a thing as the claims of the Kingdom of God we must make our choice and abide it. In all practical matters, in the domain of politics, in the conduct and critical turning-points of life, there are things which cannot be open questions. No one has a right to expect that to those who believe at all in the Kingdom of God it should be, however questioned, to them an open question. They cannot look at it simply as a matter for argument. Their whole being must be revolutionised for them to contemplate steadily the possibility of the Kingdom of God turning out a mistake or an untruth. If we, who believe in it, are wrong, it is little what the consequences will be to ourselves; for our mistake will mean a final and fatal sentence passed on all that we know of human intelligence, and, what is more, on the moral capacities of mankind. But it is not we only who must make the venture.

If, then, you find yourself dealing with the claims of the Kingdom of God, and sitting in judgment upon them, recognise what you are questioning. Recognise that you are judging the greatest spiritual and moral force in the world. And, at least, take care that you know what Christianity is before you judge it. Take it all in, not partially or by suppositions; take it all in, all that such life and reality imply, such living power, living you know not how and reaching you know not whither, but certainly living and working; take it all in, and all that would not be, if all this were not. And if you don't know it and cannot know it, as only it can be known, own to yourself that you don't know it, and be as modest and careful as all men ought to be about what they don't know. Leave it alone, if you are not prepared to be serious; leave it alone, if you are not prepared for what such inquiry involves, of steadiness, of time, of thoroughness, of sacrifice; leave it alone, if you are not prepared to deal with it as the great and tremendous reality that it is. It is not the love of being right which makes the love of truth; it is this desire to be right, planted in the heart of sincerity, of patience, of purity, of unselfishness, of humility, in a character which shrinks from indolence and negligence, which shrinks from that blinding and deadly enemy of all truth, the habit of insolence and scorn.

But on us, to whom the Kingdom of God is no dream or supposition, but the most solid of certainties, who could not, if we would, shake off the conviction and the consciousness of its existence and power, what a responsibility rests! Christianity, it is said everywhere, is not a thesis, or a system, or a school of thought, but a life answering to great certainties around us and without us. What a responsibility for being as good as our word, in sincerity, in courage, in loyalty to our King! What a note it will be against our generation if it ever shall be said that it was one in which Christians had not the moral fibre to understand and value all that they had in Christianity, and can hope for nowhere else— in which, with all that they knew, with all their experiences, they had not the courage to face the difficulties of choice, which are the common difficulties of all men—in which they gave it up, with all its powers for righteousness and all its hopes for man, cowering before the ominous aspects and prophecies of the hour. Ours is really no new and strange trial, though it seems so to us: in every age the faith and patience of the saints have had to endure the perpetual contrast between things seen and things not seen. It was this contrast which made St. John write, "This is the victory that overcometh the world, even our faith." It was this contrast which drew that burst from St. Paul, alone, against the thought and opinion of the world of his time, "But God forbid that I should glory, save in the Cross of our Lord Jesus Christ, by whom the world is crucified unto me, and I unto the world." May we not, loaded as we are by God's gifts, "enriched in all utterance, and all knowledge," be weak and poor followers of such great examples! "O Lord, in Thee have I trusted; let me never be confounded."

XVII

FAILURES IN LIFE

"For I have no man likeminded, who will naturally care for your state. For all seek their own, not the things which are Jesus Christ's."—
PHILIPPIANS ii. 20, 21.

IN these and like passages of the Epistles of St. Paul, written subsequently to his imprisonment, we may trace signs of one of the many trials of the apostle's life; one which we hardly, perhaps, estimate at its real measure. With the utter self-abandonment which was the basis of all that he was and did, with the unceasing pain and buffetings which accompanied the conflicts of his great enterprise, we are familiar. We know how, before the imprisonment, in the Epistles to the Corinthians, he spoke of the death which he died daily. But the imprisonment put an end to this activity, with all its vicissitudes of gain and loss in the warfare which he was waging for his Master. He had been passing from land to land, to extend the Kingdom of God, to gather in and build up the Church of the Gentiles, to suffer, as any one would have to suffer, in so strange and bold an invasion of the world. That course was now arrested: it closed in a prolonged imprisonment at a distance from the scenes of his work, which lasted, with some interruption, of which we know but little, till his death. That forced inactivity, with all its circumstances of restraint and isolation, which, for the most part, marked the rest of his life, opened to him a new experience of what he was called to. He had to sit still and see what came of all his work, of all his hopes : he had to sit still, no longer able to do that which was nearest to his heart, and to which he had given his life : he had to sit still with the sense that the world thought him a defeated man, whose career and whose attempts had been brought by the hand of power to an abrupt stop, and whose efforts his enemies had paralysed for good. We, who find it so hard to look beyond the low horizon of present things, should expect the attendant feelings to be those of depression and deep disappointment. We know that it was not so with St. Paul. We know from his own language of patience and resolution, of assured hope and joy prevailing over trouble, that he met this new trial as he had met his former ones. But moods of feeling come and go, even in the strongest ; and we may see, as I said, signs that he was not unmoved, when those round him evidently thought that his work had been in vain, and that all those triumphant announcements of new hopes and new interpretations of old ones, which had stirred so strongly religious minds in Greece and Asia, and had ended in the practical silencing of a Roman prison, were judged and condemned by the event. There is an undertone of deep sadness in the Epistle to the Philippians, full as it is of firm confidence and unextinguished rejoicing. He was no longer free to go where he would; yet he was at Rome, in the centre of all that was going on in the world, in that famous Roman Church, whose faith even then was "spoken of throughout the whole world," which he had so longed to see and to know. But what did he find there? What had come of that great Epistle to the Romans, his own greatest effort in interpreting his message? Do we not read between the lines, when he writes to the Philippians from Rome, that the reality was not all that he hoped for? There was energy, there was zeal, there was progress; his own troubles and bonds, he says, had fallen out rather to the furtherance of the Gospel. The majority of the brethren had received a fresh impulse of confidence from his imprisonment and his presence: Christ and His servant were spoken of among the guards and in the household of Nero: Rome was hearing, more than ever, of the name of Christ. But there was another side to this. How did he find his solemn adjuration to the Christians of Rome realised,—" I beseech you therefore, brethren, by the mercies of God, that ye present your bodies a living sacrifice, holy, acceptable unto God"? What fruit had come from those lessons of mutual forbearance and co-operation—about the strong bearing the infirmities of the weak—about the many members in the one body, all members not having the same office, but all being members one of another? What he found at Rome was that, with increasing enthusiasm in the cause of the Gospel, not without sympathy and affection among a certain number for himself, there was also in full strength the bitterness of party jealousy and of personal hostility and spite. "Some indeed preach Christ even of envy and strife." ... "The one preach Christ of contention, not sincerely, supposing to add affliction to my bonds." He makes the best of it in the nobleness and generosity of his faith—"What then? notwithstanding, every way, whether in pretence, or in truth, Christ is preached; and I therein do rejoice, yea, and will rejoice."—But what a tale does it tell, when there, in the midst of that great active Roman Church, the words escape from him, "For I have no man likeminded, ($ἰσόψυχον$) who will naturally—really, sincerely—care for your state. For all of them ($οἱ πάντες$) seek their own, not the things which are Jesus Christ's."

St. Paul's life at this time must have seemed like what we call a failure. The great work for which he lived had shattered itself against the natural obstacles of a firmly established order,—religion, law, the habits and prejudices of society, the recognised indulgences of human passion. His missionary journeys had come to an end; and he had not reconciled Jew and Gentile, his brethren after the flesh, so dear to him, his brethren after the promise, his crown and joy. The tide which had carried him so high was ebbing, and left him lonely and deserted, hardly recognised or cared for, except by his distant friends in the East. Of his public work at Rome no record remains. Of what he did in the short interval of liberty which intervened between his two imprisonments, we have only a few hints in the Pastoral Epistles. Captivity, indeed, in his case, as with others, was not unfruitful; nowhere did the seer's eye see so keenly or so far, or the man's heart of tenderness and nobleness reveal itself so completely as in the Epistles to the Philippians, Ephesians, Colossians, and the little letter to Philemon. But in these his work was not for Rome, but for old friends in Greece and Asia; and these letters show us at Rome the burden and oppression of conflict, the activity of hostile influences, the weight of an adverse public opinion, the great teacher schooling himself to lessons of resignation, hope and cheerfulness, which were plainly needed, and comforting himself that he had "not run in vain, neither laboured in vain," by his confidence in his earlier converts; they show us unexpected estrangements, waning friendships, failing sympathy. "Demas hath forsaken me"—"at my first answer no man stood with me, but all forsook me," are the words of his last Roman letter. His career, his zeal, had ended in disaster. This is what it seemed to have come to. This is what would have appeared to friend and foe, when the old man was led out along the Ostian Way to die. And yet he had laid the foundations of the Church Universal, the Church of all the nations; and had left a name, than which no earthly name is greater—than which there is no greater among the Saints of God.

To a faith like St. Paul's, these adverse appearances, though they might wring from him as they passed, a cry of pain and distress, wore a very different aspect and took very different proportions, from what they would have to the world. To him the mere vicissitudes of a mortal career would be nothing more strange than the variations in his health, or in the number of his years. They were but part of his Master's use of him; part of that Cross by which the world was crucified to him and he unto the world. What to him was the wise world's sentence on his course, or the contrast between its earlier successes and its later baffling disappointments? What was it to him, who knew in whom he had believed—to whom it was a small matter to be judged by man's judgment, yea, who judged not his own self—who knew that everything that happened to him was but a passing incident in an eternal progress which stretched far beyond the grave, and of which the end was certain? If the moment's disloyalty or bitterness stung him, and the moment's sorrow or adversity darkened his feelings, the next moment brought back the unshaken, expectant hope, the unfailing joy. To St. Paul, so that he had faithfully done what God wanted of him, the outward fortunes of that small fragment of time which we call his life, were of slight moment; it mattered little that a course which had begun triumphantly seemed to end among the breakers; it mattered little to him if when he died, the world of his day pronounced the enterprise of his life a mistake and a failure.

Centuries have passed since then, and time has judged between him and the world of his day. But the failure of life, the failure of a career or a movement, and the contrast between its opening and its close, is a spectacle to which mankind has been accustomed from the beginning. Examples of it are familiar to us now, as they were to our fathers, and they are among the facts of our experience which interest us most deeply and affect us most powerfully. They interest us as strongly as great successes. They affect us as strongly as great reverses, great overthrows of prosperity, great displays of justice. We watch them, examine them, analyse them, account for them; we moralise over them; their pathetic unexpectedness touches us: or we draw cynical inferences from them, and they give us occasion to pride ourselves on the discernment and foresight which predicted them. History is full of them; fiction is full of them; every man's experience has something to say about them, in their coarser or the infinite variety of their subtler forms. In their coarser forms, we have the evidence of them in the old cries about the cheats and broken promises of life,[1] in the discontent

---

[1] "When I consider Life, 'tis all a Cheat;
Yet, fooled with Hope, men favour the Deceit;
Trust on, and think To-morrow will repay:
To-morrow's falser than the former Day;
Lies worse; and while it says, We shall be blest

of the successful and the despair of the conqueror who has nothing more to conquer; in the falls, sudden or insensible, from goodness to evil, the resistance to temptation abandoned, and the awful plunge with the eyes open into recognised and certain sin. But these are not all the ways in which we see the failure of a life, the baffling and defeat of a great hope. Rightly or wrongly we pronounce the sentence of failure on many a life and many an effort far removed from the blame of open sin—as to which, it may be, there is nothing but good to be said of its aim, and to whose high unselfishness and purity nothing but honour is due. All our lives, indeed, have failure in them, enough and to spare. Every action which we dare examine is an instance how we have come short. Every prayer that we say is a contrast in its ideal to the thoughts and habits which we find at once taking its place in our minds, as soon as we go out of Church. Every sermon that we hear, and are moved by, places the facts of life on a level

> With some new Joys, cuts off what we possest.
> Strange Cozenage! none would live past years again,
> Yet all hope Pleasure in what yet remain;
> And, from the Dregs of Life, think to receive
> What the first sprightly Running could not give."
> > Dryden, *Aurengzebe*, iv. 1.
> > See Macaulay, *History*, iv. 131.

> "Then old Age and Experience, hand in hand,
> Lead him to Death, and make him understand,
> After a search so painful and so long,
> That all his Life he has been in the wrong."
> > Rochester's *Satyr against Mankind*,
> > quoted in Goethe's *Aus Meinem Leben*, B. xiii.

from which we descend, when we return to common intercourse and action. We see the failures of life in the ordinary incidents of our experience,—we see it when the good die young; when the bright promise is cut short or not fulfilled; when men miss their true calling, ignobly shrink from it or proudly scorn it; when a life of noble labour is wrecked within sight of the goal, as a ship sinks in sight of port; when men, who have served their brethren well grow too old for the new demands which each fresh generation brings with it, and for tasks that once were light; when, as age goes on, old friends not only are taken away from us year after year, but we who remain find ourselves drifting asunder, in judgment, in objects, in sympathies. But the failures which specially touch us are, when a man has aimed high, and has shot wide of his mark, or short of it. It is when care, and love, and toil, and hope, have been lavished on an idea or a cause; and the idea will not stand the test of conflict and time, or the cause dwindles into personal rivalries or strifes of words. It is when the purpose at starting was so honest, the thought so pure and high, but as time went on some secret mischief got entangled with them, and without any one feeling it, the enterprise was turned out of its course, and from that little angle of divergence the interval grew impassable which separated the original direction and the later one. It is when life and perhaps opportunity remain, and yet the strength is spent, just when the turning point arrives, and obstacles accumulate, and the path is confused and uncertain. It is when the successful statesman sees his policy bringing forth fruits which he did not plant or look for. It is when the teacher ceases to be in sympathy with those he speaks to,—when the leader grows too old to imagine and inspire, and only dogmatises and repeats himself. It is when the sincere reformer sees his work taken out of his hands by a second generation of disciples of meaner and narrower thoughts; still worse when he becomes himself their prey and dupe, and leaves the evils of the world greater than when he assailed them. The mark of our mortality and our weakness is set on the lives of men, the flower of our race, and on the history of institutions, founded for the highest ends. The young man whom Jesus loved goes away sorrowful, for he had great possessions. Pride, or self-will, or vanity, or the flesh, overmaster the mind which God had richly furnished for Himself with gifts, to restore a kingdom, or to purify a Church, or to lift his fellows to new heights of truth and goodness: the beginning is made with enthusiasm and hope, but long before the race is done, the gifts are wasted and spoiled, the hopes have vanished. So it has been with those wonderful, those heroic institutions, which in Christian history have one after another tried some great effort for God's glory—tried to revive in a languid and degenerate religion a sense of the realities of the Gospel faith, and to raise up, amid neglect and contradiction, the fallen banner of the Crucified. One after another they have begun in a sincerity and singleness of high purpose which none can doubt. One after another they have left their mark in the splendour of their early triumph. One after another they have flagged, and turned aside to other things than what they thought of first: they have survived in a debased and perverted form, or if they have done good, it has not been the good they were meant to do. Francis and Dominic kindled the enthusiasm of the poet of the *Paradiso*—Francis, the Royal-hearted[1] Bridegroom of the forgotten Poverty of Christ; Dominic, calling forth once more the company of the preachers to the pulpits of the silent and neglectful Church :—among their followers were great saints and great thinkers; but too soon the flock of Francis were turned into idle mendicants, and the flock of Dominic became the ministers of the Inquisition. The little company of seven, Spaniards most of them, who humbly devoted themselves to the service of Jesus in the crypt of the Church of Montmartre, swelled into that mighty order which has furnished the bravest of missionaries, but also the most daring and ambitious of political schemers, the most inveterate and most unscrupulous of political intriguers. That austere and accomplished society which the Jesuits did so much to crush, which witnessed so seriously

---

[1] "Ma regalmente sua dura intenzione
Ad Innocenzio aperse."—*Parad.* xi. 91.

and so intelligently for religion when religion had been made the cloke of frivolous vice, the solitaries of Port Royal, the friends of Pascal and Arnauld, dwindled in the second or third generation, into the soured and factious Jansenists of the eighteenth century. Wesley, if any man ever did, tried to recall the Church to its true principles, and to reanimate her care for the souls committed to her: he did awaken the thought and conscience and zeal of thousands. But as time went on, his high purpose was let slip, and gradually altered amid the difficulties of adverse circumstances. From being the inspirer of new life into a great but lukewarm Church, he was turned out of his way, to add one more to the great divisions of Christendom, to add one more spring of bitterness to its animosities.

What right have we to wonder? For all these things were done on the stage of Time, and on Time are stamped, as inexorable necessities, imperfection, decay, disappointment. What right have we to wonder that in this scene of mortality, lives, and institutions, and orders, come short of their calling and their promise, when the greatest instrument of God's grace, His Church, presents, in its reality, such a contrast to its ideal; when it can be so plausibly accused of failure; when certainly, in spite of all the wonders it has done, it has failed to do all that it ought to have done, all that was to be expected of it here? Failure, when it meets us, is bitter and hard to bear, to us who are so ambitious and so weak, so sanguine and so short-sighted. But what is it, but the inevitable incident of that mingled greatness and littleness of human life, of which, if we will only attend, every passing hour reminds us? Failure means humiliation, sorrow to ourselves; but we know not what it means in the counsels of God; we know not what it is to those whom it disappoints, when we take in that real and eternal existence which we believe to be their destiny, and of which this life is but the short opening act. The world laughs at the failure of those who have made great ventures for Christ's sake. It has good reason sometimes; and we will not pretend that the world in its irony is not often wiser than we. But there is something wiser even than the world; and that is the counsel of Him who taketh the wise in their own craftiness. St. Paul, not listened to amid the factions of the Roman Church—St. Paul, forsaken in his Roman prison, had not much to say to refute the world, which assured him that he had failed. Even he could not have convinced it then of the meaning of what he had done—of what in the immediate future, and in far-distant years, was to follow from it. He knew that the crown of faithful service was ready for him. But his justification belonged to God his Master; and God kept it in His own hands, for this world, and the next.

How shall we think, then, about what we call failure in life,—the failure even of well-ordered lives which in one way or another miss their aim and perfection—the failure of designs and efforts, which seem to us important for good and based on right and truth? What is the wise and sober way of looking at so marked a feature in the state which we are passing through—an experience which so many must recognise, as more or less their own? I cannot imagine our taking it in at all adequately, without being led to think—not hopelessly, indeed, far from it—not scornfully nor indifferently, but *very humbly*, of this human life, in which it is so severe a part of our discipline, though far from the last word in what we live for. And these lowly thoughts are enforced the more strongly when we consider the contrast, so startling and so real, between what we do as moral agents, and the success which we achieve within the range where simple intelligence works on its own suppositions of conditions and aims; between the way in which we know and the way in which we will and behave. True enough, we speak of the limitations of human knowledge. But if the *datum* line of human nature was that of the mathematician's study, or the physicist's laboratory, or the mechanic's workshop—if the world and its conditions were only those assumed and taken into account by the engineer, the navigator, the manufacturer, the economist, there certainly would be no reason for talking of failure being stamped on human work. Within that range, when once the right track has been struck, there are no steps backward, no steps thrown away. There, men can predict without mistake, can secure perfection in their skill, can verify with unfailing accuracy, can design with the certainty of fulfilment, can move steadily and without swerving through the most intricate complications of interacting forces—from one stupendous discovery to another still more amazing and fruitful. In that world man triumphs; there the race advances, conquering and to conquer, whatever becomes of the individual. But that is a world which we arbitrarily fence off from the intrusion of moral ideas and moral events, for the undisturbed play of the powers of intelligence. And all this takes another aspect as soon as we pass out of those charmed bounds, within which we confine ourselves to abstract truths, and the powers of nature, and mind which penetrates and controls them. All is changed when we pass into that other world where the great powers that rule are Love, and Duty, and Righteousness, and Pain, and Death. There we pass from clearness to perplexity, from the certain to the debateable, from the fixed to the variable, from the uniformity of law to the incalculable and the unexpected, the unsounded depths of the human will, goodness and evil equally unlooked for, the waywardness of passion and changing moods and unstable characters. In that region man reaches his greatest height—shows all that is noblest and most beautiful in what he is and does, all that is brightest or most pathetic in his fate: but it is also the region of his multiplied failures, of his average moral poverty and incompleteness, of his profoundest moral ruin. Compare what we achieve in mathematical and physical science, and by means of them, with our success in the problems of government, in dealing with the passions and ignorance of mankind, in suppressing vice and intemperance; and we see the contrast between the two great provinces of human interest and activity. It is in the most important of the two that man can least secure success; that he fails most continuously and surprisingly. Does not this read us at least the lesson of lowly thinking, which the Bible, from end to end, impresses upon man? The Bible, it has been said, which is so interested about man, yet in its whole tone holds very cheap his power and his pretensions. But it is hardly stronger than our own experience, in the rebuke which it gives to ambitious thoughts, and to that pride, which, of all our passions, is the most forgetful of the certainties and inexorable conditions of human life.

Shall we then sit still with folded hands, idle and hopeless, because in this time of our mortality, the chances of failure are so formidable—because men so often disappoint us, and we disappoint ourselves, and good causes seem to fail and come to nothing by the folly or slackness of their friends? Shall we, like the servant in the parable, bury our talent and forbear our service, because of the severity of its terms? There can be no failure worse than that.

While we are here, between the limits of birth and death, God our Master sends us forth, not to conquer, but to work—to work, it may be to be defeated, but certainly to fulfil the task which he has chosen for us, and pointed out to us. "So run that ye may obtain,"—yes, indeed, but don't be surprised if you do not always "obtain" in the way you looked for. The parable in to-day's Gospel,[1] the parable of the Sower, reminds us that God is not afraid to risk failure. God accomplishes His purposes in many ways, and one of them we know, by the highest of all examples, is the way of what seems irretrievable disaster. The followers of the Cross have no right to look, in *their own* day, for the recognition of success. And besides this, we are often bad judges of success or failure. We ought to have learned by this time how easy it is to overestimate the meaning of a success, and to exaggerate a failure. Fear, and indolence, and impatience, and despondency, are quite as false counsellors as hope; and there is the further difficulty, when things present are thronging upon us, of disengaging what is accidental and transitory from what is serious and lasting. The greatest things that man does have their trivial and commonplace accessories; and at the time the accessories often eclipse the substance.

> "We would every deed
> Perform at once as grandly as it shows
> After long ages . . .

---

[1] Sexagesima Sunday.

> It sounds so lovely what our fathers did,
> . . . . . .
> And what we do, is, as it was to them,
> Toilsome and incomplete."[1] . . .

"Toilsome and incomplete," no doubt, "compassed with infirmity," surrounded with what was poor, and mean, and miserable, appeared to many at Rome the career of the imprisoned and forlorn apostle—the man who was to outdo their own heroes in the homage of the coming times. "Toilsome and incomplete," full of pangs, and disgust, and disappointment, has often been the work of genius, as it slowly grew in the mind of its creator. "Toilsome and incomplete"—the efforts of the leader of a great movement for the overthrow of wrong, for the deliverance and happiness of a people, amid the delays and contradictions and provocations of petty adversaries and unworthy friends. "Toilsome and incomplete"—the last days of martyred saint and patriot, amid the dismal quibbles and chicane of a foregone condemnation, the punctilious, ceremonious preliminaries which led to the stake and

[1] Goethe's *Iphigenia in Tauris*, translated by Miss Swanwick, Act II. Scene i. Quoted in Lewes's *Goethe*, p. 268.
> " Unendlich ist das Werk, das zu vollführen
> Die Seele dringt. Wir möchten jede That
> So gross gleich thun, als wie sie wächst und wird,
> Wenn Jahre lang durch Länder und Geschlechter
> Der Mund der Dichter sie vermehrend wälzt.
> Es klingt so schön, was unsre Väter thaten,
> Wenn es, in stillen Abendschatten ruhend,
> Der Jüngling mit dem Ton der Harfe schlürft;
> Und was wir thun, ist, wie es ihnen war,
> Voll Müh' und eitel Stückwerk!"

the scaffold. "Toilsome and incomplete"— the labour of him who, in daily contact with all that is horrible and desperate, spends a life to bring the mercies and peace of Christ into the coarse miseries and festering vices which girdle round all our brilliant capitals, all our great seats of industry and wealth. Only in after years does their work draw itself up to its true grandeur; only then do we lose sight of partial failures, of all that made it, while it was going on, so dreary, so unspeakably depressing, —and see it, at last, as it is.

No, my brethren, don't let us be afraid, in a good cause, of the chances of failure. "Heaven is for those who have failed on earth," says the mocking proverb: and since the day of Calvary no Christian need be ashamed to accept it. But even here, men have that within them which recognises the heroic aspect of a noble failure: they own the nobleness in spite of the failure, in spite of the world's irony and amusement, which accompanies it as the jester of old accompanied what was greatest. Even here, it is better to have tried and failed, than not to have failed because we have not tried. It is better to have made the mistakes of high aspiration, of originality, of self-forgetfulness — better to have made the mistakes of the good, which it is said to be the business of the wise to correct,[1] than never

---

[1] "It may be said, with little exaggeration, that in this world a large part of the business of the wise is to counteract the efforts of the good."—Greg, *Enigmas of Life*, p. 159.

to have struck a blow for Christ and goodness, because so many before us have struck to little purpose. No one who makes the great ventures of duty and conscience can be so sure of himself as not to risk defeat, perhaps deserved defeat—but no one who does so in sincerity and humbleness knows what purpose he may be fulfilling beyond his own. If the great or the saintly life has been incomplete, at least there has been the great or the saintly life. If the great effort against error and sin and sloth has waxed feeble, at least there has been a new beacon of warning set up in the world's dangerous way. The world would have missed some of its highest examples, if men had always waited till they could make a covenant with success. *Here*, we can only give what we have to give,—our faithfulness, our honesty, our singleness of purpose, our best powers of thought and endeavour, our life, in this short stage of the endless line of our being, which we call *to-day*. *There*, in the light beyond the veil, and not here, we shall really know which are the "lost causes," and which are the victorious ones. Not till then shall we know what our work is worth, even the best of it—what is the "gold, silver, precious stones," and what the "wood, hay, stubble." There, we shall know, even as also we are known. There, those who have not been afraid to be like Him *here*, shall at last know what they shall be. They shall be like Him *there*; for they shall see Him as He is.

XVIII

SERVANTS OF GOD

"Paul, a servant of God."—TITUS, i. 1.

"SERVANT of God," "Servant of Jesus Christ," this is the title by which each one of the writers of the Epistles of the New Testament, in one place or another, describes himself. Like the title Apostle, sometimes combined with it, it indicates their work in life, the place they hold in the world, the definite object to which all their powers and activity are devoted. They have appropriated it from the language of the older dispensation, but with a special and definite meaning.

The phrase, "servant of God," then as now, had, also, a wider and looser meaning. All who honoured the name of God, and obeyed His will, and came before Him in worship, might be spoken of as servants of God. All of the race of Abraham claimed to be servants of God, and under this title their allegiance was appealed to. It is the title of the saints in heaven. It is the title of the baptized on earth. It is the liturgical expression of the Church for all her members, whether she blesses them in confirmation, or consecrates their marriage rite, or visits them in their sickness, or parts from them at the grave. And all whom God employs in His manifold ministries—angels and prophets, patriarchs like Abraham, kings like David—are spoken of under the title: in devotion, or humiliation, or gratitude, it marks their sense of their relation to Him; it is the natural recognition of the all-embracing sovereignty of God. And like all great words, it went through the process of becoming something conventional, customary, official. It passed into perhaps the greatest example of irony in history. The contrast between words and things was never carried higher than in the profoundly lowly title of the loftiest of human pretensions—"*Servus servorum Dei.*"

But when St. Paul, St. James, St. Peter, called themselves servants of God, they meant something more than this. They meant something more than what was true of all good Christians, of all religious men. They meant something very definite—a vocation and business, different from that of men in general—a very severe and exacting one. We know what is meant when we speak of a servant of the State, or a servant of the cause of learning, or science, or philanthropy. It means an employment of life, and time, and labour, as distinct as any of the crafts and trades and professions of men. It means that a man sees a great and paramount object, and devotes himself to it. It is a devotion which fills up his life, and kindles passion and enthusiasm, and gives shape and character to his labour, as well marked, as well bounded off from vague aims and competing interests, as the calling of the soldier, or the banker, or the artist. So to describe such work, in worthy hands and in an adequate character, is to make use of no loose phrase: a great servant of the State, a great servant of knowledge,—a man need desire no nobler title here. All recognise what responsibilities, what toil, what self-dedication it implies. And it is in such a definite sense as this that the Apostles called themselves, and meant to be, the servants of God and Jesus Christ.

It meant that, for that service they had absolutely separated themselves from the common aims of human life, the ordinary pursuits, the usual course and stream of activity all round them. They had to work apart from all this, and for this service alone they lived. It had a special call upon them, not shared with other men. Other men were, in their useful and innocent occupations, doing their duty, maintaining the state of the world, and thus serving their Master. They were servants of God indeed; but they were not servants of God in that difficult and eminent sense in which St. Paul and his fellows were called upon to be. For them, God had greater and more comprehensive tasks, which could only be fulfilled under very definite conditions. They were tasks as much above the common tasks and trials of Christians as the tasks of a great servant of the State are above the responsibilities and employments of those whom the State embraces and protects. For the mass of good people, nothing from the very first can be clearer and more striking than the teaching of the Epistles; with all the mysterious greatness of their calling, their duty was to do each man his work in a religious spirit, in faithfulness and truth—" To study to be quiet and to do " their " own business "—to carry into all the details of life, at home and abroad, the fear of God, and the charity and lowliness of Christ. A holy and blessed life, indeed, if they could so live. But that imperfectly represents what his Master required of St. Paul. He was the servant of God in the sense that in him the whole man was demanded for, and absorbed in, his Master's business, as another man might be absorbed in ambition, or in learning. For him, life had no other object. He had parted company with what men care for and work for here, as the enthusiast for distant travel parts company with his home. I need not remind you of the language in which he describes this death to the world. In him, certainly, it was not exaggerated.

This, then, is a definite character put before us in Scripture—a servant of God—in the sense that there are men who have, or who aim at having, no other service; who here on earth, consciously, and of set purpose, devote life to one great, engrossing employment, not for themselves, but for Him; a service as hard and trying to flesh and blood, as it yet fills and satisfies the soul. Such service is distinguished, on the one hand, from the service which all good men render to God in their several callings in the world; on the other, from the service done by men, who are rather God's instruments than His servants. While the world lasts, its manifold work has to be carried on; and it is God's work and service, when what we call its most secular occupations, and what are in themselves its natural and most earthly ties, are consecrated by His fear, and the spirit of loyalty to Him. And, again, that service is done, too, with doubtful motives, with, perhaps, fatal mixtures of pride, or selfishness, or impurity, by men whose work is better than themselves—men of whom Scripture gives us the type, in Solomon abusing his glorious gifts; by iconoclasts like Jehu, and reformers like Joash. But when we speak of St. Paul as God's servant, we mean something more than that he was the instrument of a great change, or that he followed his trade as a tent-maker in a religious spirit, or even that he fulfilled the lessons of ministerial faithfulness, which he taught to the bishops and presbyters whom he left in Ephesus or Corinth.

That distinct, definite character, which Scripture presents to us when St. Paul calls himself the servant of God, may be shown under most opposite outward conditions. But under all different forms it has essential and common features. (1) It is exclusive in its object, and complete in its self-dedication. (2) It contemplates as the centre of all interest and hope, the highest object of human thought and human devotion, a presence beyond the facts of experience, the presence of the invisible God. (3) It accepts as the measure of its labour and its endurance, the cross of Jesus Christ.

1. St. Paul's surrender of himself to his Master was absolute and unreserved. That complete self-abandonment, which was imposed in terms by some famous monastic rules, was with him the natural unforced attitude of the soul. We are most of us, in our lives, divided between different interests, different claims, different, perhaps clashing, duties. It is what must happen, even with a dominant and guiding purpose, to those who are called to deal with the world's infinite variety. And to struggle against distraction and disturbance, against being overpowered by pressing influences which in our serious moments we fear or dislike, is part of our recognised trial in the world. St. Paul certainly had his trials; but he had not this one. In him the troubles of a divided service, and of an uncertain will, did not exist. Once for all, the overwhelming power of a great conviction had carried him over all obstacles, had swept him out of the customary and familiar into a new world of thought and aims and affections. Once for all, never looking behind him, keeping back nothing from his offering, he had made himself God's servant; he knew no other interests here but the immense ones of his Master's purpose in the world; this scene of experience, of pain and pleasure, of life and death, was as if it had ceased to

be, except as the field on which he was to "spend and be spent," in persuading men of what his Master meant for them. No singleness of aim, no concentration of will, no absorbing passion, no burning enthusiasm, no devouring ambition ever possessed a human heart, as his devotion to the work for which he had been chosen possessed the heart of St. Paul.

2. And what was that overpowering object which made the common recognised interests of men seem so pale and unattractive? What was that sovereign affection, which, unless it could assimilate all other affections to itself, or make them part of its own energy, knew nothing of them, and had no room for them? What he lived for, so whole-hearted, so singleminded, was to be one with the will and purpose of Him who had chosen him from the millions of mankind, to bear his name before the world—to approve himself to that unseen Master, the Most Holy, the Most Merciful—to be a fellow labourer with God, it is his own repeated expression, in will always, in act in all that he could, in impressing on human souls and human life the lessons of the first and great commandment, and of the second that was like it, and of the love that had remedied and retrieved the sins of the world against them. And that affection, so boundless, so transporting, was one which dared to rise up and to answer in its measure to the Eternal Love which ruled on the throne of the worlds—dared with such powers as the creature has, to respond to those "unsearchable riches" of wisdom

and righteousness and loving-kindness, which no thought could measure, which no time could exhaust. There was nothing on earth to match or to rival that affection. There was none among the great objects of human life to compare in grandeur and interest to that one which had taken possession of his short passing term of years. In that short eager passage there was time for nothing else. The clouds and mists of our present state had rolled off his mind, and with open eye he saw, what is, what must be—the things which are not seen, but are eternal. Think of what God is, and to have Him for your Master; think of what Jesus Christ has been to us, and what it is to be one with Him, even on the cross. St. Paul had seen that; and the vision never faded. Wherever he turned, however his fortunes went, in weakness and suffering and disappointment, in fightings without and fears within, and, with it all, the "care of all the Churches," his soul met everywhere the thought of the God who loved him; in the doomed ship in Adria, in the darkness and despair of the tempest, in the prison and the Council Chamber, at Cæsar's judgment-seat, the Lord stood by him to strengthen him; his eye fell, amid the storms and disorder of the world, on the infinite compassion of Christ crucified, on the infinite victory of Christ risen and ascended. We need not wonder, that with all this clear before his soul, to be such a servant of God and Christ was the utmost, the highest, the sweetest, that life could offer.

3. But for such a life, a price had to be paid. In such a life of complete devotion to any engrossing object, a price has to be paid in any case. With St. Paul's purpose and object, the price was the acceptance, in its fullest meaning, of the fellowship of the cross of Christ. The likeness of that cross pervades every life of duty and earnestness. All brave and true men know it, and endure it patiently, in some shape or other: in lifelong trouble, in bereavement, in misunderstanding, in the alienation of friends, in unpopularity and mistrust, in privation, in weakness and pain, in unjust suffering, in weary labour, in failure and defeat—God's proof and test of strength is laid upon us all. But we must not confound with this, that partnership in their Master's sufferings which was the portion of servants like St. Paul, and which they accepted as a matter of course, without regret, without complaint, almost without surprise. The complete break which was necessary in his case with all the accepted ideas, the passions, the interests, the sympathies of the great world which confronted him, involved a continuity and a pressure of toil and pain, such as few of us have seen or can realise, and for which he, high-hearted and triumphant as he was, sought expression in the awful language recalling the Passion. "God forbid that I should glory, save in the cross of our Lord Jesus Christ, by whom the world is crucified unto me, and I unto the world." "I have been crucified with Christ: nevertheless I live: yet not I, but Christ liveth in me." I "fill up

that which is behind of the afflictions of Christ in my flesh." "Always bearing about in the body the dying of the Lord Jesus." This, then, is what St. Paul took to be a servant of God and Jesus Christ, a life of definite and undivided purpose, lived in God's presence, never shrinking even from His cross. Our use of Scriptural words is often so lax and unthinking, that we become deadened to the sense of their meaning, so real, so piercing, often so tremendous. But certainly, in the New Testament, over and above the ordinary and true Christian life, the life of those who innocently use this world without abusing it, and live soberly, righteously, and godly in it,—who, in honest duty and self-discipline and self-denial, willingly accept their Master's yoke and bear whatever comes on them of His cross,— there is exhibited a pattern of life, and type of character, in which the common interests and objects which attract and occupy us are not only subordinated, but given up and put aside, for the sake of a greater and more exacting service.

We ask, many of us, is such a character possible, conceivable now? Can such an entire devotion to objects not of this world be a real one, like ambition, or the life of pleasure, or the building up of a fortune? Or is it only something which we read of in books, and imagine in stories, a primitive and uncritical estimate of human nature, which breaks up and fades away under the solvent of our analysis of character, as merciless to high pretensions, as it is indulgent to the imperfect and faulty? Have we learned that it is a fiction permitted only to simpler times, to imagine a man really living his daily life as the servant of an unseen Master; living only to please, if it may be, and do the work of the unseen Power who brought him into existence, and whom he believes to be his Preserver, and Redeemer, and Saviour, who loves him better than he can ever know and realise here, for whom he never can do service enough, and for whom he is willing to give up what men most care for, to endure trouble and hardship, so that in his inner and secret experience, he may live the life of joy, and hope, and trust, and liberty of the heart, which is expressed in all its shades and contrasts in the Book of Psalms?

If this were so, the history of the Christian religion would be, indeed, a dream. That history has been in many ways a poor commentary on the Founder's teaching, and a very imperfect following of His footsteps, in what He did and suffered. But one thing the Christian Church has never lost hold of. It has never lost hold of the idea of the consecrated life, of the unreserved self-surrender to God's service, as its highest and most adequate standard; and the time has never been, whether in days of darkness or in days of the brightest thought and highest culture, when there have not been Christians who felt the full force of that simple but awful saying, standing in the forefront of their Master's plan of life, "No man can serve two masters." In the roll of saints of the Old dispensation, in the Epistle to the Hebrews, the characteristic attribute of life raised to its highest power is faith : the great ruling idea in the saints of the New dispensation goes beyond it ; it is the imitation of the self-sacrifice of Jesus Christ. These servants of God pass before men in various forms, and their service is of many kinds. It may be most romantic, or most prosaic. It may be heroic, or in the last degree commonplace and uninteresting. It may be plain before the world—it may be the man's own secret, unsuspected, unrevealed, till his course is run. There are the great commanding figures of history, and the great multitude of the obscure and the forgotten. But the degrees and accidents of service, the curious or touching details of individual history, the lights and shades of individual character, are of small account; they are lost and disappear, in the great self-surrender, however made, of him who really has no Master but one, and who has given life and all that he had to Him who gave him life and more than life ;—of him who in serious earnest has chosen, among the many paths of life, that one in which he follows most closely Him who laboured and suffered for us all.

Many, I suppose, are thinking this morning, among the changes since the University was last assembled, of one name [1] which since then has disappeared from its roll of members—a great and illustrious name, a name which was the special

[1] Dr. Pusey.

possession of Oxford, but belonged scarcely less to England and to Christendom. One of our great men has passed away from us. I hope it is pardonable, even when I cannot be sure of all sympathies, if I allow myself to remember that only within the last month we were many of us standing about the grave where the toils of his long life ended, and where he still sleeps among us, in the Oxford which he so deeply loved. Merely as the end of a career, without its match in modern Oxford, the ceasing from among us of that long, familiar life must touch us all. Few here present saw the outset of it in the Oxford honour schools, just over sixty years ago; few of those who saw it beginning could look forward to its surprising and eventful course. They could not imagine through what vicissitudes it would pass—all that it would see of what stirs and tries the soul—what persistent, unwearied industry, what unabated energy of public interest and sympathy, up to the very week of death, what deep, inconsolable sorrows, what piercing wounds, what profound disappointments, what strange chequered successes, what unlooked-for revolutions, what alternations of disgrace and honour, of unchecked obloquy and wanton insult, of boundless reverence and trust. No man was more variously judged, more sternly condemned, more tenderly loved. Of course that means that his was a time of great and prolonged conflict, of great changes and great reverses; that in it all he took a foremost part; that he had to deal largely with foes as well as with friends. But now, all is over—hardly yet weary, hardly exhausted, he rests from his labours of more than half a century. What is the judgment upon him, not on the representative of ideas, or the champion of a cause, or the worker in the field of knowledge, but on the man? I think that there is but one answer, from those whose hearts thrill at the memory of all that he was to them, and from most of those—from many, I am sure—who stood against him, disapproved, resisted him. First and foremost, he was one who lived his life, as above everything, the servant of God. He takes rank with those who gave themselves, and all that they had, and all that they wished for, their unsparing trouble, their ease, their honour, their powers, their interests, to what they believed to be their work for God; who spared nothing, reserved nothing, shrank from nothing, in that supreme and sacred ambition to be His true and persevering servant. The world will remember him as the famous student, the powerful leader, the wielder of great influence in critical times, the man of strongly marked and original character, who left his mark on his age. Those who knew and loved him will remember him, as long as life lasts with them, as one whose boundless charity was always looking out to console and to make allowance, as one whose dauntless courage and patient hopefulness never flagged, as one to whose tenderness and strength they owed the best and the noblest part of all that they have felt and all that they have done. But when our confusions are still, when our loves and enmities and angers have perished, when our mistakes and misunderstandings have become dim and insignificant in the great distance of the past, then his figure will rise in history as one of that high company who really looked at life as St. Paul looked at it. All who care for the Church of God, all who care for Christ's religion, even those— I make bold to say—who do not in many things think as he thought, will class him among those who in difficult and anxious times have witnessed, by great zeal, and great effort, and great sacrifices for God, and truth, and holiness; they will see in him one who sought to make religion a living and mighty force over the consciences and in the affairs of men, not by knowledge only and learning, or wisdom and great gifts of persuasion, but still more by boundless devotedness, by the power of a consecrated and unfaltering will.

Is it too much to say that our times still need such examples—need the lessons of such a life? Am I going beyond what is fitting for this place, and, much more, fitting in my mouth, on a day when so many careers take, as it were, a new departure, so many young men are starting with life before them, and I am sure in many hearts, with longings to make it true and noble, if I bid them remember that, apart from all the thronging claims of modern interests, besides all the varying forms of useful and honourable employment, there is still such a thing as the distinct, the separate calling of a servant of God—of a man who holds that his life is not his own; that whatever other men rightly and innocently are, he was sent into the world to pass through life for a definite service, of which, with all the difference between the first century and the nineteenth, St. Paul is the model? It is true, indeed, that there is no business too secular or too distracting, no trade too mean or place too high, to be used as a means of serving God: no one has taught it more strongly than St. Paul: it has become a commonplace, sometimes a too-easily accepted one. It is true also that we have come to realise more vividly than formerly the fact of mixed characters; our poets and novelists, as well as our preachers, have taught us to observe how strongly opposite elements and tendencies can co-exist in the same person, that "the human soul is hospitable, and will entertain conflicting sentiments and contradictory opinions with much impartiality."[1] It was easier in former days than now, to conceive of, to believe in, the homogeneous and consistent in character. Yet, for all this, I venture to think that such a life may still be realised as that which St. Paul meant, when he spoke of a "servant of God," a life consciously, deliberately, exclusively given to work for God.

I venture, too, to think that it is still wanted. If the Church of Christ is still to do its great offices among mankind, surely it is becoming more and

---

[1] George Eliot, *Romola*, p. 5.

more manifest every year, that that sharp edge and point of its instrument of warfare, that originality and adventurous daring which accepts religious service in the spirit familiar enough to us in the soldier, is a thing which the Church needs. There is an atmosphere of opinion and feeling round the soldier, which, without his knowing it, stimulates and supports him in a life which he holds on sufferance: in which, as a matter of course, every gift life has to offer must be surrendered, everything appalling to flesh and blood has to be encountered, at any moment's call: in which he is expected to unite the utmost of obedient self-sacrifice with the boldest spirit of enterprise. Is it extravagant to say that we want something of an atmosphere like this? Is it incompatible with a calm and just measure of things, with what is manly and wise and serious and self-commanding, that a man should start in life, seeking nothing for himself of what are called its prizes, going out not knowing whither he goes, bent only on doing what facts and reason and the calls of conscience invite him to do, but bent also on not letting his own interests, his own pleasure, his own life, stand in the way of doing it? Is it too high a thing for a Christian to conceive of the possible claims of his service, as the soldier ordinarily thinks of what he is bound to—a service which may at any time call him from home and peace, to the battlefield and the still more dreadful hospital; but in which the fear of them must never for a moment affect his decisions.

For the days that are before us, we want a condition of public feeling and opinion like this in the Church :—which, without affecting to exact impossible sacrifices from all men alike, as the only test of faithfulness and standard of obedience, should soberly and distinctly recognise that God still calls for men who will give Him their lives as St. Paul gave his : which no more holds it absurd, or dangerous, or quixotic in a clergyman than in a soldier, that he should give up an easy life for a hard one. There is no reason why, without extravagance, without overstrained and foolish enthusiasm, we should not still believe that a life like St. Paul's is a natural one for a Christian to choose. We still reverence his words; and his words have all along the history of the Church found echoes in many hearts. There is a great past behind us : a past, which is not dead, but lives—lives in every thought we think, and every word we speak; lives in our achievements and in our hopes; lives in our confidence and joy in life; lives in those high feelings which thrill and soothe us at the grave. May we not be unworthy of such a past!

XIX

THE IMPERFECTIONS OF RELIGIOUS MEN

"Salt is good: but if the salt have lost his savour, wherewith shall it be seasoned?"—St. Luke xiv. 34.

THREE times, and in three different connections, this memorable proverb is recorded in our Lord's teaching; in each case in reference to the failure of that which was excellent and hopeful. In St. Matthew it is applied generally to the influence of His new people on the world: in St. Mark to the danger to ourselves of the careless or selfish use of our personal influence: in St. Luke to the conditions of sincere discipleship. But, in all cases, it contemplates the possible failure of religion to do its perfect work.

The Bible, which is God's great instrument to show us what is true religion and its importance, is also the record of the imperfections of religion. By this, I do not mean the perversions and false forms of religion, the idolatries and superstitions which superseded or obscured the truth, the deliberate unfaithfulness and falls of those whom God had trusted. I mean, the shortcomings, the failures, the faults of character, of those who were, on the whole, His sincere and accepted servants: not merely their faults as men, but as religious men, the faults of their religion itself.

Indeed, it may be said, that as the one great theme of its severe and awful pages is the imperfection and sin of man, and all that was necessary of God's mercy and judgment to remedy them, so in this imperfection of man is included—it is one of its most prominent and formidable parts—the imperfection of religion in the best men, the imperfection of their best and holiest side.

It is a subject so real and so grave, and, though so obvious, so little attended to in our controversies and our dealings with our own minds and souls, that it may be worth while to reflect on it a little. There seem to be special reasons for it at this time. I think it may be said with truth, that never since the two great efforts at reformation, the attempt to reform life in the thirteenth century, and the attempt to reform doctrine in the sixteenth, has religion so filled the thoughts of men. On the one hand, it has never been so serious, so energetic, so earnest in trying to get to the root of things, and so enterprising in carrying out convictions. And on the other hand, religion has never been so seriously and resolutely questioned as now. For the sake of those whom religion interests, and for the sake of those whom it repels, and who are alive to all that seem its weak points and failures, it is desirable to reflect on the mistakes and defects, to which, even when genuine and sincere, it has shown itself liable in the hands of imperfect man.

We, at least, who trust the teaching of the Bible, ought not to be surprised at this. It might have been surmised beforehand, that when God gave men a religion, and shaped it, and encouraged His creatures to think of Him and trust Him, and allowed them to lift their affections and hopes to Him and to His blessedness, He would have guarded His great gift from being spoiled by man. But such an anticipation would only have been another instance of our inadequate measure of His ways and counsels. His first and primary gift to man is that he is a free moral agent: and with that, He has given nothing to man, not power, not knowledge, not love, not remedies, which man may not, if he will, abuse and spoil. And the history of religion in the Bible presents, notwithstanding all its achievements, no other spectacle. It is a mere commonplace now that it is not the history of perfect saints. In its calm, passionless display of them, so emphatic in its general approval, so severely true in its witness of their shortcomings, it shows us how men of like passions with ourselves have both pleased and disappointed their Master. Think of those who are singled out in what is the nearest approach in the Bible to a roll of canonisation,—the great martyrology, in the Epistle to the Hebrews, of the elders who had obtained a good report through faith,—and as soon as the record begins to show in detail the light and shades of character, each great name from Abraham downwards suggests and recalls some flaw, till the great catalogue closes in such a list as this, of the representatives of the noblest victories of religion—" and what shall I more say? for the time would fail me to tell of Gedeon, and of Barak, and of Samson, and of Jephthae; of David also, and Samuel, and of the prophets." In the New Testament, character and its variations become still more distinct and intelligible to us. There, men, singly or in bodies, seem more like ourselves. And there, as in the Old Testament, there is the same frank, unreserved disclosure of the real working out of religious principles in human nature, in strength and weakness, in their purity and in their alloy. The Epistles testify to the deep, self-devoted religion of the followers of St. Peter and St. Paul and St. John. They also prove how full of dark and strange shadows was the light of that first generation of Christians. It was after the gifts of Pentecost that we hear of the weak compromise of St. Peter, of the sharp contention and estrangement of the two great leaders of the first mission to the Gentiles on a personal question. It was after they had received the gift of the Spirit that we hear of the fickleness and superstitious bigotry of the Galatians, of the childish ostentation and partisanship of the Corinthians, and their tendency to their old licentiousness. We may be prepared, then, to find that the reality of religious history, both in Churches and individuals, has often been very different from what we, in our narrowness, and often with our misdirected logic, may have wished to imagine.

It has been one of the idols both of the "market-place" and of the "theatre" to construct, *à priori*, the ideal of the Christian Church. Prophets and Apostles have been appealed to. Isaiah had seen in vision the untroubled glory of that Kingdom of Righteousness which was to be. St. Paul fears not to speak of a "glorious Church, not having spot, or wrinkle, or any such thing." St. John saw the Bride of the Lamb coming down from heaven, the Holy City into which nothing unclean can enter. If that had been all, there might have been ground to look for, even here, the perfection of the Christian Church—if there had not been, alongside of all those wonderful promises, a current of warning as strong and clear, of the limitation of them here by the sins and perversity of men. The ideal of sanctity, of infallibility, of consistency, of unity, is what ought to have been; what *has* been, is matter of history: it is not to be settled by theory; it is what the world has seen, in the interrupted and partial struggles after that unattainable ideal.

We look back with reverence and admiration—just reverence and admiration—to those early days, when the great idea of another life had burst in certainty on men's minds, and when the strange, overwhelming, unutterable love of God, the incredible, inconceivable love of the Passion, had broken down all habits, all traditions, all fashions, all lusts, all fears, in the souls of men. They were days, indeed—we can faintly understand them—when to live was Christ, and to die was gain. If ever religion was a reality, it was then—a reality in the sacrifice of all things, a reality in the victorious joy of doing so, a reality in its witness to a frowning or a mocking world, a reality in the power of duty and in the boundless love of the brethren, a reality before the might of the Cæsars, before the Proconsul's alternative—the few grains of incense, or the sword, the amphitheatre, the wild beasts. O, my brethren, those days *were* once; and men like ourselves went through them for the love of Christ. How shall we dare to sit in criticism on such extreme trials of the soul —its steadfastness, its sincerity, its singleness of motive? And yet, even while we read with tears, and with a thrill of awe and joy, the *Acta Martyrum*, can we help wishing sometimes that things had been different; that sometimes there had been more self-restraint, less defiance, more command over the overwrought and overstrained heart, more quietness and calm in the very eye of the storm, amid the provoking of all men? Are we not compelled to see, amid so much that was universal, so much that was loftier and wider than anything the world had known, the occasional narrowness, the occasional fierceness, the occasional self-satisfaction and despising of others, which was the natural growth of circumstances, when the greatest and most divine of societies was forced into the apparent position of a little sect? Are we not forced to see, in the questions raised among them, that their very realising of truth drove them sometimes into an excess of minute care for the accessories of it, like the Paschal controversy; that the earnestness of their moral zeal and sense of purity led into what to us seem the tremendous exaggerations of their penances, into the bitter controversies respecting the treatment of the lapsed and the "traditores" in the persecutions? Can we help feeling that even then religion was not perfect in some of its noblest examples?

Can we wonder, as we descend the course of the centuries, that what we see in the history of the Bible, what we see in the age of the Apostles, we see, also, in the history of the Church—in the Church of the Fathers, in the Church of the Middle Ages, in the Church of the Reformation, in the Church of modern times? Can we wonder that when the faith of Christendom as to the supreme object of its hope and worship was in the balance, when it was shaken from end to end for centuries by persistent attempts to make that faith just a little something other than it was, the great teachers, the great champions, to whom we owe its preservation in the extremest peril, were carried away by the eagerness of their interest and conviction, by their sense of the issues at stake, into a zeal and vehemence which to us, in our easier days, seems disproportionate and excessive, and which led them sometimes to forget other equally important parts of religion? Can we wonder that, later on, in the honest earnestness of faith and morality, that impatient intolerance of supposed evil and insidious corruption, which even now is very strong in some of the most sceptical and most liberal minds, betrayed the conscience of religious men into terrible acts of harshness and cruelty? Can we wonder that when the great conflicts about true religion arose in the fifteenth and sixteenth centuries, good men on all sides thought that they were doing God service by destroying His enemies, the corrupters of His truth, the seducers of His people? Every party claims, in those days, choice representatives of high and pure religion: yet this charge of unrelenting severity and unforgiving bitterness, though it may be with great differences of degree, lies against them all—Churchman and Lollard, Catholic and Hussite, Roman and Protestant, Leaguer and Huguenot, Anglican and Puritan;—against Gerson and Savonarola, as against their unworthy opponents; against More, and Cranmer, and Pole; against Calvin, as against the men of the same stern mould, who ruled at Rome as he ruled at Geneva; against the Pilgrim Fathers of New England, who sacrificed home and country for conscience and liberty, and who, in their new home across the ocean, were as merciless to Anabaptists, witches, and Quakers as if they had been learners in the school of the Inquisition itself. We, at our greater distance, cannot help believing that we can see at once how the sincerest zeal for truth ruled their unmercifulness, and also how the dreary blindness of ignorance and the self-deceit of passion mingled with and tainted their religion.

We cannot look back on any great and interesting tract of religious history, without seeing how, with the wheat, the tares were also sown in the hearts and souls of men. A strong development of religious earnestness is at once attended with its common and familiar weaknesses, with its special and characteristic faults. There is scarcely a true principle of religious faith, there is scarcely a natural and pure instinct of worship, there is scarcely a noble work of self-devotion and usefulness, there is scarcely a wisely planned and generous institution, on which the mistakes of good men have not brought discredit, perhaps at last extinguished and abolished it. And so with some of our fiercest controversies—how can we help seeing how onesidedness and misunderstandings have been kept alive by good men on account of the supposed necessities of a position; how from very fidelity to conscience and truth, from the sincerest fear of betraying or endangering some justly prized principle, from self-distrust as to motives, where plain wisdom and charity counselled concession and explanation and conciliation, the exaggerations of controversy have become incurable. The honest Protestant shudders at the very name of the Mass, knowing only the abuses—often intolerable—connected with it; knowing nothing of what the service is in itself, or its words, or its history; not knowing, or forgetting, that it is the perpetual, the daily memorial which has kept up for centuries the memory, the consolations of the Passion, before the thoughts, and hopes, and love of millions. The honest Roman Catholic believes that the only motive which caused the revolt of Protestantism was impatience of true doctrine, and that lawlessness and selfishness and the lusts of the flesh are the real reasons which even now keep men from the Church. The honest Protestant looks on the Roman Catholics as idolaters of the flock of anti-Christ. The honest Roman Catholic, at least abroad, looks on all outside his pale as little better than infidels; without creed, without sacraments, without a Church, almost without a conscience. Both are equally honest in their dreadful hatreds—thanks, not only to the sins and follies of their fathers, but to their virtues also; to the depth and sincerity of their convictions, to the seriousness and loyalty of their religion.

With such an experience, can we be quite easy as to what our own religion may be? I do not mean our professed, conventional religion, but what is, as far as it goes, genuine, real, operative in our religion. Of course we know that there are shows and "shadows of religion." We know that there is such a thing as religion, occupying a large part in a man's character, which is absolutely neutralised and paralysed as to all good, by gross moral perversions. The world has seen a religion, on a large scale, powerful and absorbing, without morality—religion without honesty in business, religion combined with pride, harshness, self-seeking worldliness, with hardly the pretence of a check or restraint—the strange but most certain combination of a fervid devotional temper with sensual tendencies and even sin. But I am not speaking of these fatal wrecks of character. We may all gaze on such moral ruin with misgivings and self-distrust; but besides these terrible failures there are others more subtle, but very real. They may not kill our religion, but they weaken and disfigure it.

For there are temptations and mischiefs arising out of our religion itself; out of the position in which it places us, and the things which it encourages in us. Let me take two or three examples.

1. "Who loved me," says St. Paul, "the Son of God, who loved me, and gave Himself for me." There are hardly more affecting words in the New Testament, and they describe what must thrill through any man's mind, who believes in the Cross of Christ, just in proportion as he grasps its meaning. A religious man feels that he, his soul, his salvation, is the centre of a great interposition of God's mercy and love. It is as if all were for him: as if there were no one else in the universe whom God so loved, for whom God had done such wonderful things, as if he were the one lost sheep whom Christ had sought and saved and died for. But it is not without reason that we are told that what should kindle his boundless devotion may be full of peril. It may touch the subtle springs of selfishness. There may be a feverish,

faithless selfishness, in the anxiety to save one's soul, to be sure that all is right within, to be sure that all is safe. Or, a man may be tempted, while he realises what he has been, and is, to God, into a sense of self-importance, into a hard self-complacency. He may be, as men have been, tempted to think of himself as the favourite of heaven, allowed liberties forbidden to other men, forgiven, when others are not excused. Or again, he may be thrown inward on himself, to watch and study with unhealthy eagerness the vicissitudes of what is to him the most interesting of histories, the history of his religious experience. Watching all this, comparing himself with others, finding checks and differences, he becomes querulous, captious, censorious. It is not every one who can dare to repeat the experiment of St. Augustine's confessions. Religious autobiography is not without warnings that the true and awful words—"What shall a man give in exchange for his soul?"—may be perverted into a narrow and timid care for it, worried with petty fears and scruples; a care ignoble and degrading, because without interest in God's great purposes, without a generous trust in His wisdom and mercy, without sympathy for others.

2. Again, religion must be active; and towards the evils which are in the world it is bound to be hostile and aggressive. And yet this necessity shows us too often a religion, a very sincere and honest religion, which cannot avoid the dangers which come with activity and with conflict. It sometimes seems

to lose itself and its end in the energy with which it pursues its end. The zeal for a great cause, the fear of being idle and inactive, may pass insensibly but too easily into a passionate longing for immediate results and visible success : a man becomes entangled in a whirl of business arrangements, in questions of machinery and agitation, in secular details with religious names, in keen excitement, or a love of management and contrivance, which subtly eat into the best part of a man's nature ; and with the great duty of resisting evil may come other evils too natural to men, veiled, sanctioned, guaranteed as the friends and allies of religion—that host of evil things which sin against charity and truth. We cannot shut our eyes to what the history of religion shows but too clearly—that with religion may come very uncongenial elements—the habit of hasty and harsh and ungenerous judgment ; the freedom given to antipathies and detraction ; the heavy fault of unfairness, of having a different moral measure for our friends and our opponents. I say nothing of party spirit, dangerous as it is, because there is a great deal of thoughtless and unreal talking about it. People talk about it glibly, who are blindly led by it. When men are together under strong convictions, opponents will always call them partisans. What is wanted is, not that men should not be partisans, but that they should be just and considerate and generous partisans. I am afraid that real religion on all sides has been compatible with insolence, with violence, with flattery—with the pride of being on the right side, of being able to look down on our neighbours—with love of importance, with the temper of contempt and scorn; nay, at last, the inconsistency has ended in a gradual lowering of our religious ideal, with increasing narrowness and meanness of thought, with increasing readiness to seek our own advantage, as our due and reward for our religious zeal and service. We have seen this sometimes in others. Can we doubt that we are in danger from this ourselves?

3. Again, religion is a matter of the affections: and men may be led astray by their affections, in religion as in other things. We read the proof of it at large in the vast and double-sided history of mysticism in various ages of the Church. It shows us in endless forms the deep passion of the human soul to fulfil the "First and Great Commandment" of the Son of God: it shows us with what beauty and glory these supreme heights of devotion, of adoration, of divine love, have been reached: it shows us also what fearful dangers encompassed the attempt—how easily the true point was passed, and then how, like an exquisite but transient flower, or a generous but too delicate wine, the perfection, which was but for a moment, vanished, and corruption set in, irresistible and hopeless. We see it in those deplorable disputes on the love of God, its measures, its motives, its reward, in which even such men as Bossuet and Fénélon hardly found their way. These

are almost the most incomprehensible chapters in Christian history — strange above measure that, in desiring to know and to realise the love of God, devout souls should have gone astray: but we know it has been so, and that in times far separated and outwardly most different from one another. These are not, I suppose, our special dangers: mysticism, in its best and in its worst form, is not in much honour now, except perhaps in poetry. But our religion is not therefore safe on its emotional side. Our dangers lie another way—not in detachment from the world and effort to rise above it and above self, but in what is sentimental and fanciful and effeminate; in artificial frames of mind, combined with loose or technical views of duty; in a self-pleasing and self-indulgent devotion; in unreal words, and affectations, perhaps unconscious, and exaggerations of feeling— talking lightly because it is the fashion, in advance of what we really feel, beyond what we really think. These are formidable dangers; and they are dangers to those who yet are very serious about religion, and think that they are acting on its call.

This is what we see in others, what we see in the history of religion, clearly enough. I venture to appeal to the consciences and memory of religious men, and ask them whether, in proportion as they have come to know themselves, and to judge themselves honestly, they have not found some things of the same kind reflected in their own lives? Do they not recognise the humbling, but undeniable fact, that their religion has not protected them as it ought, from things most opposed to it? Do not misgivings sometimes visit them, whether the faults which they most condemn and hate, do not perhaps mingle with their religion more than they think—nay, perhaps to a degree which would shock and terrify them, if they were to become adequately conscious of them? The call to be religious is not stronger than the call to see of what sort our religion is. It does not take so much to avoid its grosser shortcomings. The opinion and feeling round us, to speak of nothing else, help to protect us from things which disfigured it in times gone by. We have the beacons of their experience to warn us. But will any time arise when we shall be safe against the subtler mischiefs, which cripple and spoil even earnest and serious religion? Even now, may there not be a religion of intelligence and honesty and manly purpose, but wanting in sympathy, in tenderness, in spiritual and devotional elevation, in patience and considerateness for the weak? Even now, may there not be a religion of warmth and self-devotion, but without light, without self-knowledge, incapable of greatness of thought and action, narrow, short-sighted, poor-spirited? Even now, may there not be a religion, robust, active, powerful, energetic, but imperious, loving power, unchastened in temper, sensibly, painfully wanting in all that makes character beautiful and attractive, in self-forgetfulness, in care for others, in calmness, in modesty? Even now, may there not be a religion of charity and self-denial and self-sacrifice, which yet cannot always resist the impulses to self-will and " holy obstinacy,"—which lets itself be enfeebled by overstrained sentiment and excitement? These alloys have been the great damage of religion in all ages. They are not to be got rid of by the *à priori* supposition that such combinations are impossible: and we may depend upon it, they are at work among us still. "*Thou* to wax fierce in the cause of the Lord," *thou*, " sin's slave," [1] —is a terrible adjuration. But the warning it conveys ought never to be out of our remembrance.

Of the sins of which our conscience is afraid when we think of the judgment-seat of Christ, some affect specially our own character; others go beyond ourselves, and affect the character, the innocence, the belief, the fate of others. We know not what will be done at that tremendous seat of eternal justice; and in these two great classes of sins, the particular instances of both vary infinitely in the degrees of guilt. But when we think of the infinite mercy and infinite remedies of God, the forgiveness and cure of that which affects our own character are not beyond what we can conceive of. It is harder to conceive how those sins will be dealt with, which by our fault have corrupted and dragged down the character of others, perhaps ruined their salvation. Awful words come into our minds about the millstone hanged about the neck, about anything being better than offending one of these little ones. Your own experience, your

[1] Newman's *Verses on Various Occasions*, XXV.

own imagination, will supply too plentifully the memories of such cases: I will not speak of them. But when we think of the faults of really religious men, of the faults having their roots in their very religion, of the religious faults of which we are ourselves conscious,—and when we are inclined to treat them tenderly,—we must remember what these faults do, outside of ourselves, outside of religion. They may be of such a kind as not to destroy our own whole-heartedness towards God. They may be consistent with very great sincerity, very great unselfishness, a very deep sense of eternal things, a very profound and awful gratitude for the love and mercy of Jesus Christ, a very true zeal and charity for our brethren, for whom He died. From those in whom such things are, we cannot imagine the Judge turning His face away. Surely, for faults which affect themselves only, He will, we may hope, have not only pardon, but help and purifying. The sight of His countenance may burn them away for ever; may accomplish and crown in a moment the long work of honest, and painful, but only partially successful self-discipline. But what of the effects of the sins and faults of religious men on the world without? Who can undo that? The writer of an immoral and polluting book, who comes in after years to the deepest penitence, cannot call back the mischief which he has done, and which is for evermore out of his reach. And so, though the mischief may not be so shocking and palpable, the man whose imperfect and inconsistent religion has alienated and disgusted souls perhaps seeking the light, must stand responsible for a great evil left behind him in the world. It is, indeed, idle to forecast, how, from the next world, we shall look back upon the present. But if regret can enter into the thoughts and memories of the blessed, how can those irretrievable legacies of evil ever be forgotten? How must good and holy men, for there were such—who slew one another in the old time, in the name of Christ, and for the honour of His Cross—look back on the hideous consequences of their folly, on the sanction which they gave to the cruelty of the cruel, on the dreadful error of having put it into the power of God's enemies to say so plausibly, that this religion of love is really a religion of hatred, and strife, and blood? And, in a lesser yet real degree, what agony will surely pass through the heart of all, who, by any fault in their religion, by undervaluing for any cause the great natural virtues which all men reverence, of truth, and justice, and equity, and generosity, by any selfishness and narrowness which they have imported into their personal religion, by the pettiness and the bitterness of their contentions, by their want of sympathy and breadth of soul, by their scorn of self-discipline and self-command, by obstinately insisting on their own will and opinion, have "perverted that which was right," have caused "the way of truth" to "be evil spoken of," and "the name of God" to be "blasphemed." St. Paul wished himself anathema, so that his brethren after the flesh might be saved. What will our thoughts be, in that kingdom of charity, which Christ left to save the world, when we realise that it is because of us and our poor, our inconsistent religion, that our brethren have lost their way and their hope?

"If the salt have lost his savour, wherewith shall it be salted?" May we carry the remembrance of this awful saying with us, not only in our hours of relaxation and enjoyment, but when we believe ourselves to be most intent and most sincere in doing our Master's service. May it keep before our thoughts the extent of what we shall have to give account for. May it make us distrust ourselves when we feel most secure in our convictions and our zeal. And may our prayer be that, wherever we have done mischief by the faults of our religion, we may have grace to see it, and time and opportunity to repair it, before we die.

XX

HUMAN LIFE IN THE LIGHT OF IMMORTALITY

"For our light affliction, which is but for a moment, worketh for us a far more exceeding and eternal weight of glory; while we look not at the things which are seen, but at the things which are not seen: for the things which are seen are temporal; but the things which are not seen are eternal."—2 CORINTHIANS iv. 17, 18.

THERE is no part of the New Testament in which the contrast appears more strongly between the two theories of life—life bounded by time, and life here as the road to something inconceivably greater—than in the Epistles to the Corinthians. The contrast, of course, is the foundation of every view of life in the New Testament. But from the circumstances under which these Epistles were written, it is more prominent and recurs more continually in them than almost anywhere else. For these Epistles were written just at the crisis when this contrast was about to disturb and move human society outside the Jewish world with its tremendous significance. It was at Corinth that it first came fairly into contact with the Greek mind, that is, with the thought and serious belief of civilised mankind. St. Paul had preached to the mixed Gentile multitudes in Antioch, in Asia

Minor. He had passed through Greek cities on the continent — Philippi, Thessalonica, Athens — and memorable things had happened in them: but he had only passed through them. But at Corinth, the most important of them all at this time, he had halted; and he had made a deep impression. Here, before these active-minded, pleasure-loving people, the great alternative had broken upon them—broken upon them by a surprise which it must be absolutely beyond our power now to realise adequately—this world only, or, also indeed, the next. For here, a received view, the practical assumption of man's absolute mortality, had possession of the ground: and the next world, if there was a next world, what had they heard of it? With all their past wonderful history, with all their roll of the cleverest and wisest of mankind, with all their captivating mythology and splendid solemnities of worship, with all their inheritance of sharpened intellect and traditions of successful thinking—what had they really heard of it? Their mythology spoke of Elysian fields, and rivers of flame and woe, and Minos, the judge. Their lyric and dramatic poetry spoke, as no literature has ever spoken, of mysterious laws of duty and retribution. Their philosophy speculated, among other things, on the soul and its immortality. Their serious thinkers looked with vague wistfulness into the darkness, beyond the impenetrable fact of death: the primary difficulties of religion, as old as human thought, were as familiar to them as to us: and they had no answer. The popular phraseology, when off its guard, named the name of God, *testimonium animæ naturaliter Christianæ*. But what serious man, in his most serious thinking, ever dreamt of looking forward, in his real hopes and practical purposes, beyond what he could see and know of life? The utmost that he attempted was to prepare himself with good sense, with dignity, with manly courage, with resigned cheerfulness, to its inevitable though uncertain end; and to make the best use he could of it, the wisest, the happiest, while it lasted. How could he do anything else? The incomparable death-scene of the *Phædo* stands alone in its heroic temerity of faith. The barbarian mysticism or asceticism of Asia might employ life in wild preparation for an unknown and unimaginable future. But what could a countryman of Hippocrates, of Sophocles, of Socrates, of Plato, of Aristotle, of Epicurus, of Zeno, do more than accept it, with all its limitations but with all its opportunities, with all its uncertainties but with all its facts, with all its pains but with all its joys, and after having done his best in it, close his eyes in silence, and wait patiently without complaint to die. That is what we may suppose of the best of the chiefs of Greek society. What would be thought of life and death by the commonplace world, such as we see it represented in the older or later comedy, in Theophrastus or Lucian? "The crowd," as has been said, "played with the imagery of another world, but it had no place as a truth in their hearts;

nobody lived for it. How could anybody live for a future such as this?"[1]

And now St. Paul came saying, and saying in a way which made these Greeks listen: "The question of human life goes far beyond all we can see and know here. The life which has hitherto, both in theory and much more practically, seemed all to you, about which you have exhausted your grandest and most pathetic language, is but a part of what concerns you, and as respects duration and perfection, the least part. It is as critical, as decisive, as the life of the unborn child; but it is in itself as poor and passing a fragment of your existence. The true, the great life, is to come: will you have it, will you take in the thought of it, will you strive for it, will you sacrifice everything to it?" Imagine what it must have been to them to come to this belief, after having lived all their days under the accepted customary conviction that men really existed only up to their death. Make all allowance for that dulness and slowness which, with men in general, even under the strongest emotion, keeps them from seeing a great change as it really is. But to those who accepted it in earnest, and felt what it meant, the shock must have been as if the familiar world were indeed turned upside down. The conversion of a worldly or unbelieving spirit to a sense of the reality of eternal things, may be something like it still, in the case of an individual. But the awful surprise of an indi-

---

[1] Dr. Mozley's *Lectures and other Theological Papers*, p. 38.

vidual is no measure of a revolutionised view of things, of human pursuits and human prospects, in a quick-witted and sympathetic society. And this was one of the results of St. Paul's preaching at Corinth. These were people, Greeks, who had hitherto lived all their lives as if time and nature were all, to whom he could now speak as if they now believed in a life which swallowed up time and nature. There was a society on whom his convictions and prospects, not without resistance and inconsistency, yet with overmastering force, had impressed themselves.

How had such a thing come about? What was the history of this profound, amazing change—the more and more amazing the more and the longer we think about it? Is any one, can any one be content with the paltry, the cheap account of enthusiasm? There is the enthusiasm of folly, but there is the enthusiasm of soberness and strength; and if ever there was the enthusiasm of a man with his eyes open, it was the enthusiasm of St. Paul—the enthusiasm kindled by the clearest and deepest conviction of a great and certain fact—a long unwelcome and long resisted, but at last overpowering certainty. By what right but that did St. Paul pretend to offer such a view of life to the shrewdness and good sense and wisdom of the Greeks—to force such a view of all its aspects and all its duties on an unwilling society—what justified him in daring to upset and invert men's ideas on so important a subject, and trouble their quiet by claims that cut so deep? St.

Paul recognised to the full his responsibility. It was not merely that he could appeal to the natural arguments for immortality, or to the general evidence of miracles as such. To the Corinthians, he put everything on one decisive, incontestable fact. One who announced himself as the Conqueror of Death, and the Giver of Life Eternal, had verified his words, had done what no living man had done. He had come back to earth from among the dead. He was dead, and He was alive once more. There was another world, and One had actually appeared among us— men had seen Him, and touched and handled Him, and heard His voice—who belonged to both worlds, and put this one in relation to the next. Jesus Christ, the crucified, was risen from the dead; on that foundation, the only one that could bear it, St Paul built his contrast between the two worlds.

Naturally, this contrast, this strange new thing for such as Greeks to accept and to care for, is interwoven with the whole texture of these Epistles. He is perfectly conscious of the enormous change, and all its consequences, social and moral, to which his preaching had led the Greeks of Corinth. He recognises the wonderful thing it must have been for the Gospel of another life, with its tremendous and unheard of condition, Jesus Christ crucified for human sin, to have taken a real place in minds accustomed to the usual grooves of Greek thought and feeling. He acknowledges, he insists upon its disturbing effect on all estimates of the objects of human action. The old view and the new view, each was inconceivable, each was pure madness to the other. Of course, on the old view, his position, his aims, his labours were those of a fool, self-condemned to wretchedness and weakness. Of course, on the old view, the preacher of the Cross of Christ, of the Son of God crucified to save the world, was an insane and reckless assailant of all that had been most wisely and most kindly arranged to make the most of a short life which ended for ever in the grave. What was there in the Cross to throw light on such a life? What was there in it to bring hope or strength, to make it such a gospel, such good news to the world? To a society, based solely on a mortal life, to a scheme of conduct, adapted solely to what meets us here, and reasonably, beneficently solicitous about its improvement, about extending and perfecting the *commoda vitæ*, the preaching of the Cross and Resurrection could not but be— whatever word will most express the extremity of human unreason. On such an assumption, even God was foolish, even God was weak, if He sent such a message to men who had no end but to perish, who had but these short years to be happy in or to be wretched. But strength and weakness, wisdom and folly, human ambition and greatness and glory, took another measure, when the thought, the conviction, came in of another world than this. Nothing could be more intelligible to a believer in the Lord's resurrection than that God should have chosen what must seem folly to this world "to confound the wise;" chosen weakness—amid the towering ambitions and iron forces of this world—"to confound" at last "the strong;" chosen characters, paths of life, stations which were at the lowest point of the accepted social scale, to put to shame in the end those who had won the magnificent prizes of the world, to shake the settled maxims and fixed habits of society. It was not wonderful, if God indeed rules over the world, and if the purposes of God extend beyond the limits of time and nature, and throw all things of time and nature into that almost inexpressible insignificance, which must appear when the transitory is seen side by side with the eternal.

And so, with this contrast ever at hand, he pursues life into its practical details. What inconceivable childishness were the Corinthian disputes about favourite Apostles, Paul and Cephas and Apollos, when "all things are yours . . . life or death, or things present or things to come!" How monstrous seemed all premature and ignorant judgments, now that they knew of the final tribunal of Jesus Christ, which should "bring to light the hidden things of darkness, and make manifest the counsels of the hearts!" How inevitable the sharply contrasted lot and fortunes of the Apostolic benefactors of the world on their errand of blessing and hope—"We are fools . . . but ye are wise . . . being reviled, we bless; being persecuted, we suffer it: being defamed, we entreat: we are made as the filth of the world, the offscouring of all things unto this day," a spectacle "unto the world, and to angels, and to men!" How shameful that believers in such a future should look on unconcerned on license more daring than that even named among the Gentiles! What meanness and "shortness of thought," that those who look forward to rule angels should go to law about trifles before those who only believed in this life, the "unbelievers" in God and immortality! Nay, the changed horizon and prospect changed too the aspect of the most innocent and beautiful portions of human life. It changed what had been the most perfect fruit of human society, the love of the family. For if "the fashion of this world passeth away," it would soon be that earthly ties were as though they were not, the joy and the sorrow, the keenness and interest of this life, all passed into forgetfulness; and there was something, not to pass away, greater than these to think of. And thus, throughout the Epistles, questions about old religious scruples, questions about the internal economy of the Church, questions about Church customs and privileges, questions about spiritual gifts, questions about due arrangement for the sacraments, all are lifted to a different level, all appear in a different light and in different proportions according as we think of them, or do not think of them, in relation to that changed view of life;—till all practical questions end in the law of charity, and all human ideas and hopes of life are wound up in that great chapter which we read from at the grave. All are governed by axioms and principles, not only new in Greek life, but, in their certainty and peremptoriness, new in the world. "All things are yours ... and ye are Christ's, and Christ is God's." "Judge nothing before the time." "Know ye not that the unrighteous," in a long catalogue of pleasant and familiar vices, "shall not inherit the kingdom of God?" "We must all appear before the judgment-seat of Christ." "So run, that ye may obtain." "Henceforth know we no man after the flesh." "The things which are seen are temporal; but the things which are not seen are eternal." "I suppose that this is good for the present distress ... the time is short." "Now we see through a glass, darkly ... now I know in part." "Then cometh the end." "The last enemy that shall be destroyed is death." "Charity"—charity only—"never faileth." "If in this life only we have hope in Christ, we are of all men most miserable." "We shall all be changed ... for this corruptible must put on incorruption, and this mortal must put on immortality."

St. Paul's view of life was a simple and consistent one. The contrast between this life and the other was ever before him. He accepted with perfect naturalness all that this life brought, its inevitable troubles and annoyances, its pains and sorrows, its harmless customs, its instinctive maxims, as a traveller passing through a strange land accepts its ways and language, and puts up with its inconveniences. But he was only a traveller, and his thoughts and purposes went far beyond it. This was his view: what is ours?

Our case is different from his in many ways. What he had to bring, we have to keep, or to give up and throw away. He had a truth to impress for the first time on the world, which has since been for centuries "current coin" with the humblest souls in Christendom. They have been taught, and they have learned, to "look for the resurrection of the dead, and the life of the world to come." In such a work as he had undertaken, all that could stamp the least importance upon it, all that men do and go through when they are most in earnest, all was not too much. "I die daily" was the natural sentiment of one whose mission was to persuade men the strange thing that death in very truth was only the road to another and eternal life. It was a day of storm and earthquake; a day of overthrow and catastrophe, such as the moral world had never yet seen. Whatever may be happening now under the comparatively smooth surface of our civilisation, in this great estimate of life, we have entered into his labours; we inherit them, if we will, in peace. And further, human life, in its developments and aspect, has altered. Put as high as we please all that had been attained to by ancient art and social achievement, yet life then presented a very different scene from what it does to us. It was simpler, it was narrower, it was ruder and coarser. It was more brutal. It was the age of slavery. It was the age of the amphitheatre. It was an age of blood. Doubtless there were those to whom life was very noble, and many more to whom it was very enjoyable: but what was it to the poor, what was it to the crowds? But cast your eyes over the infinitely complicated field of human life, where the voices of St. Paul and his Master have been listened to. I do not underrate all that still remains unchanged, unremoved, from those days to these: the sin, the shame, the misery, the blindness, the despair: the multitudes that know not their right hand from their left, the frightful, irremediable contrasts between wealth and poverty, the numbers to whom, from birth to death, life seems to bring no one good thing, not even one good chance. I do not underrate the pathetic spectacle which steals into the imagination, when you look in the faces of a great crowd, and think of the separate history behind each of those faces, and ask yourself, how many are really happy, what each has seen, what each has lost. Yet for all that, compared with what St. Paul knew, the life which men have by this time worked out for themselves seems what a trained and serious manhood is to wild and stormy and crude boyhood. It is indeed different, that manifold and richly coloured scene which modern life presents, with its endless diversity of interests, with its growing refinements of spiritual and intellectual faculty, with its infinite unfoldings and types of character, its recognition of the intricacies and complexities of mind and soul, its depth and penetration, its aspirations, its vast ideas, its insoluble problems, its inextinguishable hopes. True, it is all of the earth, earthy. But you may as well deny the magnificence of nature, because it must perish, as deny how wonderful is that human life which our eyes have seen, and which men in each age, as each age has come, have felt to be more wonderful than what their fathers saw.

What shall we say, then, to life as we know it?

1. We may surrender ourselves to what we see, and choose to ask no further questions. We may go back to that view of life which was in possession of the crowd when St. Paul came to Corinth, and deliberately choose to dispense with all encouragement, all hopes, all sanctions, outside the familiar bounds of birth and death. And for a while, now at least, it is not so difficult to live on such a faith. For life never demanded more seriously the utmost strain of attention and endeavour; and its whole machinery, science, business, law, government, art, war, literature, the vast industries of communication and trade, all that huge interlocked system, apart from which we could not live a day, and which returns to us every morning with the sun, and works so smoothly and so irresistibly, all this goes on, on the simple unquestioning supposition that what we know as time and nature are the only real conditions of human existence.

Yes, we may surrender ourselves, and we are loudly told to do so; and all that fills ear and mind around us conspires to enforce the advice. Look, they say, at the real facts of life, acknowledge, and be honest, the stress and charm of action, of knowledge, of success. Yes, that is one side, a great side of human life. It seems to show the overflowing rewards of pains and industry, its triumphant energy, its unending conquests. It is a real side. You see with your own eyes the achievements of science and art and business. But as truly as this is, so truly there is another side. What, when the dark days come, when the brain refuses to think, and the hand to ply its cunning? You talk of the real facts of life. There is another witness to the real facts of life. You may find it in those awful—alas! shall we say unanswerable pages, in which the poets of disappointment and despair—Byron, Obermann, Heine, Leopardi—have concentrated feelings not confined to themselves, about the cruelties and treacheries of nature, about the "breaking of dreams," and the emptiness of having lived—about the dreadfulness of a world in which the mightiest power is pain, and the only certainty the perishing of the fairest and best. You may find it in those majestic strains, in which Lucretius, solemnly and serenely closing the door of religion for ever on mankind, reveals, in spite of himself and his professions of content, the unutterable sadness of a noble spirit, which can see no intelligible upshot to the destinies of men. It is not enough to think of life as the strong and the successful think of it, in the hour of victorious labour. You must also think of it when their victories are over, and there are no more to win. You must also think of it, as the miserable and the dying think of it; as they think of it who have found in it no good, who have found it ensnare and delude them.

I do not deny that there may be a tragic grandeur in the call upon man to die, in the face of all this, with the steady refusal to look beyond, with the deliberate rejection of a hope which he once believed he had. A view of life, which exacts the utmost of nobleness and unselfish duty from man, and lands him in the grave and leaves him there—which requires him to push on to the utmost the development of his powers, and still more of his character, only that having reached their excellence they may end in nothing—which adjusts no wrong, and sees without pity or marvel the ultimate blowing out, like the flame of a candle, of the highest human goodness and work—which summons the soldier, the philanthropist, the servant of the State, the friend, to give up to honour the most precious thing that men possess, and refuses them the slightest shred not merely of hope but of sanction—this is, indeed, as stern, and dark, and terrible a faith as man can have. But to think to do this; to think to make men live righteously and soberly, with clean hands, and a pure heart, after you have taken from them the last, the utmost which they hoped, and feared, and tried to love; to proclaim a life of duty, owning no sanction from on high, looking for no reward, grateful for no benefits; to expect to maintain the moral level of Christianity after you have exploded Christianity, with all its tenderness and all its charities, as a long imposture of cruelty and ignorance—it may be a magnificent and imposing audacity, but it does not reckon with human nature. It does not reckon with its passion, with its selfishness, with its shrewdness; and as little with what it has learned and knows of the heights to which it may be raised. It is too late. Man has heard of a life to come,—of the key to the mystery of his existence, not as a guess, but as a truth. It is not because some men say that they can do without it that he will lightly let himself be sent once more adrift, wandering without hope on the waste of circumstance. Their negations only bring home more vividly what man is asked to resign. We have too often carelessly and thanklessly taken for granted "the blessed hope of everlasting life." Now, we find in good earnest what it would be to lose it. If now at the end of the world we had finally to give up our fathers' hopes and promises, we should be, in a sense more deep than even St. Paul's, of all generations of men the most miserable. But if there is anything serious and solid in this existence of ours, if there is any probability in human history, if there is anything of weight in the judgment of successive ages, if any trust is to be reposed on evidence, accumulated and manifold, and again and again tested, if there is any reasonable hope in the goodness of God and His care for men, if there is any substance and value in human virtue and human character, if any meaning in man's longing for perfection, if anything real in the tragedy and pathos of human affections in the presence of the grave—then, woe is me, if I play with such a subject; if I dare to deal with it lightly, treacherously, insincerely; if I ever think of it without reverent awe as the dearest and last hope of suffering man; if I betray to the speculations and perplexities of the hour, the inheritance, now in my hands, of generations to come, to whom my faithlessness, my trifling, may make faith more difficult.

2. And yet, how plausibly is it said that in all our lives, we at least who live in the world, live practically as if this were all. We are told that we profess immortality in words, but we live in fact as the resigned, nay contented slaves of mortality—that we waste our breath in talking against the absorbing and satisfying interests of our present condition. Yes, it is hard for most of us to imagine, what, and whom, we shall meet when we are dead. It is difficult to remember, to believe in, immortality, in the rush of our crowded streets, in our luxurious drawing-rooms, in the turmoil and din of the "world's debate." It is hard to think that in these short and busy days of time, a preparation is going on for that which is beyond time; a preparation the results of which will one day find us out, as surely as the examination finds out the student, or the war finds out the soldier.

And as we are bound to work, as there is so much to be done for human life, and no man can stand idle with impunity, and it is certain that if we are to do anything, we must give our whole mind to our work, whether it deals with matter or spirit—how is it to be expected that we should keep in our thoughts what is so alien to all present things that occupy us?

It is hard: but there is nothing in its hardness which is not of a piece with our general experience. It rests with us—with our choice and tendencies, with what goes on in the secret recesses of the will, amid the springs of its decisions and its strength—whether the present shall obliterate or eclipse the future. The future has before now overwhelmed the present, it did so with St. Paul: it did so, because he willed that it should. Doubtless, there are feelings which kill all other feelings—interests, which absorb and extinguish all other interests—ideas or an atmosphere of thought, which make it impossible to admit other ideas, or to conceive of another manner of reasonable thinking. Many of us know what it is to be for a time under the spell and glamour of a new and imposing aspect of men and things, revealing itself with all its claims and proofs, in all its consistency and majesty; how other things dwindle and are dwarfed beside it; how familiar life, and what we once thought the highest life, becomes tame and commonplace and repulsive; how the light upon it darkens everything else; how the new conceptions, scientific, historical, religious, seem to justify themselves, and make any rival theory appear irrational and impossible. And we know perhaps how under the influences of time and experience, this onesidedness has given way; we can see now, that it was not reason only, but subtle attractions to imagination and will, which so monopolised us. It is on our own responsibility, that we are, as we say, taken up with by the present. We can break away, if we will, it may be with trouble and sacrifice, from the enchanted bounds. We speak of a life occupied exclusively by work which leaves no room for other things. But our words make life a much simpler thing than it is. The same man may lead, naturally and rightly lead, not one, but several distinct lives. He may lead one life in his profession and business. He leads another life in his family and among his friends. He may lead another, quite as absorbing, quite as characteristic, in the pursuit of some favourite line of literature, or science, or art; and he has time, and interest, and serious thought for all, without sacrificing, even without subordinating, one to the other. And besides, the most occupied and eager life has its reserved moments, its pauses and retirements, when the man is, and feels himself, alone. They may be for many uses. They may be for dreams, for ambitions, for regrets. They may be for his secret sins, his hatreds, his impurities, his pride. But they may be, too, for the discipline and forethought of another and greater life. The thing is that the busiest life, the life which makes the most of the opportunities and conditions of the present time, and aims the highest at its object, is not incompatible, unless we choose, with the most resolute preparation for another life to come. "The world is not nothing, because it is transient."[1] And the faithful servant is he who uses to the utmost whatever talent has been assigned him in the manifold system of visible things, uses it with his whole heart and strength and enthusiasm; uses it as if it were all he had to do; and yet is ever conscious that all that he is passing through here is but the antechamber of what is to be his real life, and that to be fitted for all that he may meet *there*, all its tasks, all that will make demands on his character and will and affections, is the real reason why he is here.

For the truth is that there is but one conceivable preparation for the life to come; and that is, the discipline and building up of character—the only thing, in which we can imagine ourselves under training for what is to be. Knowledge, accomplishments, inventiveness, power, all that fills the daily scene of human action—we cannot imagine them in any relation to the future world, except as they are exercises and proofs of character. Except as they require and call forth moral qualities—patience, industry, faithfulness, honesty, justice, truth, self-command, sincere dealing with oneself, they can make no difference to us there, where we are to go:

---

[1] Dr. Mozley's *University Sermons*, p. 82.

we cannot carry them with us, any more than we can carry with us the equipments and ornaments, and the ways and customs of this life. But it is because no human activity is excluded from this office, because of the vast field which human business and interests present for the growth and correction and establishment of character, that this world becomes the school of another. This can go on under the most opposite conditions. This brings the most opposite pursuits together, and makes their votaries one. We sometimes wonder what St. Paul would have thought if suddenly plunged into our modern life; what he could have thought of our command over nature, our hunger and thirst for knowledge, our complicated systems of social order, our refined and ever improving methods of work, our inventions, our provisions for human comfort. Little enough, in comparison with those great certainties which he had to impress upon mankind; but he would, I suppose, have told us to make an "apostolical use" of what was given into our hands to use; he would have welcomed those, who in another time and with other necessities than his, having received the truth into their hearts which he was sent to teach, were using this world's business to perfect in themselves that which only they could carry with them when they die, the moral qualities required in a world of righteousness. He who laid such stress on the duty of the slave, on the obligation and the worth of labour, on the homely conditions which sanctify domestic life, would have found no difficulty in seeing his own lofty conceptions of human life beyond the grave, carried into our keenest and most exacting work—producing its lasting, its immortal fruits, in the council-chamber in the camp, in the school, in the counting-house, in the artist's studio, the engineer's workshop, the lecture-room of the man of science, as well as in the careers of missionaries like Henry Martyn and Bishop Steere, or in the patient continuance in well-doing of the humblest Christian labourer. Indeed, it is no imagination of theory. Unhappy, indeed, is he who, if he has lived the time of man's ordinary life, has not seen how possible it is to keep that awful vision of the life to come ever before the soul, in the thick and pressure of secular affairs, in riches and poverty, in joy and in sorrow, in strength and power, as in weakness and decay.

The work of the present life is great, is often glorious, is beneficent, is ennobling. It is the work which God appointed. Men may well be enthusiastic about its triumphs, for they are wonderful. They may well be sanguine about the steps of its progress, for with all its failures and with so much still to do, they are real steps. Whether, if we knew no more, it might satisfy such as we are, in spite of that awful blight of sin and death which is upon it all, I cannot tell—it is not our case. But when all that is to pass here *has* passed, then comes that which throws it all into infinite insignificance. The hour shall come, for the sake of which, once upon this earth, our Lord rose from the dead; and "the dead shall be raised incorruptible, and we shall be changed." And long before that hour arrives, all that we are now every day accustomed to, will have changed too. All that each generation has most valued, will have become old and out of date. The processes of decay which we see, will have gone over us. Successes are exhausted. Reputations wane and are forgotten. Schemes have their hour and come to naught. The science of one age is superseded in the next. The taste of one age is unintelligible in the next. All will have retired into the distance of the past, all will seem what to old men are the prizes they won at school, the honours they strove for at college. One thing only, in that hour, we can imagine remaining. Only character remains: it remains in the defeated as well as in the victorious, in the forgotten as in the best remembered—not what a man had or knew, but what he is, his honesty, his unselfishness, his purity, his fortitude, his justice, his charity, his hatred of what is false and vain and base and mean and cruel. To them, not to what we call here knowledge and deep thought and power and genius, are the promises of the future made. To them alone, unless they are empty words, the creation and idols of our fancy, belong the hopes of immortality—that new wonder which came down on earth, into our time of mortality and ignorance, with the Resurrection of Jesus Christ and with that alone—the knowledge, the assured certainty of everlasting life.

"Who shall ascend into the hill of the Lord, and who shall rise up in His holy place?

"Even he that hath clean hands and a pure heart; and that hath not lift up his mind unto vanity, nor sworn to deceive his neighbour.

"He shall receive the blessing from the Lord, and righteousness from the God of his salvation."

THE END

MESSRS. MACMILLAN & CO.'S PUBLICATIONS.

BY THE SAME AUTHOR.

ADVENT SERMONS, 1885. Crown 8vo. 4s. 6d.

THE DISCIPLINE OF THE CHRISTIAN CHARACTER. Second Edition. Crown 8vo. 4s. 6d.

THE GIFTS OF CIVILISATION, and other sermons and lectures delivered at Oxford and at St. Paul's. Second Edition. Crown 8vo. 7s. 6d

GUARDIAN.—" A suggestive and fascinating volume."

HUMAN LIFE AND ITS CONDITIONS. Sermons preached before the University of Oxford in 1876-1878, with three Ordination Sermons. Second Edition. Crown 8vo. 6s.

VILLAGE SERMONS. Preached at Whatley. Crown 8vo. 6s.

THE CHURCH QUARTERLY REVIEW, July 1892.—" Both the matter and diction of these exquisite sermons are within the compass of the most unlettered congregation. . . . But the more cultured a reader is the more clearly will he perceive that the sermons are the composition of a highly trained intellect. There are traces all through them of the art that conceals art . . . a closer study shows the scholar and the divine in every page, nay, in every sentence."

CATHEDRAL AND UNIVERSITY SERMONS. Crown 8vo. 6s.

Sermons preached in St. Paul's Cathedral or in the University Pulpits at Oxford and Cambridge.

BRITISH WEEKLY.—" The last volume of Dean Church's sermons we admire so much that we almost fear to say all we think. To say that it is the grandest expression of the most cultured and the most completely Christian mind of the generation is to say much. We deliberately go further, and venture to affirm that these are the most magnificent sermons in the English language."

SPECTATOR.—" Dean Church's seem to us the finest sermons published since Newman's, even Dr. Liddon's rich and eloquent discourses not excepted,—and they breathe more of the spirit of perfect peace than even Newman's. They cannot be called High Church or Broad Church, much less Low Church sermons; they are simply the sermons of a good scholar, a great thinker, and a firm and serene Christian."

PALL MALL GAZETTE.—" Such sermons as Dean Church's really enrich the national literature. We may well hope they do more."

THE SACRED POETRY OF EARLY RELIGIONS. Two Lectures delivered in St. Paul's Cathedral, Jan. 27 and Feb. 3, 1874. Pott 8vo. 1s.

MISCELLANEOUS WRITINGS. Collected Edition. 6 Vols. Globe 8vo. 5s. each.

- Vol. I. MISCELLANEOUS ESSAYS.
- Vol. II. DANTE; and other Essays.
- Vol. III. ST. ANSELM.
- Vol. IV. SPENSER.
- Vol. V. BACON.
- Vol. VI. THE OXFORD MOVEMENT. Twelve Years, 1833-1845.

TIMES.—" Will quickly take its place among the most interesting of the many extant accounts of what is called 'The Oxford Movement.' . . . The volume as a whole is an historical and critical survey of the highest interest, full of the delicate quality of Dean Church's mind. The characteristics of all his best writings are here, as is only natural."

GLOBE.—" Will certainly rank next in interest to Newman's autobiography itself."

MANCHESTER GUARDIAN.—" It is not only far away the best and probably also the final account of the Oxford Movement; it is also the only complete one that has yet appeared from the Anglican point of view. . . ."

MACMILLAN AND CO., LONDON.

MESSRS. MACMILLAN & CO.'S PUBLICATIONS.

WORKS BY BISHOP WESTCOTT.

THE GOSPEL OF LIFE. Thoughts Introductory to the Study of Christian Doctrine. By BROOKE FOSS WESTCOTT, D.D., Bishop of Durham. Crown 8vo, Cloth, 6s.

ESSAYS ON THE HISTORY OF RELIGIOUS THOUGHT IN THE WEST. By BROOKE FOSS WESTCOTT, D.D., D.C.L., Lord Bishop of Durham, Honorary Fellow of Trinity and King's Colleges, Cambridge. Globe 8vo, 6s.

TIMES.—"Their scholarly execution, their graceful style, their devout temper, and their wealth of suggestion and instruction, should render these masterly essays as welcome as if they were new to all serious readers."

SCOTSMAN.—"Readers of all shades of opinion will recognise in the volume a work of high excellence, and find in it everywhere evidence of copious learning and sympathetic and penetrative insight."

8vo, Cloth.

THE EPISTLES OF ST. JOHN. The Greek Text, with Notes, Third Edition. 12s. 6d.

THE EPISTLE TO THE HEBREWS. The Greek Text, with Notes and Essays. Second Edition. 14s.

CLASSICAL REVIEW.—"It would be difficult to find in the whole range of exegetical literature a volume at the same time so comprehensive and so compact. It possesses characteristics which will command for it the permanent attention of scholars."

Crown 8vo, Cloth.

GENERAL SURVEY OF THE HISTORY OF THE CANON OF THE NEW TESTAMENT DURING THE FIRST FOUR CENTURIES. Sixth Edition. 10s. 6d.

INTRODUCTION TO THE STUDY OF THE FOUR GOSPELS. Seventh Edition. 10s. 6d.

THE GOSPEL OF THE RESURRECTION. Sixth Edition. 6s.

THE BIBLE IN THE CHURCH. Tenth Edition, 18mo. 14s. 6d.

THE CHRISTIAN LIFE, MANIFOLD AND ONE. 2s. 6d.

ON THE RELIGIOUS OFFICE OF THE UNIVERSITIES. Sermons. 4s. 6d.

THE HISTORIC FAITH. Third Edition. 6s.

THE REVELATION OF THE RISEN LORD. Fourth Edition. 6s.

THE REVELATION OF THE FATHER. 6s.

CHRISTUS CONSUMMATOR. Second Edition. 6s.

SOME THOUGHTS FROM THE ORDINAL. 1s. 6d.

SOCIAL ASPECTS OF CHRISTIANITY. 6s.

GIFTS FOR MINISTRY. Addresses to Candidates for Ordination. 1s. 6d.

THE VICTORY OF THE CROSS. Sermons Preached during Holy Week, 1888, in Hereford Cathedral. 3s. 6d.

FROM STRENGTH TO STRENGTH. Three Sermons (in Memoriam, J. B. D.). 2s.

WESTCOTT AND HORT'S GREEK TESTAMENT.

Crown, 8vo.

THE NEW TESTAMENT IN THE ORIGINAL GREEK. Revised Text. 2 vols. 10s. 6d. each. Vol. I. Text. Vol. II. The Introduction and Appendix.

18mo.

THE NEW TESTAMENT IN THE ORIGINAL GREEK. An Edition for Schools. The Text revised by Bishop WESTCOTT and Dr. HORT. 4s. 6d.; roan, 5s. 6d.; morocco, 6s. 6d.

MACMILLAN AND CO., LONDON.

January 1893

A Catalogue

of

Theological Works

published by

Macmillan & Co.

Bedford Street, Strand, London

CONTENTS

THE BIBLE—
    History of the Bible
    Biblical History
    The Old Testament
    The New Testament

HISTORY OF THE CHRISTIAN CHURCH

THE CHURCH OF ENGLAND

DEVOTIONAL BOOKS

THE FATHERS

HYMNOLOGY

SERMONS, LECTURES, ADDRESSES, AND THEOLOGICAL ESSAYS

January 1893.

MACMILLAN AND CO.'S THEOLOGICAL CATALOGUE

The Bible

HISTORY OF THE BIBLE

THE ENGLISH BIBLE: An External and Critical History of the various English Translations of Scripture. By Prof. JOHN EADIE. 2 vols. 8vo. 28s.

THE BIBLE IN THE CHURCH. By Right Rev. Bishop WESTCOTT. 10th Edition. 18mo. 4s. 6d.

BIBLICAL HISTORY

BIBLE LESSONS. By Rev. E. A. ABBOTT. Crown 8vo. 4s. 6d.

SIDE-LIGHTS UPON BIBLE HISTORY. By Mrs. SYDNEY BUXTON. Illustrated. Crown 8vo. 5s.

STORIES FROM THE BIBLE. By Rev. A. J. CHURCH. Illustrated. Two Series. Crown 8vo. 3s. 6d. each.

BIBLE READINGS SELECTED FROM THE PENTATEUCH AND THE BOOK OF JOSHUA. By Rev. J. A. CROSS. 2nd Edition. Globe 8vo. 2s. 6d.

CHILDREN'S TREASURY OF BIBLE STORIES. By Mrs. H. GASKOIN. 18mo. 1s. each. Part I. Old Testament; II. New Testament; III. Three Apostles.

A CLASS-BOOK OF OLD TESTAMENT HISTORY. By Rev. Canon MACLEAR. With Four Maps. 18mo. 4s. 6d.

A CLASS-BOOK OF NEW TESTAMENT HISTORY. Including the connection of the Old and New Testament. By the same. 18mo. 5s. 6d.

A SHILLING BOOK OF OLD TESTAMENT HISTORY. By the same. 18mo. 1s.

A SHILLING BOOK OF NEW TESTAMENT HISTORY. By the same. 18mo. 1s.

THE OLD TESTAMENT

SCRIPTURE READINGS FOR SCHOOLS AND FAMILIES. By C. M. YONGE. Globe 8vo. 1s. 6d. each; also with comments, 3s. 6d. each.—First Series: GENESIS TO DEUTERONOMY.—Second Series: JOSHUA TO SOLOMON.—Third Series: KINGS AND THE PROPHETS.—Fourth Series: THE GOSPEL TIMES.—Fifth Series: APOSTOLIC TIMES.

The Old Testament—*continued.*

WARBURTONIAN LECTURES ON THE MINOR PROPHETS. By Rev. A. F. KIRKPATRICK, B.D. Crown 8vo. [*In the Press.*

THE PATRIARCHS AND LAWGIVERS OF THE OLD TESTAMENT. By FREDERICK DENISON MAURICE. New Edition. Crown 8vo. 3s. 6d.

THE PROPHETS AND KINGS OF THE OLD TESTAMENT. By the same. New Edition. Crown 8vo. 3s. 6d.

THE CANON OF THE OLD TESTAMENT. An Essay on the Growth and Formation of the Hebrew Canon of Scripture. By Rev. Prof. H. E. RYLE. Crown 8vo. 6s.

THE EARLY NARRATIVES OF GENESIS. By Rev. Prof. H. E. RYLE. Cr. 8vo. 3s. net.

The Pentateuch—

AN HISTORICO-CRITICAL INQUIRY INTO THE ORIGIN AND COMPOSITION OF THE HEXATEUCH (PENTATEUCH AND BOOK OF JOSHUA). By Prof. A. KUENEN. Translated by PHILIP H. WICKSTEED, M.A. 8vo. 14s.

The Psalms—

THE PSALMS CHRONOLOGICALLY ARRANGED. An Amended Version, with Historical Introductions and Explanatory Notes. By Four Friends. New Edition. Crown 8vo. 5s. net.

GOLDEN TREASURY PSALTER. The Student's Edition. Being an Edition with briefer Notes of "The Psalms Chronologically Arranged by Four Friends." 18mo. 3s. 6d.

THE PSALMS. With Introductions and Critical Notes. By A. C. JENNINGS, M.A., and W. H. LOWE, M.A. In 2 vols. 2nd Edition. Crown 8vo. 10s. 6d. each.

INTRODUCTION TO THE STUDY AND USE OF THE PSALMS. By Rev. J. F. THRUPP. 2nd Edition. 2 vols. 8vo. 21s.

Isaiah—

ISAIAH XL.—LXVI. With the Shorter Prophecies allied to it. By MATTHEW ARNOLD. With Notes. Crown 8vo. 5s.

ISAIAH OF JERUSALEM. In the Authorised English Version, with Introduction, Corrections, and Notes. By the same. Cr. 8vo. 4s. 6d.

A BIBLE-READING FOR SCHOOLS. The Great Prophecy of Israel's Restoration (Isaiah xl.-lxvi.) Arranged and Edited for Young Learners. By the same. 4th Edition. 18mo. 1s.

COMMENTARY ON THE BOOK OF ISAIAH, Critical, Historical, and Prophetical; including a Revised English Translation. By T. R. BIRKS. 2nd Edition. 8vo. 12s. 6d.

THE BOOK OF ISAIAH CHRONOLOGICALLY ARRANGED. By T. K. CHEYNE. Crown 8vo. 7s. 6d.

Zechariah—

THE HEBREW STUDENT'S COMMENTARY ON ZECHARIAH, Hebrew and LXX. By W. H. LOWE, M.A. 8vo. 10s. 6d.

THE NEW TESTAMENT

APOCRYPHAL GOSPEL OF PETER. The Greek Text of the Newly-Discovered Fragment. 8vo. Sewed. 1s.

THE NEW TESTAMENT. Essay on the Right Estimation of MS. Evidence in the Text of the New Testament. By T. R. BIRKS. Crown 8vo. 3s. 6d.

THE SOTERIOLOGY OF THE NEW TESTAMENT. By W. P. DU BOSE, M.A. Crown 8vo. 7s. 6d.

THE MESSAGES OF THE BOOKS. Being Discourses and Notes on the Books of the New Testament. By Ven. Archdeacon FARRAR. 8vo. 14s.

THE CLASSICAL ELEMENT IN THE NEW TESTAMENT. Considered as a Proof of its Genuineness, with an Appendix on the Oldest Authorities used in the Formation of the Canon. By C. H. HOOLE. 8vo. 10s. 6d.

ON A FRESH REVISION OF THE ENGLISH NEW TESTAMENT. With an Appendix on the last Petition of the Lord's Prayer. By Bishop LIGHTFOOT. Crown 8vo. 7s. 6d.

DISSERTATIONS ON THE APOSTOLIC AGE. By Bishop LIGHTFOOT. 8vo. 14s.

THE UNITY OF THE NEW TESTAMENT. By F. D. MAURICE. 2nd Edition. 2 vols. Crown 8vo. 12s.

A COMPANION TO THE GREEK TESTAMENT AND THE ENGLISH VERSION. By PHILIP SCHAFF, D.D. Cr. 8vo. 12s.

A GENERAL SURVEY OF THE HISTORY OF THE CANON OF THE NEW TESTAMENT DURING THE FIRST FOUR CENTURIES. By Right Rev. Bishop WESTCOTT. 6th Edition. Crown 8vo. 10s. 6d.

THE NEW TESTAMENT IN THE ORIGINAL GREEK. The Text revised by Bishop WESTCOTT, D.D., and Prof. F. J. A. HORT, D.D. 2 vols. Crown 8vo. 10s. 6d. each.—Vol. I. Text; II. Introduction and Appendix.

THE NEW TESTAMENT IN THE ORIGINAL GREEK, for Schools. The Text revised by Bishop WESTCOTT, D.D., and F. J. A. HORT, D.D. 12mo, cloth, 4s. 6d.; 18mo, roan, red edges, 5s. 6d.; morocco, gilt edges, 6s. 6d.

THE GOSPELS—

THE COMMON TRADITION OF THE SYNOPTIC GOSPELS, in the Text of the Revised Version. By Rev. E. A. ABBOTT and W. G. RUSHBROOKE. Crown 8vo. 3s. 6d.

SYNOPTICON: An Exposition of the Common Matter of the Synoptic Gospels. By W. G. RUSHBROOKE. Printed in Colours. In Six Parts, and Appendix. 4to.—Part I. 3s. 6d. Parts II. and III. 7s. Parts IV. V. and VI. with Indices, 10s. 6d. Appendices, 10s. 6d. Complete in 1 vol., 35s. Indispensable to a Theological Student.

INTRODUCTION TO THE STUDY OF THE FOUR GOSPELS. By Right Rev. Bishop WESTCOTT. 7th Ed. Cr. 8vo. 10s. 6d.

THE COMPOSITION OF THE FOUR GOSPELS. By Rev. ARTHUR WRIGHT. Crown 8vo. 5s.

Gospel of St. Matthew—
  THE GOSPEL ACCORDING TO ST. MATTHEW. Greek Text as Revised by Bishop WESTCOTT and Dr. HORT. With Introduction and Notes by Rev. A. SLOMAN, M.A. Fcap. 8vo. 2s. 6d.
  CHOICE NOTES ON ST. MATTHEW, drawn from Old and New Sources. Crown 8vo. 4s. 6d. (St. Matthew and St. Mark in 1 vol. 9s.)

Gospel of St. Mark—
  SCHOOL READINGS IN THE GREEK TESTAMENT. Being the Outlines of the Life of our Lord as given by St. Mark, with additions from the Text of the other Evangelists. Edited, with Notes and Vocabulary, by Rev. A. CALVERT, M.A. Fcap. 8vo. 2s. 6d.
  CHOICE NOTES ON ST. MARK, drawn from Old and New Sources. Cr. 8vo. 4s. 6d. (St. Matthew and St. Mark in 1 vol. 9s.)

Gospel of St. Luke—
  THE GOSPEL ACCORDING TO ST. LUKE. The Greek Text as Revised by Bishop WESTCOTT and Dr. HORT. With Introduction and Notes by Rev. J. BOND, M.A. Fcap. 8vo. 2s. 6d.
  CHOICE NOTES ON ST. LUKE, drawn from Old and New Sources. Crown 8vo. 4s. 6d.
  THE GOSPEL OF THE KINGDOM OF HEAVEN. A Course of Lectures on the Gospel of St. Luke. By F. D. MAURICE. 3rd Edition. Crown 8vo. 6s.

Gospel of St. John—
  THE CENTRAL TEACHING OF CHRIST. Being a Study and Exposition of St. John, Chapters XIII. to XVII. By Rev. CANON BERNARD, M.A. Crown 8vo. 7s. 6d.
  THE GOSPEL OF ST. JOHN. By F. D. MAURICE. 8th Ed. Cr. 8vo. 6s.
  CHOICE NOTES ON ST. JOHN, drawn from Old and New Sources. Crown 8vo. 4s. 6d.

THE ACTS OF THE APOSTLES—
  THE ACTS OF THE APOSTLES. Being the Greek Text as Revised by Bishop WESTCOTT and Dr. HORT. With Explanatory Notes by T. E. PAGE, M.A. Fcap. 8vo. 3s. 6d.
  THE CHURCH OF THE FIRST DAYS. THE CHURCH OF JERUSALEM. THE CHURCH OF THE GENTILES. THE CHURCH OF THE WORLD. Lectures on the Acts of the Apostles. By Very Rev. C. J. VAUGHAN. Crown 8vo. 10s. 6d.

THE EPISTLES of St. Paul—
  ST. PAUL'S EPISTLE TO THE ROMANS. The Greek Text, with English Notes. By Very Rev. C. J. VAUGHAN. 7th Edition. Crown 8vo. 7s. 6d.
  A COMMENTARY ON ST. PAUL'S TWO EPISTLES TO THE CORINTHIANS. Greek Text, with Commentary. By Rev. W. KAY. 8vo. 9s.

Of St. Paul—*continued.*

ST. PAUL'S EPISTLE TO THE GALATIANS. A Revised Text, with Introduction, Notes, and Dissertations. By Bishop LIGHTFOOT. 10th Edition. 8vo. 12s.

ST. PAUL'S EPISTLE TO THE PHILIPPIANS. A Revised Text, with Introduction, Notes, and Dissertations. By the same. 9th Edition. 8vo. 12s.

ST. PAUL'S EPISTLE TO THE PHILIPPIANS. With translation, Paraphrase, and Notes for English Readers. By Very Rev. C. J. VAUGHAN. Crown 8vo. 5s.

ST. PAUL'S EPISTLES TO THE COLOSSIANS AND TO PHILEMON. A Revised Text, with Introductions, etc. By Bishop LIGHTFOOT. 9th Edition. 8vo. 12s.

THE EPISTLES OF ST. PAUL TO THE EPHESIANS, THE COLOSSIANS, AND PHILEMON. With Introductions and Notes. By Rev. J. LL. DAVIES. 2nd Edition. 8vo. 7s. 6d.

THE EPISTLES OF ST. PAUL. For English Readers. Part I. containing the First Epistle to the Thessalonians. By Very Rev. C. J. VAUGHAN. 2nd Edition. 8vo. Sewed. 1s. 6d.

ST. PAUL'S EPISTLES TO THE THESSALONIANS, COMMENTARY ON THE GREEK TEXT. By Prof. JOHN EADIE. 8vo. 12s.

The Epistle of St. James—

THE EPISTLE OF ST. JAMES. The Greek Text, with Introduction and Notes. By Rev. JOSEPH MAYOR, M.A. 8vo. 14s.

The Epistles of St. John—

THE EPISTLES OF ST. JOHN. By F. D. MAURICE. 4th Edition. Crown 8vo. 6s.

THE EPISTLES OF ST. JOHN. The Greek Text, with Notes. By Right Rev. Bishop WESTCOTT. 3rd Edition. 8vo. 12s. 6d.

The Epistle to the Hebrews—

THE EPISTLE TO THE HEBREWS IN GREEK AND ENGLISH. With Notes. By Rev. FREDERIC RENDALL. Crown 8vo. 6s.

THE EPISTLE TO THE HEBREWS. English Text, with Commentary. By the same. Crown 8vo. 7s. 6d.

THE EPISTLE TO THE HEBREWS. With Notes. By Very Rev. C. J. VAUGHAN. Crown 8vo. 7s. 6d.

THE EPISTLE TO THE HEBREWS. The Greek Text, with Notes and Essays. By Right Rev. Bishop WESTCOTT. 8vo. 14s.

REVELATION—

LECTURES ON THE APOCALYPSE. By F. D. MAURICE. 2nd Edition. Crown 8vo. 6s.

LECTURES ON THE APOCALYPSE. By Rev. Prof. W. MILLIGAN. Crown 8vo. 5s.

THE REVELATION OF ST. JOHN. By Rev. Prof. W. MILLIGAN. 2nd Edition. Crown 8vo. 7s. 6d.

REVELATION—*continued.*
  LECTURES ON THE REVELATION OF ST. JOHN. By Very
  Rev. C. J. VAUGHAN. 5th Edition. Crown 8vo. 10s. 6d.

  THE BIBLE WORD-BOOK. By W. ALDIS WRIGHT. 2nd Edition.
  Crown 8vo. 7s. 6d.

Christian Church, History of the

Church (Dean).—THE OXFORD MOVEMENT. Twelve
  Years, 1833-45. Globe 8vo. 5s.
Cunningham (Rev. John).—THE GROWTH OF THE CHURCH
  IN ITS ORGANISATION AND INSTITUTIONS. 8vo. 9s.
Dale (A. W. W.)—THE SYNOD OF ELVIRA, AND CHRIS-
  TIAN LIFE IN THE FOURTH CENTURY. Cr. 8vo. 10s. 6d.
Hardwick (Archdeacon).—A HISTORY OF THE CHRISTIAN
  CHURCH. Middle Age. Ed. by Bishop STUBBS. Cr. 8vo. 10s. 6d.
  A HISTORY OF THE CHRISTIAN CHURCH DURING THE
  REFORMATION. Revised by Bishop STUBBS. Cr. 8vo. 10s. 6d.
Hort (Dr. F. J. A.)—TWO DISSERTATIONS. I. On
  ΜΟΝΟΓΕΝΗΣ ΘΕΟΣ in Scripture and Tradition. II. On the
  "Constantinopolitan" Creed and other Eastern Creeds of the
  Fourth Century. 8vo. 7s. 6d.
Killen (W. D.)—ECCLESIASTICAL HISTORY OF IRE-
  LAND, FROM THE EARLIEST DATE TO THE PRESENT
  TIME. 2 vols. 8vo. 25s.
Simpson (W.)—AN EPITOME OF THE HISTORY OF THE
  CHRISTIAN CHURCH. Fcap. 8vo. 3s. 6d.
Vaughan (Very Rev. C. J., Dean of Llandaff).—THE CHURCH
  OF THE FIRST DAYS. THE CHURCH OF JERUSALEM. THE
  CHURCH OF THE GENTILES. THE CHURCH OF THE WORLD.
  Crown 8vo. 10s. 6d.
Ward (W.)—WILLIAM GEORGE WARD AND THE
  OXFORD MOVEMENT. Portrait. 8vo. 14s.

The Church of England

Catechism of—
  A CLASS-BOOK OF THE CATECHISM OF THE CHURCH
  OF ENGLAND. By Rev. Canon MACLEAR. 18mo. 1s. 6d.
  A FIRST CLASS-BOOK OF THE CATECHISM OF THE
  CHURCH OF ENGLAND, with Scripture Proofs for Junior
  Classes and Schools. By the same. 18mo. 6d.
  THE ORDER OF CONFIRMATION, with Prayers and Devo-
  tions. By the Rev. Canon MACLEAR. 32mo. 6d.

Collects—
COLLECTS OF THE CHURCH OF ENGLAND. With a Coloured Floral Design to each Collect. Crown 8vo. 12s.

Disestablishment—
DISESTABLISHMENT AND DISENDOWMENT. What are they? By Prof. E. A. FREEMAN. 4th Edition. Crown 8vo. 1s.

DISESTABLISHMENT: or, A Defence of the Principle of a National Church. By GEORGE HARWOOD. 8vo. 12s.

A DEFENCE OF THE CHURCH OF ENGLAND AGAINST DISESTABLISHMENT. By ROUNDELL, EARL OF SELBORNE. Crown 8vo. 2s. 6d.

ANCIENT FACTS & FICTIONS CONCERNING CHURCHES AND TITHES. By the same. 2nd Edition. Crown 8vo. 7s. 6d.

Dissent in its Relation to—
DISSENT IN ITS RELATION TO THE CHURCH OF ENGLAND. By Rev. G. H. CURTEIS. Bampton Lectures for 1871. Crown 8vo. 7s. 6d.

Holy Communion—
THE COMMUNION SERVICE FROM THE BOOK OF COMMON PRAYER, with Select Readings from the Writings of the Rev. F. D. MAURICE. Edited by Bishop COLENSO. 6th Edition. 16mo. 2s. 6d.

BEFORE THE TABLE: An Inquiry, Historical and Theological, into the Meaning of the Consecration Rubric in the Communion Service of the Church of England. By Very Rev. J. S. HOWSON. 8vo. 7s. 6d.

FIRST COMMUNION, with Prayers and Devotions for the newly Confirmed. By Rev. Canon MACLEAR. 32mo. 6d.

A MANUAL OF INSTRUCTION FOR CONFIRMATION AND FIRST COMMUNION, with Prayers and Devotions. By the same. 32mo. 2s.

Liturgy—
A COMPANION TO THE LECTIONARY. By Rev. W. BENHAM, B.D. Crown 8vo. 4s. 6d.

AN INTRODUCTION TO THE CREEDS. By Rev. Canon MACLEAR. 18mo. 3s. 6d.

AN INTRODUCTION TO THE THIRTY-NINE ARTICLES. By the same. 18mo. [*In the Press.*

A HISTORY OF THE BOOK OF COMMON PRAYER. By Rev. F. PROCTER. 18th Edition. Crown 8vo. 10s. 6d.

AN ELEMENTARY INTRODUCTION TO THE BOOK OF COMMON PRAYER. By Rev. F. PROCTER and Rev. Canon MACLEAR. 18mo. 2s. 6d.

TWELVE DISCOURSES ON SUBJECTS CONNECTED WITH THE LITURGY AND WORSHIP OF THE CHURCH OF ENGLAND. By Very Rev. C. J. VAUGHAN. 4th Edition. Fcap. 8vo. 6s.

Devotional Books

Brooke (S. A.)—FORM OF MORNING AND EVENING PRAYER, and for the Administration of the Lord's Supper, together with the Baptismal and Marriage Services, Bedford Chapel, Bloomsbury. Fcap. 8vo. 1s. net.

Eastlake (Lady).—FELLOWSHIP: LETTERS ADDRESSED TO MY SISTER-MOURNERS. Crown 8vo. 2s. 6d.

IMITATIO CHRISTI, LIBRI IV. Printed in Borders after Holbein, Dürer, and other old Masters, containing Dances of Death, Acts of Mercy, Emblems, etc. Crown 8vo. 7s. 6d.

Kingsley (Charles).—OUT OF THE DEEP: WORDS FOR THE SORROWFUL. From the writings of CHARLES KINGSLEY. Extra fcap. 8vo. 3s. 6d.

DAILY THOUGHTS. Selected from the Writings of CHARLES KINGSLEY. By his Wife. Crown 8vo. 6s.

FROM DEATH TO LIFE. Fragments of Teaching to a Village Congregation. With Letters on the "Life after Death." Edited by his Wife. Fcap. 8vo. 2s. 6d.

Maclear (Rev. Canon).—A MANUAL OF INSTRUCTION FOR CONFIRMATION AND FIRST COMMUNION, WITH PRAYERS AND DEVOTIONS. 32mo. 2s.

THE HOUR OF SORROW; OR, THE OFFICE FOR THE BURIAL OF THE DEAD. 32mo. 2s.

Maurice (Frederick Denison).—LESSONS OF HOPE. Readings from the Works of F. D. MAURICE. Selected by Rev. J. LL. DAVIES, M.A. Crown 8vo. 5s.

RAYS OF SUNLIGHT FOR DARK DAYS. With a Preface by Very Rev. C. J. VAUGHAN, D.D. New Edition. 18mo. 3s. 6d.

Service (Rev. John).—PRAYERS FOR PUBLIC WORSHIP. Crown 8vo. 4s. 6d.

THE WORSHIP OF GOD, AND FELLOWSHIP AMONG MEN. By FREDERICK DENISON MAURICE and others. Fcap. 8vo. 3s. 6d.

Welby-Gregory (The Hon. Lady).—LINKS AND CLUES. 2nd Edition. Crown 8vo. 6s.

Westcott (Rt. Rev. B. F., Bishop of Durham).—THOUGHTS ON REVELATION AND LIFE. Selections from the Writings of Bishop WESTCOTT. Edited by Rev. S. PHILLIPS. Crown 8vo. 6s.

Wilbraham (Frances M.)—IN THE SERE AND YELLOW LEAF: THOUGHTS AND RECOLLECTIONS FOR OLD AND YOUNG. Globe 8vo. 3s. 6d.

The Fathers

Cunningham (Rev. W.)—THE EPISTLE OF ST. BARNABAS. A Dissertation, including a Discussion of its Date and Authorship. Together with the Greek Text, the Latin Version, and a New English Translation and Commentary. Crown 8vo. 7s. 6d.

Donaldson (Prof. James).—THE APOSTOLICAL FATHERS. A Critical Account of their Genuine Writings, and of their Doctrines. 2nd Edition. Crown 8vo. 7s. 6d.

Lightfoot (Bishop).—THE APOSTOLIC FATHERS. Part I. ST. CLEMENT OF ROME. Revised Texts, with Introductions, Notes, Dissertations, and Translations. 2 vols. 8vo. 32s.

THE APOSTOLIC FATHERS. Part II. ST. IGNATIUS to ST. POLYCARP. Revised Texts, with Introductions, Notes, Dissertations, and Translations. 3 vols. 2nd Edition. Demy 8vo. 48s.

THE APOSTOLIC FATHERS. Abridged Edition. With Short Introductions, Greek Text, and English Translation. 8vo. 16s.

Hymnology

Brooke (S. A.)—CHRISTIAN HYMNS. Edited and arranged. Fcap. 8vo. 2s. net.

This may also be had bound up with the Form of Service at Bedford Chapel, Bloomsbury. Price complete, 3s. net.

Palgrave (Prof. F. T.)—ORIGINAL HYMNS. 18mo. 1s. 6d.

Selborne (Roundell, Earl of)—

THE BOOK OF PRAISE. From the best English Hymn Writers. 18mo. 2s. 6d. net.

A HYMNAL. Chiefly from *The Book of Praise*. In various sizes.—A. Royal 32mo. 6d.—B. Small 18mo, larger type. 1s.—C. Same Edition, fine paper. 1s. 6d.—An Edition with Music, Selected, Harmonised, and Composed by JOHN HULLAH. Square 18mo. 3s. 6d.

Woods (M. A.) — HYMNS FOR SCHOOL WORSHIP. Compiled by M. A. WOODS. 18mo. 1s. 6d.

Sermons, Lectures, Addresses, and Theological Essays

(*See also* '*Bible,*' '*Church of England,*' '*Fathers.*')

Abbot (Francis)—

SCIENTIFIC THEISM. Crown 8vo. 7s. 6d.

THE WAY OUT OF AGNOSTICISM: or, The Philosophy of Free Religion. Crown 8vo. 4s. 6d.

Abbott (Rev. E. A.)—

CAMBRIDGE SERMONS. 8vo. 6s.

OXFORD SERMONS. 8vo. 7s. 6d.

PHILOMYTHUS. An Antidote against Credulity. A discussion of Cardinal Newman's Essay on Ecclesiastical Miracles. 2nd Edition. Crown 8vo. 3s. 6d.

NEWMANIANISM. A Reply. Crown 8vo. Sewed, 1s. net.

Ainger (Rev. Alfred, Canon of Bristol).—SERMONS PREACHED IN THE TEMPLE CHURCH. Extra fcap. 8vo. 6s.

Alexander (W., Bishop of Derry and Raphoe).—THE LEADING IDEAS OF THE GOSPELS. New Edition, Revised and Enlarged. Crown 8vo. 6s.

Baines (Rev. Edward).—SERMONS. With a Preface and Memoir, by A. BARRY, D.D., late Bishop of Sydney. Crown 8vo. 6s.

Bather (Archdeacon).—ON SOME MINISTERIAL DUTIES, CATECHISING, PREACHING, ETC. Edited, with a Preface, by Very Rev. C. J. VAUGHAN, D.D. Fcap. 8vo. 4s. 6d.

Binnie (Rev. William).—SERMONS. Crown 8vo. 6s.

Birks (Thomas Rawson)—
 THE DIFFICULTIES OF BELIEF IN CONNECTION WITH THE CREATION AND THE FALL, REDEMPTION, AND JUDGMENT. 2nd Edition. Crown 8vo. 5s.
 JUSTIFICATION AND IMPUTED RIGHTEOUSNESS. Being a Review of Ten Sermons on the Nature and Effects of Faith, by JAMES THOMAS O'BRIEN, D.D., late Bishop of Ossory, Ferns, and Leighlin. Crown 8vo. 6s.
 SUPERNATURAL REVELATION : or, First Principles of Moral Theology. 8vo. 8s.

Brooke (Rev. Stopford A.)—SHORT SERMONS. Cr. 8vo. 6s.

Brooks (Phillips, Bishop of Massachusetts)—
 THE CANDLE OF THE LORD, and other Sermons. Crown 8vo. 6s.
 SERMONS PREACHED IN ENGLISH CHURCHES. Crown 8vo. 6s.
 TWENTY SERMONS. Crown 8vo. 6s.
 TOLERANCE. Crown 8vo. 2s. 6d.
 THE LIGHT OF THE WORLD. Crown 8vo. 3s. 6d.

Brunton (T. Lauder).—THE BIBLE AND SCIENCE. With Illustrations. Crown 8vo. 10s. 6d.

Butler (Rev. George).—SERMONS PREACHED IN CHELTENHAM COLLEGE CHAPEL. 8vo. 7s. 6d.

Butler (W. Archer)—
 SERMONS, DOCTRINAL AND PRACTICAL. 11th Edition. 8vo. 8s.
 SECOND SERIES OF SERMONS. 8vo. 7s.

Campbell (Dr. John M'Leod)—
 THE NATURE OF THE ATONEMENT. 6th Ed. Cr. 8vo. 6s.
 REMINISCENCES AND REFLECTIONS. Edited with an Introductory Narrative, by his Son, DONALD CAMPBELL, M.A. Crown 8vo. 7s. 6d.
 THOUGHTS ON REVELATION. 2nd Edition. Crown 8vo. 5s.
 RESPONSIBILITY FOR THE GIFT OF ETERNAL LIFE. Compiled from Sermons preached at Row, in the years 1829-31. Crown 8vo. 5s.

THEOLOGICAL CATALOGUE

Canterbury (Edward White, Archbishop of)—
  BOY-LIFE: its Trial, its Strength, its Fulness. Sundays in Wellington College, 1859-73. 4th Edition. Crown 8vo. 6s.
  THE SEVEN GIFTS. Addressed to the Diocese of Canterbury in his Primary Visitation. 2nd Edition. Crown 8vo. 6s.
  CHRIST AND HIS TIMES. Addressed to the Diocese of Canterbury in his Second Visitation. Crown 8vo. 6s.

Carpenter (W. Boyd, Bishop of Ripon)—
  TRUTH IN TALE. Addresses, chiefly to Children. Crown 8vo. 4s. 6d.
  THE PERMANENT ELEMENTS OF RELIGION: Bampton Lectures, 1887. 2nd Edition. Crown 8vo. 6s.

Cazenove (J. Gibson).—CONCERNING THE BEING AND ATTRIBUTES OF GOD. 8vo. 5s.

Church (Dean)—
  HUMAN LIFE AND ITS CONDITIONS. Crown 8vo. 6s.
  THE GIFTS OF CIVILISATION, and other Sermons and Lectures. 2nd Edition. Crown 8vo. 7s. 6d.
  DISCIPLINE OF THE CHRISTIAN CHARACTER, and other Sermons. Crown 8vo. 4s. 6d.
  ADVENT SERMONS. 1885. Crown 8vo. 4s. 6d.
  VILLAGE SERMONS. Crown 8vo. 6s.
  CATHEDRAL AND UNIVERSITY SERMONS. Crown 8vo. 6s.
  CLERGYMAN'S SELF-EXAMINATION CONCERNING THE APOSTLES' CREED. Extra fcap. 8vo. 1s. 6d.

Congreve (Rev. John).—HIGH HOPES AND PLEADINGS FOR A REASONABLE FAITH, NOBLER THOUGHTS, LARGER CHARITY. Crown 8vo. 5s.

Cooke (Josiah P., Jun.)—RELIGION AND CHEMISTRY. Crown 8vo. 7s. 6d.

Cotton (Bishop).—SERMONS PREACHED TO ENGLISH CONGREGATIONS IN INDIA. Crown 8vo. 7s. 6d.

Cunningham (Rev. W.)—CHRISTIAN CIVILISATION, WITH SPECIAL REFERENCE TO INDIA. Cr. 8vo. 5s.

Curteis (Rev. G. H.)—THE SCIENTIFIC OBSTACLES TO CHRISTIAN BELIEF. The Boyle Lectures, 1884. Cr. 8vo. 6s.

Davies (Rev. J. Llewelyn)—
  THE GOSPEL AND MODERN LIFE. 2nd Edition, to which is added Morality according to the Sacrament of the Lord's Supper. Extra fcap. 8vo. 6s.
  SOCIAL QUESTIONS FROM THE POINT OF VIEW OF CHRISTIAN THEOLOGY. 2nd Edition. Crown 8vo. 6s.
  WARNINGS AGAINST SUPERSTITION. Extra fcap. 8vo. 2s. 6d.
  THE CHRISTIAN CALLING. Extra fcap. 8vo. 6s.
  ORDER AND GROWTH AS INVOLVED IN THE SPIRITUAL CONSTITUTION OF HUMAN SOCIETY. Crown 8vo. 3s. 6d.

Davies (Rev. J. Llewelyn)—*continued.*
BAPTISM, CONFIRMATION, AND THE LORD'S SUPPER, as interpreted by their Outward Signs. Three Addresses. New Edition. 18mo. 1s.

Diggle (Rev. J. W.)—GODLINESS AND MANLINESS. A Miscellany of Brief Papers touching the Relation of Religion to Life. Crown 8vo. 6s.

Drummond (Prof. James).—INTRODUCTION TO THE STUDY OF THEOLOGY. Crown 8vo. 5s.

ECCE HOMO. A Survey of the Life and Work of Jesus Christ. 20th Edition. Globe 8vo. 6s.

Ellerton (Rev. John).—THE HOLIEST MANHOOD, AND ITS LESSONS FOR BUSY LIVES. Crown 8vo. 6s.

FAITH AND CONDUCT: An Essay on Verifiable Religion. Crown 8vo. 7s. 6d.

Farrar (Ven. F. W., Archdeacon of Westminster)—
THE HISTORY OF INTERPRETATION. Being the Bampton Lectures, 1885. 8vo. 16s.

Collected Edition of the Sermons, etc. Crown 8vo. 3s. 6d. each.

SEEKERS AFTER GOD.
ETERNAL HOPE. Sermons Preached in Westminster Abbey.
THE FALL OF MAN, and other Sermons.
THE WITNESS OF HISTORY TO CHRIST. Hulsean Lectures.
THE SILENCE AND VOICES OF GOD.
IN THE DAYS OF THY YOUTH. Sermons on Practical Subjects.
SAINTLY WORKERS. Five Lenten Lectures.
EPHPHATHA: or, The Amelioration of the World.
MERCY AND JUDGMENT. A few last words on Christian Eschatology.
SERMONS AND ADDRESSES delivered in America.

Fiske (John).—MAN'S DESTINY VIEWED IN THE LIGHT OF HIS ORIGIN. Crown 8vo. 3s. 6d.

Forbes (Rev. Granville).—THE VOICE OF GOD IN THE PSALMS. Crown 8vo. 6s. 6d.

Fowle (Rev. T. W.)—A NEW ANALOGY BETWEEN REVEALED RELIGION AND THE COURSE AND CONSTITUTION OF NATURE. Crown 8vo. 6s.

Fraser (Bishop).—SERMONS. Edited by Rev. JOHN W. DIGGLE. 2 vols. Crown 8vo. 6s. each.

Hamilton (John)—
ON TRUTH AND ERROR. Crown 8vo. 5s.
ARTHUR'S SEAT: or, The Church of the Banned. Crown 8vo. 6s.
ABOVE AND AROUND: Thoughts on God and Man. 12mo. 2s. 6d.

Hardwick (Archdeacon).—CHRIST AND OTHER MASTERS. 6th Edition. Crown 8vo. 10s. 6d.

Hare (Julius Charles)—
  THE MISSION OF THE COMFORTER. New Edition. Edited by Dean PLUMPTRE. Crown 8vo. 7s. 6d.
  THE VICTORY OF FAITH. Edited by Dean PLUMPTRE, with Introductory Notices by Prof. MAURICE and Dean STANLEY. Crown 8vo. 6s. 6d.
Harper (Father Thomas, S. J.)—THE METAPHYSICS OF THE SCHOOL. In 5 vols. Vols. I. and II. 8vo. 18s. each. Vol. III. Part I. 12s.
Harris (Rev. G. C.)—SERMONS. With a Memoir by CHARLOTTE M. YONGE, and Portrait. Extra fcap. 8vo. 6s.
Hutton (R. H.)—
  ESSAYS ON SOME OF THE MODERN GUIDES OF ENGLISH THOUGHT IN MATTERS OF FAITH. Globe 8vo. 6s.
  THEOLOGICAL ESSAYS. Globe 8vo. 6s.
Illingworth (Rev. J. R.)—SERMONS PREACHED IN A COLLEGE CHAPEL. Crown 8vo. 5s.
  UNIVERSITY AND CATHEDRAL SERMONS. Crown 8vo. [*In the Press.*
Jacob (Rev. J. A.)—BUILDING IN SILENCE, and other Sermons. Extra fcap. 8vo. 6s.
James (Rev. Herbert).—THE COUNTRY CLERGYMAN AND HIS WORK. Crown 8vo. 6s.
Jeans (Rev. G. E.)—HAILEYBURY CHAPEL, and other Sermons. Fcap. 8vo. 3s. 6d.
Jellett (Rev. Dr.)—
  THE ELDER SON, and other Sermons. Crown 8vo. 6s.
  THE EFFICACY OF PRAYER. 3rd Edition. Crown 8vo. 5s.
Kellogg (Rev. S. H.)—THE LIGHT OF ASIA AND THE LIGHT OF THE WORLD. Crown 8vo. 7s. 6d.
  THE GENESIS AND GROWTH OF RELIGION. Cr. 8vo. 6s.
Kingsley (Charles)—
  VILLAGE AND TOWN AND COUNTRY SERMONS. Crown 8vo. 3s. 6d.
  THE WATER OF LIFE, and other Sermons. Crown 8vo. 3s. 6d.
  SERMONS ON NATIONAL SUBJECTS, AND THE KING OF THE EARTH. Crown 8vo. 3s. 6d.
  SERMONS FOR THE TIMES. Crown 8vo. 3s. 6d.
  GOOD NEWS OF GOD. Crown 8vo. 3s. 6d.
  THE GOSPEL OF THE PENTATEUCH, AND DAVID. Crown 8vo. 3s. 6d.
  DISCIPLINE, and other Sermons. Crown 8vo. 3s. 6d.
  WESTMINSTER SERMONS. Crown 8vo. 3s. 6d.
  ALL SAINTS' DAY, and other Sermons. Crown 8vo. 3s. 6d.
Kirkpatrick (Prof. A. F.)—THE DIVINE LIBRARY OF THE OLD TESTAMENT. Its Origin, Preservation, Inspiration, and Permanent Value. Crown 8vo. 3s. net.

Kirkpatrick (Prof. A. F.)—*continued.*
    THE DOCTRINE OF THE PROPHETS. Warburtonian Lectures 1886-1890. Crown 8vo. 6s.

Kynaston (Rev. Herbert, D.D.)—SERMONS PREACHED IN THE COLLEGE CHAPEL, CHELTENHAM. Crown 8vo. 6s.

Lightfoot (Bishop)—
    LEADERS IN THE NORTHERN CHURCH: Sermons Preached in the Diocese of Durham. 2nd Edition. Crown 8vo. 6s.
    ORDINATION ADDRESSES AND COUNSELS TO CLERGY. Crown 8vo. 6s.
    CAMBRIDGE SERMONS. Crown 8vo. 6s.
    SERMONS PREACHED IN ST. PAUL'S CATHEDRAL. Crown 8vo. 6s.
    SERMONS PREACHED ON SPECIAL OCCASIONS. Crown 8vo. 6s.
    A CHARGE DELIVERED TO THE CLERGY OF THE DIOCESE OF DURHAM, 25th Nov. 1886. Demy 8vo. 2s.
    ESSAYS ON THE WORK ENTITLED "Supernatural Religion." 8vo. 10s. 6d.
    DISSERTATIONS ON THE APOSTOLIC AGE. 8vo. 14s.
    BIBLICAL MISCELLANIES. 8vo. [*In the Press.*

Maclaren (Rev. Alexander)—
    SERMONS PREACHED AT MANCHESTER. 11th Edition. Fcap. 8vo. 4s. 6d.
    A SECOND SERIES OF SERMONS. 7th Ed. Fcap. 8vo. 4s. 6d.
    A THIRD SERIES. 6th Edition. Fcap. 8vo. 4s. 6d.
    WEEK-DAY EVENING ADDRESSES. 4th Ed. Fcap. 8vo. 2s. 6d.
    THE SECRET OF POWER, AND OTHER SERMONS. Fcap. 8vo. 4s. 6d.

Macmillan (Rev. Hugh)—
    BIBLE TEACHINGS IN NATURE. 15th Ed. Globe 8vo. 6s.
    THE TRUE VINE; OR, THE ANALOGIES OF OUR LORD'S ALLEGORY. 5th Edition. Globe 8vo. 6s.
    THE MINISTRY OF NATURE. 8th Edition. Globe 8vo. 6s.
    THE SABBATH OF THE FIELDS. 6th Edition. Globe 8vo. 6s.
    THE MARRIAGE IN CANA. Globe 8vo. 6s.
    TWO WORLDS ARE OURS. 3rd Edition. Globe 8vo. 6s.
    THE OLIVE LEAF. Globe 8vo. 6s.
    THE GATE BEAUTIFUL AND OTHER BIBLE TEACHINGS FOR THE YOUNG. Crown 8vo. 3s. 6d.

Mahaffy (Rev. Prof.)—THE DECAY OF MODERN PREACHING: AN ESSAY. Crown 8vo. 3s. 6d.

Maturin (Rev. W.)—THE BLESSEDNESS OF THE DEAD IN CHRIST. Crown 8vo. 7s. 6d.

Maurice (Frederick Denison)—
    THE KINGDOM OF CHRIST. 3rd Ed. 2 Vols. Cr. 8vo. 12s.
    EXPOSITORY SERMONS ON THE PRAYER-BOOK; AND ON THE LORD'S PRAYER. New Edition. Crown 8vo. 6s.

Maurice (Frederick Denison)—*continued.*
  SERMONS PREACHED IN COUNTRY CHURCHES. 2nd Edition. Crown 8vo. 6s.
  THE CONSCIENCE. Lectures on Casuistry. 3rd Ed. Cr. 8vo. 4s. 6d.
  DIALOGUES ON FAMILY WORSHIP. Crown 8vo. 4s. 6d.
  THE DOCTRINE OF SACRIFICE DEDUCED FROM THE SCRIPTURES. 2nd Edition. Crown 8vo. 6s.
  THE RELIGIONS OF THE WORLD. 6th Edition. Cr. 8vo. 4s. 6d.
  ON THE SABBATH DAY; THE CHARACTER OF THE WARRIOR; AND ON THE INTERPRETATION OF HISTORY. Fcap. 8vo. 2s. 6d.
  LEARNING AND WORKING. Crown 8vo. 4s. 6d.
  THE LORD'S PRAYER, THE CREED, AND THE COMMANDMENTS. 18mo. 1s.
  SERMONS PREACHED IN LINCOLN'S INN CHAPEL. In Six Volumes. Crown 8vo. 3s. 6d. each.
  Collected Works. Monthly Volumes from October 1892. Crown 8vo. 3s. 6d. each.
  CHRISTMAS DAY AND OTHER SERMONS.
  THEOLOGICAL ESSAYS.
  PROPHETS AND KINGS.
  PATRIARCHS AND LAWGIVERS.
  THE GOSPEL OF THE KINGDOM OF HEAVEN.
  GOSPEL OF ST. JOHN.
  EPISTLE OF ST. JOHN.
  LECTURES ON THE APOCALYPSE.
  FRIENDSHIP OF BOOKS.
  SOCIAL MORALITY.
  PRAYER BOOK AND LORD'S PRAYER.
  THE DOCTRINE OF SACRIFICE.

Milligan (Rev. Prof. W.)—THE RESURRECTION OF OUR LORD. Fourth Thousand. Crown 8vo. 5s.
  THE ASCENSION AND HEAVENLY PRIESTHOOD OF OUR LORD. *Baird Lectures*, 1891. Crown 8vo. 7s. 6d.

Moorhouse (J., Bishop of Manchester)—
  JACOB: Three Sermons. Extra fcap. 8vo. 3s. 6d.
  THE TEACHING OF CHRIST. Its Conditions, Secret, and Results. Crown 8vo. 3s. net.

Mylne (L. G., Bishop of Bombay).—SERMONS PREACHED IN ST. THOMAS'S CATHEDRAL, BOMBAY. Crown 8vo. 6s.
NATURAL RELIGION. By the author of "Ecce Homo." 3rd Edition. Globe 8vo. 6s.
Pattison (Mark).—SERMONS. Crown 8vo. 6s.
PAUL OF TARSUS. 8vo. 10s. 6d.
PHILOCHRISTUS. Memoirs of a Disciple of the Lord. 3rd Ed. 8vo. 12s.

Plumptre (Dean). — MOVEMENTS IN RELIGIOUS THOUGHT. Fcap. 8vo. 3s. 6d.

Potter (R.)—THE RELATION OF ETHICS TO RELIGION. Crown 8vo. 2s. 6d.

REASONABLE FAITH: A Short Religious Essay for the Times. By "Three Friends." Crown 8vo. 1s.

Reichel (C. P., Bishop of Meath)—
 THE LORD'S PRAYER, and other Sermons. Crown 8vo. 7s. 6d.
 CATHEDRAL AND UNIVERSITY SERMONS. Crown 8vo. 6s.

Rendall (Rev. F.)—THE THEOLOGY OF THE HEBREW CHRISTIANS. Crown 8vo. 5s.

Reynolds (H. R.)—NOTES OF THE CHRISTIAN LIFE. Crown 8vo. 7s. 6d.

Robinson (Prebendary H. G.)—MAN IN THE IMAGE OF GOD, and other Sermons. Crown 8vo. 7s. 6d.

Russell (Dean).—THE LIGHT THAT LIGHTETH EVERY MAN: Sermons. With an introduction by Dean PLUMPTRE, D.D. Crown 8vo. 6s.

Salmon (Rev. Prof. George)—
 NON-MIRACULOUS CHRISTIANITY, and other Sermons. 2nd Edition. Crown 8vo. 6s.
 GNOSTICISM AND AGNOSTICISM, and other Sermons. Crown 8vo. 7s. 6d.

Sandford (C. W., Bishop of Gibraltar).—COUNSEL TO ENGLISH CHURCHMEN ABROAD. Crown 8vo. 6s.

SCOTCH SERMONS, 1880. By Principal CAIRD and others. 3rd Edition. 8vo. 10s. 6d.

Service (Rev. John).—SERMONS. With Portrait. Crown 8vo. 6s.

Shirley (W. N.)—ELIJAH: Four University Sermons. Fcap. 8vo. 2s. 6d.

Smith (Rev. Travers).—MAN'S KNOWLEDGE OF MAN AND OF GOD. Crown 8vo. 6s.

Smith (W. Saumarez).—THE BLOOD OF THE NEW COVENANT: A Theological Essay. Crown 8vo. 2s. 6d.

Stanley (Dean)—
 THE NATIONAL THANKSGIVING. Sermons preached in Westminster Abbey. 2nd Edition. Crown 8vo. 2s. 6d.
 ADDRESSES AND SERMONS delivered during a visit to the United States and Canada in 1878. Crown 8vo. 6s.

Stewart (Prof. Balfour) and **Tait** (Prof. P. G.)—THE UNSEEN UNIVERSE; OR, PHYSICAL SPECULATIONS ON A FUTURE STATE. 15th Edition. Crown 8vo. 6s.
 PARADOXICAL PHILOSOPHY: A Sequel to "The Unseen Universe." Crown 8vo. 7s. 6d.

Stubbs (Rev. C. W.)—FOR CHRIST AND CITY. Sermons and Addresses. Crown 8vo. 6s.

Tait (Archbishop)—
THE PRESENT POSITION OF THE CHURCH OF ENGLAND. Being the Charge delivered at his Primary Visitation. 8vo. 3s. 6d.
DUTIES OF THE CHURCH OF ENGLAND. Being seven Addresses delivered at his Second Visitation. 8vo. 4s. 6d.
THE CHURCH OF THE FUTURE. Charges delivered at his Third Quadrennial Visitation. 2nd Edition. Crown 8vo. 3s. 6d.

Taylor (Isaac).—THE RESTORATION OF BELIEF. Crown 8vo. 8s. 6d.

Temple (Frederick, Bishop of London)—
SERMONS PREACHED IN THE CHAPEL OF RUGBY SCHOOL. SECOND SERIES. 3rd Edition. Extra fcap. 8vo. 6s.
THIRD SERIES. 4th Edition. Extra fcap. 8vo. 6s.
THE RELATIONS BETWEEN RELIGION AND SCIENCE. Bampton Lectures, 1884. 7th and Cheaper Ed. Cr. 8vo. 6s.

Trench (Archbishop).—HULSEAN LECTURES. 8vo. 7s. 6d.

Tulloch (Principal).—THE CHRIST OF THE GOSPELS AND THE CHRIST OF MODERN CRITICISM. Extra fcap. 8vo. 4s. 6d.

Vaughan (C. J., Dean of Llandaff)—
MEMORIALS OF HARROW SUNDAYS. 5th Edition. Crown 8vo. 10s. 6d.
EPIPHANY, LENT, AND EASTER. 3rd Ed. Cr. 8vo. 10s. 6d.
HEROES OF FAITH. 2nd Edition. Crown 8vo. 6s.
LIFE'S WORK AND GOD'S DISCIPLINE. 3rd Edition. Extra fcap. 8vo. 2s. 6d.
THE WHOLESOME WORDS OF JESUS CHRIST. 2nd Edition. Fcap. 8vo. 3s. 6d.
FOES OF FAITH. 2nd Edition. Fcap. 8vo. 3s. 6d.
CHRIST SATISFYING THE INSTINCTS OF HUMANITY. 2nd Edition. Extra fcap. 8vo. 3s. 6d.
COUNSELS FOR YOUNG STUDENTS. Fcap. 8vo. 2s. 6d.
THE TWO GREAT TEMPTATIONS. 2nd Ed. Fcap. 8vo. 3s. 6d.
ADDRESSES FOR YOUNG CLERGYMEN. Extra fcap. 8vo. 4s. 6d.
"MY SON, GIVE ME THINE HEART." Extra fcap. 8vo. 5s.
REST AWHILE. Addresses to Toilers in the Ministry. Extra fcap. 8vo. 5s.
TEMPLE SERMONS. Crown 8vo. 10s. 6d.
AUTHORISED OR REVISED? Sermons on some of the Texts in which the Revised Version differs from the Authorised. Crown 8vo. 7s. 6d.
LESSONS OF THE CROSS AND PASSION. WORDS FROM THE CROSS. THE REIGN OF SIN. THE LORD'S PRAYER. Four Courses of Lent Lectures. Crown 8vo. 10s. 6d.
UNIVERSITY SERMONS. NEW AND OLD. Cr. 8vo. 10s. 6d.

Vaughan (C. J., Dean of Llandaff)—*continued.*
 NOTES FOR LECTURES ON CONFIRMATION. Fcap. 8vo. 1s. 6d.
 THE PRAYERS OF JESUS CHRIST: a closing volume of Lent Lectures delivered in the Temple Church. Globe 8vo. 3s. 6d.
 DONCASTER SERMONS. Lessons of Life and Godliness, and Words from the Gospels. Cr. 8vo. 10s. 6d.
 RESTFUL THOUGHTS IN RESTLESS TIMES. Crown 8vo. [*In the Press.*

Vaughan (Rev. D. J.)—THE PRESENT TRIAL OF FAITH. Crown 8vo. 9s.

Vaughan (Rev. E. T.)—SOME REASONS OF OUR CHRISTIAN HOPE. Hulsean Lectures for 1875. Crown 8vo. 6s. 6d.

Vaughan (Rev. Robert).—STONES FROM THE QUARRY. Sermons. Crown 8vo. 5s.

Venn (Rev. John).—ON SOME CHARACTERISTICS OF BELIEF, SCIENTIFIC AND RELIGIOUS. 8vo. 6s. 6d.

Warington (G.)—THE WEEK OF CREATION. Cr. 8vo. 4s. 6d.

Welldon (Rev. J. E. C.)—THE SPIRITUAL LIFE, and other Sermons. Crown 8vo. 6s.

Westcott (B. F., Bishop of Durham)—
 ON THE RELIGIOUS OFFICE OF THE UNIVERSITIES. Sermons. Crown 8vo. 4s. 6d.
 GIFTS FOR MINISTRY. Addresses to Candidates for Ordination. Crown 8vo. 1s. 6d.
 THE VICTORY OF THE CROSS. Sermons preached during Holy Week, 1888, in Hereford Cathedral. Crown 8vo. 3s. 6d.
 FROM STRENGTH TO STRENGTH. Three Sermons (In Memoriam J. B. D.) Crown 8vo. 2s.
 THE REVELATION OF THE RISEN LORD. Cr. 8vo. 6s.
 THE HISTORIC FAITH. 3rd Edition. Crown 8vo. 6s.
 THE GOSPEL OF THE RESURRECTION. 6th Ed. Cr. 8vo. 6s.
 THE REVELATION OF THE FATHER. Crown 8vo. 6s.
 CHRISTUS CONSUMMATOR. 2nd Edition. Crown 8vo. 6s.
 SOME THOUGHTS FROM THE ORDINAL. Cr. 8vo. 1s. 6d.
 SOCIAL ASPECTS OF CHRISTIANITY. Crown 8vo. 6s.
 ESSAYS IN THE HISTORY OF RELIGIOUS THOUGHT IN THE WEST. Globe 8vo. 6s.
 THE GOSPEL OF LIFE. Cr. 8vo. 6s.

Wickham (Rev. E. C.)—WELLINGTON COLLEGE SERMONS. Crown 8vo. 6s.

Wilkins (Prof. A. S.)—THE LIGHT OF THE WORLD: an Essay. 2nd Edition. Crown 8vo. 3s. 6d.

Wilson (J. M., Archdeacon of Manchester)—
 SERMONS PREACHED IN CLIFTON COLLEGE CHAPEL. Second Series. 1888-90. Crown 8vo. 6s.
 ESSAYS AND ADDRESSES. Crown 8vo. 4s. 6d.
 SOME CONTRIBUTIONS TO THE RELIGIOUS THOUGHT OF OUR TIME. Crown 8vo. 6s.

www.ingramcontent.com/pod-product-compliance
Lightning Source LLC
Chambersburg PA
CBHW030315240426
43673CB00040B/1178